After Wallace

Photo credit: Amy Kilpatrick.

After Wallace

The 1986 Contest for Governor and Political Change in Alabama

Patrick R. Cotter and James Glen Stovall

The University of Alabama Press

Tuscaloosa

The University of Alabama Press
Tuscaloosa, Alabama 35487-0380

Manufactured in the United States of America

Hardcover edition published 2009.
Paperback edition published 2013.
eBook edition published 2013.

Cover photographs: (L) Small-town rallies such as this one for Charles Graddick in Evergreen during the primary election were a staple of the 1986 election. (Mike Casey, Courtesy of the *Press Register* © All rights reserved. Reprinted with permission.) (R) Bill Baxley shakes hands with a voter at an airport rally on the day before the Democratic runoff election. (Roy McAuley, Courtesy of the *Press Register* © All rights reserved. Reprinted with permission.)
Cover design: Kate E. K. Barber

∞
The paper on which this book is printed meets the minimum requirements of American National Standard for Information Science–Permanence of Paper for Printed Library Materials, ANSI Z39.48-1984.

Paperback ISBN: 978-0-8173-5754-2
eBook ISBN: 978-0-8173-8727-3

A previous edition of this book has been catalogued by the Library of Congress as follows:

Library of Congress Cataloging-in-Publication Data

Cotter, Patrick R.
After Wallace : the 1986 contest for governor and political change in Alabama / Patrick R. Cotter and James Glen Stovall.
p. cm.
Includes bibliographical references and index.
ISBN 978-0-8173-1660-0 (cloth : alk. paper) 1. Alabama—Politics and government—1951– 2. Wallace, George C. (George Corley), 1919–1998—Influence. 3. Governors—Alabama—Election—History—20th century. 4. Elections—Alabama—History—20th century. 5. Political campaigns—Alabama—History—20th century. 6. Social change—Alabama—History—20th century. I. Stovall, James Glen. II. Title.
F330.C67 2009
324.9761'063—dc22

2009003363

Contents

Illustrations

Figures

Photos

Tables

Preface

When George Wallace was wheeled into the state House of Representatives chamber in Alabama's old state capitol building on April 2, 1986, his face was gaunt, his hands shook, his hearing had dissipated, and he had not been able to walk for nearly fourteen years. Wallace was quite familiar with the house chamber. His almost forty-year involvement with Alabama state government had begun when he was elected to the state house. Since then he had lost one election for governor and won four others. His wife was elected governor in still another contest. Many of his State of the State addresses as governor had been delivered from the chamber's podium.

On this April morning, a crowd of three hundred or so had gathered. The makeup of the crowd reflected Wallace's long and varied career. Included were members of the state and national media, prominent officials associated with a range of interests and concerns, black civil rights leaders and their white opponents, and other, less famous, longtime Wallace supporters representing most of the varied components of the Alabama electorate. The presence of these supporters, many of whom wore "In Alabama, we Luv our Gov" buttons and waved signs showing Wallace's picture, made the atmosphere within the house chamber more like a campaign rally than a time for a serious speech.

Wallace's entry into the chamber was greeted with long applause. He was coming to the end of his fourth term as governor, and there were two days left before the candidate filing deadline—the time when he would have to declare whether or not he was running for a fifth term. Alabama's political world had speculated for months about whether or not he would mount another campaign. He cagily allowed that speculation to grow. Now, the gathered crowd was eager to hear Wallace's decision.

But Wallace, as ever, remained the master of the moment. He carried two speeches with him—one declaring his candidacy, the other his retirement.

Some of his closest advisers later said that they did not know which of the two speeches Wallace would give that morning. Others thought they knew what Wallace would do, but even they felt some uncertainty.

In the end, Wallace told the gathered crowd that he would not seek reelection. "I have climbed my last political mountain," he said. It was now time "to pass the rope and pick to another climber, and say, climb on to higher heights." He ended by declaring that his "heart will always belong to Alabama." To the citizens of Alabama, he bid "a fond and affectionate farewell."

Tears and later more applause greeted Wallace's announcement. Many in the crowd tried to touch the governor and shake his hand as he left the chamber.[1]

Wallace's decision that day marks the official beginning of the "post-Wallace" era of Alabama politics. What followed was one of the most interesting and important elections for governor in the state's political history. The strange developments and unexpected outcome of the campaign make its story seem more like fiction than real life. The election year began with the question of whether or not Wallace would retire. The contest ended with the election of one of the most unlikely persons, Republican Guy Hunt, ever selected governor of any state. Between Wallace's retirement and Hunt's election there occurred many elements of modern campaigns, as well as some that are unique to Alabama and this particular contest. These elements included dedicated and concerned office seekers, political opportunists, policy debates between powerful sets of interests holding strongly opposing views concerning what Alabama and its government should be like, candidate name-calling, personal scandals, stolen documents, legal challenges and hearings, and charges of a biased press.

Interesting as all of these events were, there was a more important outcome to the election than simply a rollicking good political story. The 1986 campaign for governor brought profound changes in Alabama's state politics. Before 1986, Democrats thoroughly controlled Alabama's state government; no Republican had been elected governor in more than a century. Other state constitutional offices, such as the state's lieutenant governor or attorney general, had also remained in Democratic hands since the end of Reconstruction. Entering 1986, the GOP held only about 10 percent of the seats in Alabama's state legislature. A spring 1986 survey of the state's population found that Democrats outnumbered Republicans by 43 to 27 percent.[2]

The 1986 election ended the solid Democratic control over Alabama's state politics. Since then the GOP has won four of the state's last five gubernatorial elections. During this same period, a Republican has been elected at least once to each state constitutional office. While still a minority, Republicans have gained considerable strength in the state legislature, currently holding more than one-third of the seats. Our latest reading (spring 2005) of party identification shows an even balance between Democrats (38 percent) and Republicans (38 percent) within Alabama.[3]

These two decades of GOP victories do not mean that Republicans now dominate the state. In fact, both parties have won recent statewide elections. The margin of victory in most of these contests has also been quite narrow. Rather, the 1986 election marks the beginning of a period of closely balanced partisan politics in Alabama. As a result, since 1986 Alabama's state elections have been more closely and consistently contested than they have been at any other time during the last century and perhaps at any other time in the state's history.

Since the completion of the election, we have often thought about the intriguing questions raised by the 1986 campaign. Why was the campaign conducted the way it was? Why did this type of contest occur when it did? Why did the election have such a large impact on Alabama's partisan politics? Given the rarity of such interesting and important elections, finding answers to these questions about the 1986 campaign should increase understanding of both Alabama's politics and the more general topic of political change.

The first goal of this book is to tell the story of the 1986 election—a truly intriguing political tale. The second, more important goal is to provide at least partial answers to the questions raised by the Alabama's 1986 election for governor. The result of our analysis, in short, suggests that the conduct, outcome, and impact of the 1986 election was the product of a confluence of regionwide forces that undermined the Solid South, the political vacuum created by Wallace's retirement, and the emergence of a viable alternative to continued Democratic control. Thus, our analysis argues, significant partisan political change requires not only the presence of resources encouraging the undermining of established conditions but also an opportunity for these resources to come into play, and, finally, the availability of a viable alternative to the status quo.

We first became involved, sometimes more closely than we wished, in the 1986 election through the positions we then held as co-directors of the University of Alabama's Capstone Poll. During 1985 and 1986 the Capstone Poll was commissioned by the *Birmingham News* to conduct a series of surveys concerning the election. As the events of the campaign unfolded, the number of surveys we conducted grew, and we eventually completed eleven election-related surveys for the *News*. In addition, during the summer of 1986 we conducted a survey for the *Anniston Star* examining the career and legacy of Alabama's four-time governor, George Wallace.

In telling the story of the 1986 election, and analyzing its outcome, we relied upon the results of these surveys. (Details about the methods used in conducting the surveys are presented in appendix A.) We have also taken advantage of the extensive news coverage given to the 1986 election by Alabama newspapers. In particular, we relied heavily, though not exclusively, upon reports presented in the *Birmingham News* (the state's largest-circulation newspapers), the *Montgomery Advertiser* (the state's capital city newspaper), and the *Anniston Star* (which, as one of the few family-owned daily newspapers in the state, devoted considerable to covering the gubernatorial election).[4] As we mentioned earlier, we were sometimes close to or present at the events referred to in this book, and we have used those observations as much as possible. Finally, in the years since, we conducted interviews with many of the major participants in the 1986 election.[5]

We hope that we have used the information collected from these various sources to tell the story of the 1986 Alabama gubernatorial election in a manner it deserves. Any shortcomings or errors in this regard are, of course, our responsibility.

As with any project (particularly one extending for almost twenty years), there are many people who contributed to its outcome. Our good friends at the *Birmingham News*, particularly Glenn Stephens, Michele MacDonald, Tom Gordon, and Dave White, afforded us a front-row seat to many of the events of 1986, almost as they were occurring. Their hard work as journalists is apparent in the reports we have used to reconstruct this story, and their keen analysis of the race—and even their part in it—proved invaluable for us. We have many good friends at the University of Alabama without whose support and encouragement this manuscript would not have been produced; they include Ed Mullins, Barbara Chotiner, and Jim Oakley. Sam Fisher, our good friend and colleague at the University of South Alabama, and Kandis Steele, who is now working, teaching, and going to school in Birmingham, deserve special mention and special thanks. Our efforts with the Capstone Poll was greatly aided by the hard work of Annie and Rosa Johnson. Many of the participants in the 1986 election campaign were generous with their time and thoughts, including Bill Baxley, Charles Graddick, Sam Duvall, John Baker, Chris Grimshawe, Tom Coker, Paul Hubbert, and Jack Drake.

Mike Marshall, editor of the *Mobile Register,* was kind enough to grant permission to use many of the photographs of the campaign included in this book.

Joseph Aistrup and Anne Permaloff reviewed this manuscript as it was being considered for publication by the University of Alabama, and we found their comments insightful and consistently helpful. We thank them both for the close reading they gave the manuscript for helping us make it better.

Finally, our wives, Barbara Cotter and Sally Stovall, and the other members of our families, Ed Cotter, Anna Cotter, and Jefferson Stovall, are the real unsung heroes of this book.

After Wallace

1
The Dominance of George Wallace

To talk about Alabama politics during the second half of the last century is to talk about George Wallace. He dominated the political arena of the state for almost three decades, holding an almost mystical grip on a substantial portion of the state's electorate.

For those who opposed him, Wallace represented the dark side of American politics—a demagogue who played on the people's fears and prejudices with simple answers to complex problems. He symbolized southern resistance to integration, vowing "Segregation forever!" in his 1962 inaugural speech, standing in the schoolhouse door at the University of Alabama in 1963, and failing to protect marchers in Selma from the onslaught of state troopers in 1965.

For many others throughout the state and nation, Wallace was the little man who stood against the encroachment of the federal government and who voiced their frustrations at the "pointy-headed bureaucrats" and "limousine liberals."

No matter how he was viewed, Wallace actively participated in the turbulence of American politics in the 1960s and early 1970s, and as much as any other politician, he symbolized the violence to which it succumbed. The most lasting image of Wallace has him lying in a parking lot in Laurel, Maryland, the victim of an assassin's bullet, another of America's political leaders cut down by a random insanity that stalked the nation.

Often forgotten in these varying images is the fact that George Wallace was first and finally an Alabamian. Wallace never forgot this fact. For all of his activity on the national scene, he always tended the political fences at home and maintained a dominance in state politics that ensured his survival. In fact, while his national image may have remained unchanged, his ability to shift with the changing Alabama electorate demonstrated his extraordinary acumen as a politician.

Beginnings of a Political Reign

George Corley Wallace was born on August 25, 1919, in Clio, Alabama, a small farming community in southern Alabama's Barbour County.[1] Politically, the Alabama into which Wallace was born was solidly Democratic. As every student of the region's history knows, in the years following the Civil War, Reconstruction, and the decline of the Populist Party, each of the southern states developed a one-party, solidly Democratic electoral system. Election laws that disenfranchised large segments of the population, particularly black citizens, and social taboos against supporting Republicans, the party of Lincoln, Emancipation, and Reconstruction aided in both the development and maintenance of this one-party politics.

During the era of the Solid South, Democratic candidates throughout most of the region repeatedly won elections at all levels of government by large margins, often with little opposition. This was certainly the case in Alabama. Between 1922 and 1954, no Republican candidate for governor in Alabama gathered more than 27 percent of the vote. No Republican was elected to Congress from Alabama during this period. Nor did Republicans ever hold more than a handful of seats in the state legislature.[2]

V. O. Key described the electoral politics of Alabama during the period of the Solid South as featuring a considerable degree of multifactionalism, personalism, and disorganization. "Alabama has not been dominated over a long period by a single well-disciplined machine," Key reported. "Nor have there been in recent years well-organized competing machines. Political factions form and reform. Leadership in statewide politics tends to be transient. New statewide leaders emerge, rise to power, and disappear as others take their place. Voters group themselves in one faction and then in another in the most confusing fashion." Overall, Key concluded, the state's "political process appears as a free-for-all, with every man looking out for himself."[3]

However, Key also noted that occasionally the state's disorganized politics would transform itself into a rough form of bifactionalism. When this occurred, the state's electoral politics involved intense conflict between the progressive and agrarian interests of northern and southeastern Alabama against a coalition of more conservative Black Belt planters and "Big Mule" industrialists and financiers of Birmingham and Mobile.[4] Two parallel lines divided the progressives from conservatives in this alignment. Conservatives were staunch supporters of racial segregation and opponents of active government, especially when it came to questions of government services and the taxes needed to pay for them. Progressives, while generally not pro-integration, were less concerned about segregation and more in favor of active government and its ability to provide services such as good schools, health care, and roads benefiting the common citizen. As conditions and candidates changed, followers of one side of this semi-organized conflict would replace supporters of the other side in office.

In the years immediately after World War II, Big Jim Folsom best personified the progressive tradition of Alabama politics. Folsom was the state's governor from 1946 to 1950 and from 1954 to 1958. He called himself the "little man's big friend" and sought to marshal the forces of government to help lower-income groups. His personality and programs engendered fierce loyalty to him as a politician—a loyalty that was eventually overcome by his weakness for alcohol and his less than staunch segregationist stands.[5]

As Wallace began his political career, he clearly positioned himself within the progressive tradition of Alabama politics. His grandfather was a prominent physician, but his family was not prosperous. Throughout his career, Wallace made good use of his humble beginnings. He soon recognized the advantage of remaining on the side of the "underdogs" and the "outs." He refused to join a fraternity when he attended the University of Alabama, and he remained a noncommissioned officer when he was in the army. He was an assistant state attorney general, state representative, and circuit judge in the 1940s and 1950s.

He made his first run for governor in 1958. The campaign involved the usual list of state issues such a funding for education, industrial development, health care, and state pensions. What was somewhat new to the campaign agenda in 1958 was the issue of race. For the previous half-century in Alabama and throughout the South, serious candidates had uniformly expressed support for racial segregation and the maintenance of white supremacy. What campaign debate was generated by the race issue during this period concerned which candidate was most likely to maintain and reinforce the status quo of segregation.

The politics of race, however, had changed by the beginning of the 1958 campaign. The U.S. Supreme Court's *Brown* decision outlawing racial segregation in public schools encouraged efforts to integrate the University of Alabama.[6] The Montgomery bus boycott in 1955 had brought the issue home to Alabama, and the passage of the 1957 Civil Rights Act and the crisis over school integration in Little Rock, Arkansas, also altered political calculations concerning race.[7]

In the midst of this shift in the political winds, a new way of running for office was beginning to emerge. Big Jim Folsom's campaigns transformed the way Alabama candidates sought votes. Instead of the traditional methods of traveling from county courthouse to courthouse asking for support from local political leaders, Folsom organized rallies in towns throughout the state where he could speak directly to voters. These came about with the help of "new" technology in the form of reliable cars, paved roads, and improved sound systems. To attract crowds to these rallies, Folsom provided not only political talk but entertainment in the form of country-and-western music.

Other candidates, including Wallace, quickly copied Folsom's campaign techniques. Wallace began his 1958 campaign with a rally in Ozark, Alabama, a small town near his home.[8] The weather was so cold and wintry that one of the entertainers, Minnie Pearl, wore long underwear under her dress. Miss Cornelia Ellis, Jim Folsom's niece and a future Mrs. George Wallace, was also in attendance. She offered to sing a song she had composed but was not allowed to because she was not a member of the appropriate union.

The cold weather also forced Wallace to shorten his campaign kickoff speech. Still, he managed to outline several themes that he would continue to promote through many of his political campaigns. First, like each of the thirteen other Democratic candidates who entered the contest, Wallace said he would maintain segregation.[9] What was different in this campaign was the style Wallace said he would use to maintain segregation. Unlike in his later campaigns, Wallace called for moderation and conciliation. He said he would maintain segregation "without violence or ill will." Further, he asserted, "with fairness, dignity and firmness, we can preserve our way of life." Finally, "we must never resort to maliciousness, violence or ill will—that will only compound our problems," he said.

A second theme was states' rights and the increasing intrusiveness of the national government. Speaking of the Civil Rights Commission's efforts regarding voting rights, Wallace told the crowd, "You have enough good and honest people right here in Ozark to decide on matters such as that and you sure don't have to rely on any imported federal and district judges."

Wallace presented himself as the candidate of the average citizen. He promised help to Alabamians in areas such as roads, schools, pensions, and jobs. Later in the campaign he said that if elected he would champion the cause of the "little income people."[10]

Wallace lost this initial bid for the governorship to Attorney General John Patterson. Contemporary accounts of the campaign suggest that a number of issues were important to voters during the primary and runoff campaigns.[11] These included:

- The public's unhappiness with the Folsom administration. Wallace was a former campaign and legislative leader for Folsom, while Patterson had investigated corruption charges against members of the Folsom administration.
- Crime. Patterson had become attorney general in the aftermath of his father's assassination by gangsters in his hometown of Phenix City.
- Race. During the runoff campaign, newspapers reported that the Ku Klux Klan supported Patterson.

Most post-election analysis suggests that of these issues, race was by far the most important. After the votes were counted, Wallace is reported to have sworn that he would never be defeated on the race issue again.[12]

Four years later, Wallace ran again and this time was elected governor, leading the field of seven candidates in the primary, and then defeating state senator Ryan DeGraffenreid in a runoff. In the four years between 1958 and 1962, Wallace's positions did not change, but his political style did. Wallace promised to stand in the "school house door" to prevent the integration of the state's schools. Further, he declared that "As governor of your state I will stand strong for segregation. Some people say you are too strong, but how can you be too strong in what you believe? There is no middle of the road. You are either for it or against it."[13]

Regarding the national government, Wallace said, "We have the sorriest federal court system in the world. They're telling us who we're going to live with, who we're going to swim with, who we're going to play with, who we're going to eat with. They're trying to run the country by their own rules and I'm sick and tired of it, and I'm sure you are too."[14]

In looking out for common citizens, Wallace said he would do more in education and pensions. He would also stop wasteful spending by the state government. To illustrate this concern, he said that if elected he would sell the state yacht, which was now being used by "big shots" "with high connections, who ate thick steaks, drank free liquor" and were "taken for free rides in the moonlight."[15]

Turmoil, Fame, and Republicans

During Wallace's term, the civil rights movement not only brought turmoil to Alabama but also brought the news media. Wallace quickly became a nationally recognized figure as a segregationist and launched a brief but highly effective bid for the 1964 Democratic presidential nomination. Before withdrawing he received 34 percent of the vote in the Wisconsin primary, 30 percent in the Indiana primary, and 42 percent in the Maryland presidential preference primary.[16]

Back home, the Alabama constitution prevented Wallace from succeeding himself, and he was unable to persuade the Alabama senate to allow a referendum to change this provision. Ryan DeGraffenreid's death in an airplane crash in early 1966, however, created a political vacuum within the state. Wallace soon moved to fill this opening, presenting his wife, Lurleen, as a candidate for governor.

Testifying to Wallace's popularity in the state, Mrs. Wallace won a majority of the vote in the Democratic primary, despite the presence of nine other candidates. Unlike in earlier years, however, the campaign did not end with the primary. Instead, for the first time in decades, the state's Republicans seriously contested the gubernatorial election. The GOP's candidate, Jim Martin, had almost defeated veteran U.S. senator Lister Hill in 1962, and then had won one of the state's congressional positions in the 1964 Goldwater landslide.

The presence of a potentially serious Republican gubernatorial candidate reflected the political changes that were occurring throughout the region, including Alabama. In particular, at the national level, the era of the Solid Democratic South was ending. In his two campaigns, Dwight Eisenhower easily exceeded the vote received in Alabama by most previous Republican presidential candidates, winning about 35 percent in 1952 and about 39 percent in 1956. Richard Nixon did even better in 1960, receiving about 42 percent in his race against John Kennedy. In the 1964 election, Barry Goldwater carried the state for the GOP, winning almost 70 percent of Alabama's vote.

Similarly, in congressional elections Republicans won three of the state's eight congressional seats in 1964 (in 1986 they still held two of these seats). In 1980 the Republicans elected their first U.S. senator, Jeremiah Denton, from the state in more than one hundred years. (As we will see, Denton's reelection bid became part of the story of the 1986 gubernatorial contest.)

A Shift in the Electorate

Not only was the partisan outcome of Alabama's presidential and congressional elections changing, but so was the size and makeup of its electorate. The 1965 Voting Rights Act and a number of other actions occurring in the

1950s and 1960s removed many of the barriers to voting in Alabama. As a consequence, the percentage of African Americans registered to vote within the state soared. Many white Alabamians also took advantage of the new requirements. Altogether, turnout rates, as percentages of the voting-age population, in Alabama elections about doubled between elections conducted before and after the Voting Rights Act.[17]

Accompanying these electoral changes was a shift in the position of race as an issue in Alabama politics. As noted earlier, in the days of the Solid South, candidates pledging their unqualified support for segregation and white supremacy were a common feature of Alabama elections. However, with the passage of the Voting Rights Act and the resulting massive increase in the number of African-American voters, the politics of the race issue changed. No longer did any serious candidate campaign as a defender of racial segregation.[18] Instead, many office seekers openly began to seek the support of the growing black electorate. This was particularly true of Democratic candidates. The reason for this was that once they entered the electorate in large numbers, African Americans became an important and loyal element within the state's Democratic Party. A spring 1986 University of Alabama survey, for example, found that about 85 percent of black citizens in the state were Democrats, while only 6 percent identified themselves as Republicans. (That survey found a more even distribution of party identification among whites. About 35 percent of white citizens said that they were Democrats, while 30 percent identified themselves as Republicans.)

The disappearance of segregationist candidates did not mean that race had become a non-issue. Instead, at least according to some observers, race remained a central, if not the central, issue in state and national politics, but one that was often spoken of indirectly. In particular, it is argued, racial opinions affected the views of white voters on a number of apparently nonracial issues such as crime, taxes, or states' rights.[19] Talking about such issues is, in the minds of many white voters, really a discussion of race. Thus, according to this view, a politician's promise to "get tough on crime" is seen by many voters as a pledge to protect the social, economic, and political position of whites.

Wallace, campaigning alongside his wife, spent much of both the 1966 primary and general election campaigns portraying himself as the representative of the state's citizens. At one campaign stop he declared, "the mob of liberal beatnicks who are running this country are afraid of the Alabama movement." Further, he stated, "They don't think we in Alabama have got enough sense to go to bed at night without somebody in Washington telling us when to go and when to get up."[20] Wallace also spent considerable time attacking the national government and national politics. One report of a Wallace campaign rally held late in the campaign noted that in his speech the governor had managed to attack "both national political parties, the Supreme Court, the Department of Health, Education and Welfare, the attorney general, some 10 to 15 U.S. Senators, a sprinkling of governors and this newspaper."[21]

Because of the altered the racial makeup Alabama's electorate, Wallace no longer presented himself as a segregationist; indeed, little time was spent taking directly about race or civil rights. Nor did he spend much effort responding to Martin's campaign, a tactic clearly justified when Mrs. Wallace won well over 60 percent of the vote on election day. Martin's defeat in 1966 was a serious blow to the state's Republican Party. It showed that, despite the changes occurring at the national level, Alabama's state politics remained solidly Democratic. Not until 1982 did the GOP again make any serious, and again unsuccessful, effort in a state-level election.

Run for the Presidency

The 1966 victory gave Wallace a base from which he began the American Independent Party in 1968. He succeeded in the daunting task of getting his name on the ballot in all fifty states, and he raised enough money to conduct a viable campaign. Despite these impressive efforts, Wallace ultimately received only 9 percent of the popular vote, and he did not succeed in deadlocking the electoral balloting as he had hoped.

Wallace's success came from his ability to articulate the anger of Americans who felt the government was paying too much attention to the rich and the poor and not enough to them. His "Not a Dime's Worth of Difference" theme highlighted the feeling among his adherents that neither the Republicans nor the Democrats offered much relief to the alienated middle class. Wallace's central message of the campaign is well illustrated by a line from one of his television advertisements—a line he used again and again in his speeches: "The big bureaucrats in Washington never ask a good cab driver what he thinks—they only ask a pointy-headed intellectual who can't park a bicycle straight—people who write guidelines for your children."

In the midst of his presidential bid in 1968, Wallace suffered a political and personal tragedy. His wife, Lurleen, died of cancer, and when the presidential election was over, Wallace found himself without a political resting place. He immediately set about regaining his old job as governor from Governor Albert Brewer, who as lieutenant governor had succeeded Mrs. Wallace.

Many believe that the 1970 gubernatorial campaign was the dirtiest in Alabama's history. It did not, however, begin that way. Indeed, in many ways Wallace's actions in the primary were simply continuations of the themes and images he had pushed during his presidential campaign. For example, he kept up his attack on the "country-club crowd, Harvard graduates, and people with long hair," as well as the courts and the national Democratic Party.[22] Similarly, he told the state's voters that national forces, like big newspapers, monied interests, top Republicans, and Hubert Humphrey Democrats were against him because "I represent you, it's you they want to shut up."[23] He also told voters to ignore his critics. "You don't have to worry about your image like the *Birmingham News* and *Post-Herald* editors say, who drink tea at the Mountain Brook Country Club with their little finger stuck out."[24]

When the primary votes were counted, Wallace unexpectedly found himself trailing. As a result, he adopted a new strategy, one that involved reviving the race issue. Wallace began talking about the black "bloc" vote. "I don't think the people of Alabama are going to allow a bloc vote to name their governor," he proclaimed.[25] Later he said that if he lost, the "bloc vote will control politics in Alabama for the next 50 years."[26] With these appeals, and the registration of some forty thousand voters between the primary and runoff election (ironically aided by the 1965 Voting Rights Act, which he had opposed), Wallace won a narrow victory over Brewer in the runoff. However, by reverting to a southern segregationist position, he employed tactics that were costly to his national ambitions.

Still, in his campaigns Wallace had demonstrated that he could communicate with voters not only in the state but also in many parts of the nation, and he remained an articulate spokesman for their concerns. With his state base secure, he began another run for the presidency in 1972, this time forsaking the independent party that he had formed and trying instead for the Democratic nomination.

Wallace found that voters still responded to his slashing message about the inabilities and inappropriateness of the federal government's involvement in social programs. He continued to voice the frustrations of those who felt that government at all levels was not doing what it could or should to maintain a peaceful and orderly society. By this time, Wallace had deleted the overtly racist rhetoric that had characterized his early days as governor and instead talked about the concerns of "farmers, small shopkeepers, cab drivers, beauticians, average citizens" in his advertisements.

As in 1968, Wallace found many willing listeners. In Florida he made school busing the most important issue of the 1972 presidential primary campaign and won a clear victory there in March. Next came strong second-place finishes in Wisconsin, Pennsylvania, and Indiana, followed by outright victories in Tennessee and North Carolina. In this campaign Wallace was asking the voters to "send them a message," and that's what many of the voters were doing.

On May 15, one day before the Maryland and Michigan primaries, Wallace was campaigning in the Washington, D.C., suburb of Laurel, Maryland, when Arthur Bremmer, a deranged drifter from Milwaukee, fired five shots from a handgun at him. One bullet pierced Wallace's stomach and lodged in his spine, putting his life in immediate danger and ultimately rendering him a paraplegic.

Wallace won remarkable victories in Maryland and Michigan the next day, but his race was over. He could no longer persuade voters of his viability as a candidate, and his campaign dried up. Wallace retreated to his home state to do what he could to restore his health and regain his national standing.

Back in Alabama, Wallace was still governor and looking forward to a reelection race in 1974 (by this time, the laws had been changed in Alabama to allow a governor two successive terms). His image as a wounded spokesman for the state's citizens made him politically untouchable. Thus for the first time he entered (and ended) a campaign with little opposition.

In 1976 he briefly ran again for the presidency. His health problems and the candidacy of fellow southerner Jimmy Carter convinced him that his days of directly influencing presidential politics had passed.

In 1978 Wallace was constitutionally barred from seeking a third consecutive term as governor. In May, however, he abruptly announced that he would not run for the U.S. Senate.[27] It was unclear if this meant the end of Wallace's career. "I didn't say I was retiring from politics, and I didn't say I wasn't. I just said I wasn't going to run for the United States Senate," Wallace said.[28] Later he told a gathering of state legislators, "I'm not going to say 'never, never' because you paint yourself in a corner that way." Still, he added, "I suppose my political career is over."[29]

2

Wallace's Final Exit

In 1978 it was hard to imagine Alabama politics without George Wallace—and few people tried. Since the assassination attempt in 1972, Wallace had lost much of his physical ability to appear as a dynamic political force. No longer could he strut around a stage, making fun of his absent opponents. His voice had lost some of his sharpness, and his zingers did not sting as badly as they once did. His attempts to be a national political force had faded with the rise of Jimmy Carter in 1976.

Still, Wallace had proved himself to be remarkably resilient in Alabama, and no one could doubt his power to communicate a clear and precise message and his ability to gather votes. His reluctance to chart a clear political course gave many state politicians pause. No one with ambitions to higher office in the state wanted—without a great deal of planning and thought—to be on the side opposing George Wallace.

So, in 1978 politicians in Alabama had a degree of freedom that they had never experienced before. George Wallace would not be running for governor, though he still might return at some future point. With that degree of freedom available, the 1978 Democratic primary contest to succeed George Wallace attracted a large field of candidates. The two who emerged from the crowded primary field to compete in the runoff were Bill Baxley and Fob James.

Bill Baxley

Baxley was the boy wonder of Alabama politics.[1] Despite his age—he was thirty-seven in 1978—Baxley had long been involved in politics. The son of a judge, he had helped in his father's political campaigns, and his political involvement continued during his undergraduate days at the University of Alabama in Tuscaloosa and later during his time at the university's law school.

He first attracted statewide attention when he became the nation's youngest district attorney, appointed to that position in 1966 at the age of twenty-five by George Wallace. In 1970 he ran for attorney general and defeated the incumbent, McDonald Gallion, who had won the office just four years before with the largest majority in the state's history.

At thirty-one, Baxley was still the youngest attorney general in the nation. He put together an exceptionally well-qualified staff, including both female and black attorneys. His performance in this office proved him to be an aggressive pursuer of civil rights offenders (successfully prosecuting one of the people responsible for the 1963 bombing of a African-American church in Birmingham that resulted in several deaths), environmental polluters, and corrupt government officials.

Baxley developed the image of an intelligent and able politician, but his personal life caused him major problems. Some of his characteristics, while peculiar, had little political impact. For example, Baxley is such a baseball fan that he has taken time in the middle of an election campaign to attend the World Series. But stories of his drinking, gambling, and connections with less-than-reputable businessmen did have their effect both in 1978 and later. Baxley's reputation was like a magnet—everything stuck to it. His early years in Montgomery found him young and single and often in the company of people not known for regular church attendance. Baxley's sandpaper-like personality never allowed for a softening of this image, even though his two terms as attorney general were considered effective and progressive.

Hailing from the Wiregrass section of the state, Baxley was a part of the progressive tradition in Alabama politics. Indeed, later, during the 1986 campaign, this connection became explicit. Then he would tell a group in his hometown of Dothan, "Two of the great governors of this state reached back to the average person—Jim Folsom and George Wallace. I don't agree with everything they did, but if I had to pick two governors I would be similar to, it would be those two. They grew up around here. They believe the obligation of state government ought to be to help the average person of this state. It should make life a little better for the average person who doesn't have a lobbyist in Montgomery."[2]

Fob James

Fob James, a Lee County native, entered the 1978 Democratic primary race as an outsider to both the Democratic Party and Alabama politics.[3] The son of a high school football coach and himself an All-American running back for Auburn University, James graduated with a civil engineering degree. In 1971 he formed Diversified Products Corporation, a manufacturer of sports equipment, particularly plastic-coated barbells. The success of this business soon made James a millionaire.

Until shortly before he announced his candidacy for the Democratic gubernatorial nomination, James was a member of the Republican Party's State Executive Committee. By the late 1970s the GOP had gained some strength within Alabama, but in its state politics Alabama remained a strongly Democratic state. Thus, like other ambitious office seekers, James realized that he needed to run as a Democrat if he was serious about winning.

In his 1978 campaign, James preached the virtues of fiscal restraint and the need to run the state government like a business. In order to emphasize his interest in education, he toured the state in a yellow school bus (the "Readin' Ritin' and 'Rithmatic Special") and poured a considerable amount of money into what was perhaps Alabama's first modern media campaign. James portrayed himself as an outsider to state government and politics. By adopting this position, he, like many other candidates, was appealing to voters on the basis of another long-standing tradition in Alabama politics: a Jacksonian/populist belief in democracy and opposition to interests or institutions interfering with popular rule.

In his midcentury analysis of Alabama politics, V. O. Key looked at the state's voters and saw "a sort of frontier independence, with an inclination to bait the interests." And in Alabama's case, the "interests" also could include the state legislature. Key notes the case of Julian Hall, editor of the *Dothan Eagle*, who once urged his readers to arm themselves "with shillelaghs, set out for Montgomery, and whale hell out of members of the state legislature."[4] Though not always expressed in such vivid terms, these same dispositions were still present in the 1980s in the form of low levels of trust in state government[5] and negative evaluations of the performance of state government institutions.[6]

In the 1978 runoff election, James won with 55 percent of the vote. Then, after, in an almost invisible general election campaign, James won the governorship by easily defeating, by a margin of 73 to 27 percent, the Republican candidate, Cullman County farmer and businessman Guy Hunt.

The 1978 election for other state offices was no kinder to Republicans. Each of the constitutional positions such as attorney general or secretary of state remained in Democratic hands. Democrats also continued to hold more than 95 percent of the seats in the state legislature.

Later, in a little-noticed action, the Democratic Party in 1979 adopted a rule that a person who voted in a Republican primary election could not "crossover" and vote in the Democratic runoff during the same year.[7] Little was noted in the press about this change. The absence of a statewide GOP primary contest in 1982 and the fact that Republican voters did not influence the outcome of the Democratic nomination contest meant this rule attracted little attention until 1986.[8]

After his defeat, Baxley moved to Birmingham and developed a successful practice as a trial lawyer. In 1982, after considering another gubernatorial campaign, he chose to run for lieutenant governor rather than possibly facing George Wallace. Baxley was elected easily.

Guy Hunt, the Republican gubernatorial nominee, returned to political oblivion. He reemerged in 1980 to head Ronald Reagan's presidential campaign in Alabama and in 1981 was appointed by Reagan to head the state's Agricultural Stabilization and Conservation Service.[9]

George McMillan and Charles Graddick

In 1978 two other politicians who would compete for governor eight years later won their first statewide campaigns. George McMillan, a Birmingham attorney and state senator, was elected lieutenant governor, and Charles Graddick won the post of attorney general.

McMillan grew up in southeastern Alabama.[10] His father was a county extension agent, and not surprisingly, McMillan attended Auburn University, the state's land grant college. There he was elected president of the Student Government Association. Following graduation from the University of Virginia Law School and a clerkship with a federal judge, McMillan opened his own law firm in Birmingham. In 1973 he was elected to the Alabama House of Representatives and a year later won an open seat in the state senate. In his 1978 campaign, McMillan projected the image of an intense, competent, and progressive leader as well as someone who had an abundance of political ambition.

Graddick, a native of Mobile, came from a solidly middle class, but not very political, background.[11] A good high school athlete and at one time a singer in a local rock band, Graddick attended the University of Alabama and Cumberland Law School. After a clerkship with an Alabama Supreme Court justice, Graddick became an assistant to the Republican Mobile County district attorney, Charles Butler, in 1971. In 1974 Butler promised to help Graddick succeed him if he would run as a Republican. Shortly after his successful campaign, Graddick switched to the Democratic

Party. This was the first evidence of Graddick's tenuous allegiance to the party, and Graddick never made any real effort to change the impression that he was only nominally a Democrat.

In 1978 Graddick ran for attorney general on an extremely tough anti-crime platform. Indeed, his outspoken support for the death penalty earned him the nickname "Charcoal Charlie." This outspokenness on emotional issues helped created an image—particularly among his enemies—of being an opportunist and demagogue. Graddick gained a reputation for having more convictions than ideas.

Graddick remained visible throughout his two terms as attorney general, often as a result of highly publicized prosecutions of "welfare cheats." He continued his tough anti-crime campaign by helping to draft the state's death penalty law, favoring the passage of a habitual offenders act that mandated sentences for those convicted of crimes several times, and opposing the state prison system's work-release program. His lack of initiative in pursuing white-collar criminals, along with his proclivity to ignore possible violations of the state ethics law, and his acceptance of two pay raises (later ruled unconstitutional) also produced many critics of his administration. His reelection in 1982 was unopposed, however.

The James Administration

Fob James's term as governor proved to be highly controversial. He showed little skill in working with the state legislature and in building the coalitions to help pass his programs. Despite a vow to improve education and to declare a "war on illiteracy," James presided over continuing funding shortfalls for the state's education system. He was forced to ask for an increase in the state's already high gasoline tax to finance road maintenance and construction. The nation's recession in the early 1980s hit Alabama particularly hard, and the state's unemployment rate climbed toward 15 percent, rivaling that of states in the North and Midwest. At one time he inadvertently pocket vetoed a set of anti-crime bills that he had proposed to a special session of the legislature.

During his last two years in office (no data are available for the first two), James's job performance ratings by the public remained exceptionally low. Typically, only about a quarter to a third of the public said he was doing an "excellent" or "good" job. Many more said he was doing a "fair" or "poor" job (table 2.1). In response to both a campaign pledge and his low level of public support, James did not seek reelection in 1982. His poor performance,

Table 2.1

Evaluations of Fob James as governor, 1980–1982

"How would you rate the job that Fob James is doing as governor—excellent, good, fair or poor?"

	Fall 1980	Spring 1981	Fall 1981	Spring 1982	Fall 1982
Excellent	4%	5%	3%	6%	4%
Good	25	19	22	21	16
Fair	41	37	41	42	34
Poor	25	34	31	26	41
Don't know/No answer	5	5	3	4	5
N	670	552	494	523	511

Source: Capstone Poll 02, 08, 13, 23, 45

however, set the stage for an event that seemed highly unlikely in 1978—the return of Alabama's political legend, George Wallace.

Wallace's Comeback

After he announced in early 1978 that he would not run for the U.S. Senate, George Wallace settled himself into a dignified retirement, living in Montgomery and working as a consultant for the University of Alabama in Birmingham, and speaking and appearing often on behalf of the handicapped. His four years out of office helped him regain some of his deteriorating health, but it also gave him the opportunity to reexamine the political landscape. Blacks, he found, were an even larger part of the electorate, but Wallace discovered—or knew innately—something about blacks in the 1980s that he had found out about union members in the 1960s. They don't always follow their leaders, especially the self-appointed leaders.

Wallace also had some luck on his side. His successor as governor, Fob James, had emerged from a political forest in 1978 with a massive and effective television advertising campaign. His new face appealed to those who had been looking toward the post-Wallace era and who were dissatisfied with the field of old-line politicians who had announced for governor. But James found that getting elected and being governor were different things. As governor James failed at many things, but possibly his most notable failure was his inability to establish himself as a strong, continuing political force—one who could effectively block the return of the Wallace era.

As the 1982 campaign began, public-opinion survey results showed that Wallace was in a strong position to mount a campaign, but they did not show him to be a certain winner.[12] Still, it was uncertain whether he would again run for office. Some believed that the potential for defeat would keep him out of the race; on the other hand, few of the state's politicians relished challenging him in a race for governor. Wallace kept his potential opponents at bay until early in 1982 when he announced that he would be a candidate for governor.[13]

In the Democratic primary, Wallace faced two major opponents, the conservative speaker of the state house of representatives, Joe McCorquodale, and the state's more progressive lieutenant governor, George McMillan. Alabama Republicans also decided it was time to mount a serious challenge for the governorship. Their candidate was Montgomery mayor Emory Folmar.

McCorquodale had been a longtime ally of Wallace.[14] He had labored quietly in the legislative vineyards for many years, and he entered the race without much going for him. His name recognition was low, he had a difficult name to pronounce and spell, and he had little flair for the media campaign that politicians of the 1980s were required to run. McCorquodale failed to ignite many followers and finished in third place. Later that year he burned many of his political bridges by endorsing the GOP's Emory Folmar.[15]

George McMillan entered the race with many of the same public-opinion numbers as McCorquodale. Few people recognized him, there were more people who thought negatively than positively of him, and most people had no opinion at all about him. McMillan, however, had won a statewide election in 1978 and was not identified with the Wallace faction of Alabama politics. He also was young and presented a fairly vigorous image. On the campaign hustling, however, McMillan proved to be much less effective than he first appeared. His rapid-fire and seemingly ceaseless speaking style, with a confusing syntax and a sometimes high-pitched voice, irritated audiences and opened him up to imitation and ridicule. He delivered long, drawn-out explanations of his positions and attacked his opponents with less than memorable phrases. Always well dressed and standing straight to his six-foot-plus height, he never seemed at ease with his audiences.[16]

Emory Folmar was the first Republican in more than a decade to be a serious challenger for governor.[17] A tough, conservative businessman and Korean War veteran, he had become known for his stand against crime. As the "pistol-packing" mayor of Montgomery, Folmar *had* also demonstrated that concerns for the civil liberties of minorities or others would not deter him. As a result, Folmar, to an extent greater than most politicians, had both his defenders and his opponents.

In his campaigning, Wallace showed signs of both a new and the old Wallace. The race issue was an area where Wallace had most clearly changed. Here, he sought to explain his past. "Our actions," he said, "in being anti-big government were translated into being racist."[18] He also sought reconciliation. Speaking to a meeting of the Alabama Democratic Conference, the state's major black political organization, Wallace said, "I'm not asking forgiveness. Everything I've done has been honest. I've made some mistakes in the past . . . I've been a good governor . . . I'm going to be the governor."[19]

In other areas, Wallace continued to express themes from his previous campaigns. The national government and other "big interests" remained targets. "I'm paralyzed in the legs, but we in Alabama knew way back yonder that the government in Washington was being run by people who were paralyzed in the head."[20] Later, at a rally featuring Tammy Wynette singing "Stand by Your Man," Wallace said that the state's voters supported him because "I have been representative of the average citizen of Alabama. I have not been the voice of the special interests in Birmingham and Montgomery. I didn't let the big-money interests run me."[21]

The main issue of the 1982 campaign was Alabama's economic development, but in Wallace's more succinct terms, it was "Jobs, jobs, jobs." While attacking the special interests and extolling the plight of the underdog, Wallace vowed to bring new industry to the state. He argued that the contacts he had made as a governor and presidential candidate would enable him to persuade new industry to come to the state.

In the final days of the fall campaign, Wallace combined several of these themes as he spoke to campaign crowd. "My friends," he said, "we are in difficult times in the state. Some people are not eating right . . . some can't take care of their children. But we overcame the Depression. You young people remember: you're going to have a bright future no matter how bleak it might seem right now. We shall overcome."[22]

Wallace led McMillan in the primary election with 43 percent of the vote to McMillan's 30; McCorquodale received about 25 percent, with the remainder going to minor candidates. McMillan was behind but within striking distance, and analysts expected a hard-fought campaign.[23]

The anticipated runoff campaign fireworks never occurred, however.[24] Instead, the race was a relatively quiet and low-key affair. On election night, as the votes began to come in, it looked good for McMillan. He was running fairly strong in some Wallace strongholds, and it was expected—even predicted by at least some Birmingham television news analysts—that McMillan would be victorious. Then some of the rural counties with large black populations began to report their vote. They showed that McMillan did not receive the overwhelming majorities for which he had hoped. In fact, Wallace received just enough of those votes to give him an overall 51 to 49 percent edge.[25] Wallace's margin of victory was so narrow that many factors can be identified as reasons for his win, but the one that has been focused on the most was the number of blacks who voted for him. Some estimates have put the black vote for Wallace at 35 to 40 percent.[26]

Following this defeat, McMillan returned to his Birmingham law firm and for the most part remained out of public view for the next two years, though he did keep close contact with his political supporters.

In the general election campaign, Wallace continued his emphasis on jobs. He also claimed that "rich Republicans" were trying to buy the governorship. Folmar ran a well-organized and well-financed campaign. He found Wallace a difficult candidate to run against, since the former governor could not be labeled as either a big spender or as someone who was "soft" on social issues such as crime.

In the election, Wallace received 58 percent of the vote and carried all ten of the state's majority black counties. In nine of these he had a two-to-one margin. Folmar managed to win in only five counties.

Altogether, the 1982 election did little to alter the conclusion that Alabama was, at least at the state level, solidly Democratic. Republicans did pick up a few seats in the state house and senate. Still, following the 1982 election, Democrats held more than 90 percent of the seats in each chamber. Further, the state's GOP had focused almost all of its effort on Folmar's ultimately losing candidacy. As a result, Democrats uniformly won easy, sometimes uncontested victories in races for other state constitutional offices. Democrats also continued to dominate local elections within the state.[27]

Wallace as Governor

The issue Wallace had used in the campaign, economic development, was a real one, and one that people were concerned about. Alabama had suffered double-digit unemployment, shortfalls in state and local government budgets, and a general economic downturn that made it seem more like part of the Rust Belt than the Sun Belt. Wallace took seriously his promise to seek out new industry for the state. He organized trips for himself and other state leaders to Europe and Asia, seeking new investments. In order to attract the General Motors Saturn plant—which eventually located in Tennessee, about fifty miles from the Alabama line—he called the legislature into special session to amend or repeal laws that seemed anti-business. He also took advantage of a turnaround in the economy and offshore oil lease funds to increase funds to schools and other state agencies.

One of the more notable political events of Wallace's administration occurred in 1983. Following the 1980 census, Alabama, like every other state, was required to redraw its state legislative district lines. The state legislature adopted a redistricting plan that was used in the 1982 election. Later, however, a federal judge rejected this plan and ordered that the state hold new legislative elections in 1983. In responding to this order, the state Democratic Party decided not to hold a new round of primary elections. Instead, citing the fact that the last election had been held less than a year earlier, the party's leadership designated the state executive committee to select the Democratic nominee in each house and senate district.

The decision to "hand pick" the party's candidates generated considerable controversy, at least among political insiders, once it became clear that the selection process was being dominated by a coalition of liberal-leaning labor leaders, teachers, trial lawyers, and black interests.[28] Unhappiness about the decision further increased when several incumbent legislators were passed over by the leadership and denied the party's nomination. Some of these officeholders, in turn, entered the race as Independent candidates. Other disgruntled Democrats ran as Republicans.

While some saw the special legislative election as a "fight for the political control of the state," its outcome had little immediate impact on the state's partisan balance.[29] In the election, the GOP picked up less than five new seats. Independent candidates won (one as a write-in candidate) in eight districts. Of these, five were Democratic incumbent officeholders who were denied renomination. Most of the Independents rejoined the Democratic Party. At the end of the special election campaign, Democrats continued to hold an overwhelming majority in each state legislative chamber.

Republicans saw the election outcomes as a sign that the state was entering an era of two-party politics. Democrats, however, reached a different conclusion. They saw the election as an indication that their party's domination over the state was unchanged, and would not change in the near future. Speaking of the election results, Jimmy Knight, the state Democratic chair, said, "I'm tickled to death, just really pleased with the outcome. I'm absolutely convinced that 95 percent of the people in Alabama are pleased with the way the Democratic Party handled the election and the nomination process." He went on to say that the election was a "vindication of the Democratic party and its actions on dealing with the election."[30]

Will He Run Again?

During the last half of 1985 and the early months of 1986, the major political question in the state was, "Will Wallace run again?" That question so dominated the political discussions—particularly among the news media—that no other candidate was able to capture the public agenda with either his issues or his personality. It was not until Wallace formally took himself out of the race in April that public support for other candidates in the field began to harden. In addition, Republicans showed little interest in developing candidates who might want to compete for the governor's chair. At this particular point, they were focused on maintaining the U.S. Senate seat held by Jeremiah Denton.[31]

Wallace, of course, was not unmindful of his position. Ever the canny politician, he allowed speculation about his political future to take on a life of its own, coyly hinting at times that he would not run and at other times that he would like to remain in the governor's mansion. In September he told the press that he might run but it would depend on "what the polls showed." He did not specify which public-opinion polls he would rely on or when that decision would finally be made.[32] As usual, Wallace maintained a great deal of control over events.

One thing Wallace could not control, however, was his health. Paralyzed from the waist down by the assassination attempt in 1972, Wallace had resumed political life in a wheelchair and had been marvelously successful. He had run for governor twice and once for the presidency. Early on, however, he had a nagging series of maladies associated with his paralysis, and people close to him reported that he was never completely free of pain.

Wallace's last term as governor was interrupted six times by a series of highly publicized hospital visits. In 1985 he was away from work for nearly three months because of spinal surgery. The surgery was one of many efforts to relieve some of the pain that he constantly suffered. Wallace's age was causing other problems, most noticeably a deterioration of his hearing. Along with this came problems with his speech, so that he could no longer deliver the fiery addresses for which he was noted. For some time, Wallace had not been able to spend more than a couple of hours a day in his office. By the fall of 1985, the question was not only "Will Wallace run?" but also "Can he campaign?"

Wallace made a career out of focusing the attention of a campaign on himself and in turning that focus to his advantage. The negative feelings he engendered because of his policies and his style were never enough to prevent his election. But with his health now an issue, that was no longer an advantage. In the fall of 1985 and the early part of 1986, Wallace found that he could not divert attention from his health problems, and that inability would cause him major problems in mounting another statewide campaign.

Wallace's ill health raised another consequential question: "Who's in charge?" Except for Billy Joe Camp, who had been a candidate in several elections, none of Wallace's aides was familiar to the public, and none successfully captured and held the limelight during his absences. The Wallace administration gave out little information about how decisions were made and how the government operated, particularly when Wallace was incapacitated. Those outside the administration complained that it was hard to know who was in charge and who, if anyone, was making decisions when Wallace was not available.

The political effects of Wallace's ill health were first examined in a statewide survey conducted in October 1985. In a hypothetical horse race with his four most likely opponents (Baxley, Graddick, James, and McMillan), Wallace led the field with 26 percent of the electorate; Baxley had 19 percent, Graddick had 15 percent, and James and McMillan had 14 percent (table 2.2). By this count, Wallace was the clear leader. Still, the public was well aware of Wallace's health problems. Nearly half (44 percent) of the October respondents said they thought his health had "a great deal" of an effect on his performance as governor. Close to a third more (32 percent) said Wallace's health had "somewhat" affected his performance as government.

As to the matter of "Who's in charge?" a majority of those interviewed (51 percent) felt that Wallace's assistants, rather than Wallace himself, were making "most of the important decisions involving state government." Thirty-one percent said they thought Wallace was still making most of those decisions.[33]

Despite the health issue, Wallace still controlled much of the state's political environment. He was in about the same position as he had been four years earlier when he was thinking about trying to regain the governor's seat. A run for a fifth term as governor was not out of the question.[34]

Wallace continued to allow speculation about his possible candidacy, and he drew some fire from the other candidates because of it.[35] The possibility of another campaign remained real until January, when two events occurred that revived all the fears about his health. Early in the month, Wallace was

Table 2.2

Democratic gubernatorial race, October 1985 and January 1986

	October 1985	January 1986
Wallace	26%	16%
Baxley	19	21
Graddick	15	15
James	14	17
McMillan	14	13
Other/Don't Know	12	18
N	416	418

Source: Capstone Poll 148, 160
Question wording:

October—"If there was a Democratic Party primary for governor and the candidates were Lieutenant Governor Bill Baxley, Attorney General Charles Graddick, former governor Fob James, former lieutenant governor George McMillan and Governor George Wallace, for whom would you vote?"

January—"If there was a Democratic party primary for governor and the candidates were Lieutenant Governor Bill Baxley, former press secretary Billy Joe Camp, Attorney General Charles Graddick, former governor Fob James, former lieutenant governor George McMillan, and Governor George Wallace, for whom would you vote?"

again hospitalized, suffering from another of the infections that plagued him. The stay was not a long one, but it was just long enough to remind the voters of his condition. The second event was Wallace's State of the State address, which was delivered to the opening session of the legislature later that month. The speech was televised across the state, and it was a glaring demonstration of Wallace's infirmities. The speech was a long, rambling address delivered in soft and slurred tones. The governor obviously had difficulty with it, and it continued to be the subject of speculation for several days afterward.[36]

The effect of these two events on Wallace's public image was immediate and devastating. During the week after the State of the State speech, a survey of 418 registered voters asked many of the same questions about the gubernatorial campaign that had been asked in October. Now, however, the survey showed that Wallace no longer led the field of possible gubernatorial

Table 2.3

Opinions about George Wallace's health, October 1985 and January 1986

"How much do you think that George Wallace's health has affected his performance as governor during the last several years—a great deal, somewhat, not very much or not at all?"

	October 1985	January 1986
A great deal	44%	61%
Somewhat	32	25
Not very much	13	10
Not at all	8	3
Don't know/No answer	3	1
N	416	418

"Do you think that at the present time most of the important decisions involving state government are being made by George Wallace himself or by his assistants?"

	October 1985	January 1986
Wallace himself	31%	21%
Assistants	51	57
Both	9	12
Don't know/No answer	8	10
N	416	418

Source: Capstone Poll 148, 160

candidates. Instead, while technically in third place, Wallace was in reality bunched with James, Graddick, and McMillan. Baxley was now the front-runner (table 2.2).

The reason for this decline in Wallace's support is apparent from the results of two of the health questions that were repeated from the October survey (table 2.3). About 61 percent of the respondents said they believed Wallace's health had "a great deal" of effect on his performance, up from 44 percent who said they believed that in October. Similarly, about 57 percent said they believed Wallace's assistants, rather than Wallace himself, were "making most of the important decisions involving state government." In October only 51 percent said they believed this.

Other results from the survey confirmed a decline in support for Wallace. In October, 43 percent of the respondents said they felt positively toward Wallace, and 30 percent said they felt negatively; in January, 34 percent said they felt positively, and 39 percent negatively.

The January events dealt a serious blow to Wallace's political standing. Late in the month, his longtime ally and current press secretary, Billy Joe Camp, resigned and announced that he was running for governor.[37] Some viewed this move as a signal that Wallace would not run, but Wallace himself continued to drop broad hints. (Eventually, Camp dropped his campaign, finding that he was unable to raise enough support or money to continue his run.)[38] After January, those already in the race felt more confident that Wallace would ultimately bow out.

Two days before the qualifying deadline on April 4, Wallace told a large crowd of supporters and state workers gathered in the chamber of the state house of representatives that he had "climbed my last political mountain." He would not be a candidate for governor again, he said, and after an emotional and rambling speech he bid his friends "a fond and affectionate farewell."

George Wallace, at times the boldest political gambler in the nation, held his last hand as long as he could. He finally folded the cards.

3
The Wallace Legacy

The most remarkable feature of George Wallace's political career was that it lasted as long as it did. For almost thirty years, Wallace was a major factor in each Alabama gubernatorial election. He won the office four times, and his wife was elected to one term. He was also a four-time presidential candidate. When Wallace finally retired, the *New York Times* noted that "his endurance as a political force is such that no voter younger than 50 can recall participating in a gubernatorial election in which George Wallace was not a candidate or, at least, a controlling influence."[1]

Wallace's longevity is remarkable for two reasons. First, before Wallace, no Alabama politician had remained at the center of the state's politics for such an extended period of time. Other southern states, such as Virginia with Harry Byrd, Tennessee with "Boss" Crump, Georgia with Eugene Talmadge, or Louisiana with Huey Long, had experienced politicians who dominated their politics for long periods of time. Such dynasties, however, were absent in Alabama until Wallace.

Second, Wallace persisted and succeeded despite the fact that during his career Alabama experienced substantial and significant demographic, economic, and political changes. In particular, the political system into which Wallace was born and which he first entered as a gubernatorial candidate—the one-party, solidly Democratic South—developed and most effectively operated at a time when the state had a rural, poor, and near racially balanced population and a predominantly agriculture-based economy.[2] Moreover, this one-party system was associated with the adoption and enforcement of restrictive suffrage laws, resulting in a relatively small and socially homogeneous electorate.[3]

During the course of Wallace's career, change occurred in each of these conditions. In particular, while Alabama was still more rural than the nation as a whole, during Wallace's life and political career it changed from an overwhelmingly rural to a predominantly urban state. At the beginning of the 1900s only about one in ten of the state's citizens lived in an urban setting. By midcentury, about the time Wallace made his first bid for governor, slightly less than half (about 43 percent) of the state's citizens lived in an urban area. By 1980, when Wallace won his last term, a majority (about 60 percent) of the state's citizens resided in an urban setting.

Shifting Populations, Demographics

Population shifts within Alabama during the time covered by Wallace's career obviously were not restricted to movements from rural to urban settings. Citizens of all types were also moving into and out of the state. One of the more politically important of these migrations involved African-American citizens leaving Alabama to settle in other parts of the country.[4] This movement significantly changed the racial composition of the state. In 1900, African Americans made up about half (about 45 percent) of the state's population. By 1950 about one-third of the state's citizens were black. By 1980, African Americans constituted about one in four Alabamians.

The "Great Migration" of African Americans from the South affected political considerations throughout the country.[5] Within Alabama, the outmigration of blacks helped to undermine a core argument for the continuation of the Solid South—that the political threat posed by African Americans required racial unity under the banner of the Democratic Party in order to maintain "white supremacy."

Similarly, while Alabama was still an economically poor area, it was far less so in the 1980s than in the years before World War II. In 1929, for example, Alabamians generally were far poorer than other citizens. Per capita income in the state was then was less than half of the national average. By the 1980s the income gap had significantly narrowed. While Alabamians in 1989 were still less wealthy than citizens living elsewhere in the country, their average per capita income was now about 80 percent of the national norm.

Accompanying these demographic and social changes was an alteration of Alabama's traditional agriculture-based economy. In 1920 more than half (about 56 percent) of the state's workforce was employed in agriculture or forestry. By 1950 only about one in four (25 percent) of the state's workers were employed in this industry. In 1980 the agriculture and forestry industry employed only 3 percent of the state's workers. As agriculture declined, an increasing number of Alabamians were employed in manufacturing, professional services, or retail and wholesale trades.

Another change, previously noted, that occurred in Alabama during Wallace's career was an expansion of the state's electorate. In the 1920s and 1930s less than 20 percent of the state's voting-age population generally voted in presidential elections—a figure far below the turnout rates found elsewhere. The lack of politically useful resources, indicated by high levels of poverty and illiteracy found within Alabama during that period, as well as the one-party system itself contributed to the low voting turnout within the state. Also important, however, were the restrictive suffrage laws—in the form of devices such as the poll tax, literacy test, and white primary—operating within the state.[6]

The rising income (and education) levels found in Alabama in the postwar years expanded the number of Alabamians able to participate in politics. Moreover, the civil rights movement encouraged actions such as the outlawing of the white primary, the elimination of a literacy test, and reform and ultimate removal of the poll tax, thereby increasing the opportunity for the state's citizens to become active in politics.[7] As a result, by the 1980s about half of the state's voting-age population was participating in presidential elections.

Much, but certainly not all, of this increased turnout reflects the enfranchisement of African-American voters.[8] In 1952 about 5 percent of Alabama's adult African Americans were registered to vote. By 1964, voter-registration rates among the state's black citizens had increased to 23 percent. This figure more than doubled with the passage of 1965 Voting Rights Act, reaching 51 percent in 1966 and 64 percent in 1970.[9] By the 1980s, voter-registration rates among blacks and whites in Alabama were about equal.[10] Then, about one in four of the state's voters was African American. In sum, during Wallace's political career, not only did the state's electorate grow, but it also became more varied in its makeup.[11]

Altogether, Alabama was quite different at the end of Wallace's career than it was when he first entered statewide politics. It had a more urban, wealthier, and economically varied population, as well as a considerably larger and more heterogeneous electorate. Politically these shifts meant that during the course of Wallace's career the types and relative size of the groups active in state politics changed. Accompanying these changes were alterations in the type of issues and divisions facing state government.

Change and Stability in Alabama's Politics

Despite these changes, and despite the absence of previous durable factions within Alabama, Wallace remained the dominating force within the state's politics for almost three decades. The key to this persistence was his ability, first, to restructure the state's traditional electoral patterns, and second, to continue altering them to fit changing political realities within the state. His success in accomplishing these tasks, in turn, rested on his exceptional political skills.

As noted earlier, V. O. Key described the politics of Alabama during the period of the Solid South as a political "free-for-all" in which there were no long-lasting political factions or leaders. What organization did occur in state politics involved occasional conflicts between economic and civil rights progressives from northern Alabama and the Wiregrass section of the state against a more economically conservative and stronger segregationist coalition involving Black Belt planters and the "Big Mule" allies.[12]

Wallace altered the politics Key described. He began his career clearly positioned within the progressive wing of the state's politics, taking liberal positions on issues like health care and state pensions while staking out a stylistically moderate (by Alabama standards) stance on segregation. He underwent a political evolution, however, following his 1958 defeat. The liberal economic positions remained, but his segregationist credentials were now emphasized. By stylistically placing himself in positions that cut across the state's previously parallel progressive-conservative division, Wallace broadened his appeal to voters, particularly when combined with his skill of identifying which dimension was most salient at any given time. As a result, in some of his campaigns he was a segregationist when being a segregationist would get him elected. In other contests, he was a populist when being a populist would get him elected.

Moreover, Wallace was particularly adept at pinpointing which issues were moving (or could be moved) to the top of voters' concerns. He also had a rare skill of talking about these issues in a language that people could understand. This allowed him continually to adapt his electoral appeals in response to the social, economical, and political changes occurring within the state. Thus as the issues of white supremacy and legally based segregation faded in Alabama, Wallace adapted his message to tap into voters' increasing sense of alienation and distrust of national institutions.

Ultimately, Wallace's success in anticipating and reacting to public opinion came not only from his perceiving what voters wanted but also in identifying with his constituents. When Wallace retired, one of his longtime political foes, H. Brandt Ayers, publisher of the *Anniston Star*, wrote that Wallace had "blood knowledge of the ancient animosities of rural and working-class Southerners, their century-old legacy of defeat, frustration and poverty and, worst of all, the scorn with which they were regarded by other Americans who had been treated more gently by history." People identified with Wallace because Wallace identified with them.[13]

More than most other politicians, Wallace was able to control the political agenda, particularly during election campaigns. He understood as well as any candidate of his era that he had to communicate not only with the audience before him but also with a large audience provided to him by the mass media. He knew what reporters wanted and when they wanted it. He knew that he did not have to get reporters to agree with his policies in order to get them to cover him. He also knew how to make other politicians react to him and to his issues in part because of his ability to use the budgetary and appointment powers of incumbency.

The "Wallace Faction"

Because Wallace appealed to voters on a variety of grounds during his career, the "Wallace faction" in Alabama politics was a heterogeneous collection of citizens and interest groups, each interpreting Wallace as the champion of their cause. These causes might be conflicting, but one of Wallace's talents as a politician was to be many things to many people. Despite the fact that his supporters might strongly disagree among themselves on racial, social, or economic issues, their disagreements were not important. That they supported Wallace and contributed to his victories—and thus had a part in those victories—was important. A similar phenomenon, though in the opposite direction, occurred among Wallace's opponents. Their only unifying element was a dislike for Wallace.

One indicator of the heterogeneity of Wallace's supporters and opponents is found in the favorable though mixed way Alabamians evaluated Wallace's political career at the time of his retirement (table 3.1). A statewide survey conducted shortly after his retirement announcement found that a substantial plurality (about 45 percent), but not a majority, of Alabama citizens said Wallace had had a generally "good" impact on the state.[14] About the same number (43 percent) said Wallace has been "both good and bad" for the state. Only about 9 percent were willing to say Wallace's influence

Table 3.1

Alabama citizens' evaluations of George Wallace, June 1986

"Now in some ways this year's election marks the end of the George Wallace era in Alabama politics. I would like to ask you some questions about this period of time, not just this current term as governor, but for all the time Wallace has been a major figure in state and national politics. Overall, how would you rate the impact which George Wallace has had on Alabama—has it been very good, good, both good and bad, bad, or very bad?"

Very good	15%
Good	30
Both good and bad	43
Bad	5
Very bad	4
Don't know/No answer	2
N	500

"Again think about the entire Wallace era. Please tell me if you strongly agree, agree, disagree, or strongly disagree with each of the following statements."

"Governor Wallace has been the best governor Alabama has ever had."

Strongly agree	14%
Agree	36
Disagree	32
Strongly disagree	10
Don't know/No answer	9
N	500

Source: Capstone Poll 178

had been "bad." Similar mixed results were found on a question that asked if Wallace was "the best governor Alabama has ever had." About 50 percent of the respondents agreed with the statement. Slightly fewer, some 42 percent, disagreed.

Somewhat more favorable judgments were found when respondents were asked about specific aspects of Wallace's career. Specifically, a majority of citizens believed that Wallace had increased the amount of pride and respect that people felt for the state (table 3.2). Some 58 percent agreed that Wallace "has made me proud to be an Alabamian," and two-thirds of the sample said they believed that Wallace "has gained respect for Alabama in the nation and the world." Close to 70 percent agreed that Wallace "has helped show the rest of the country that Alabama and the South as a whole is not a backwards and ignorant region."

The survey also found that most Alabamians believed that Wallace was their spokesman, someone who could articulate their desires when other politicians were ignoring them (table 3.3). Wallace, they said, had made these people more responsive. Nearly 60 percent of the sample agreed with the statement: "Throughout his career, George Wallace has looked out for the interests of people like me." And nearly two-thirds of the sample agreed that Wallace "has made the national government and national politicians pay attention to what people like me think."

Similarly, generally positive results were found when respondents were asked about policy-related aspects of Wallace's career (table 3.4). Most of the sample (57 percent) said that Wallace had not hindered the economic and social development of the state. About 60 percent did not believe that Wallace's success was based "only" on his ability to divide "black and white Alabamians from one another."

The heterogeneity of Wallace supporters is also seen when the type of citizens expressing positive or negative views about the former governor is examined. Specifically, that Alabamians should generally be favorable toward Wallace should come as no great shock. What is more surprising, however, is the way that blacks responded to the questions and statements in this survey (table 3.5). In general, blacks were more favorably disposed toward Wallace than whites. For instance:

- While 44 percent of the whites in the sample saw Wallace's impact on the state as either "good" or "very good," 50 percent of the blacks were willing to use these terms to describe his influence.
- Some 53 percent of the blacks in the sample, as opposed to 46 percent of the whites, agreed Wallace had been "the best governor Alabama has ever had."
- About 54 percent of the blacks and 56 percent of the whites agreed Wallace "had made me proud to be an Alabamian."
- Some 80 percent of the blacks and only 63 percent of the whites said Wallace "has gained respect for Alabama in the nation as a whole," and 79 percent of the blacks and 67 percent of the whites said Wallace

Table 3.2

Citizens' evaluations of George Wallace's effect on image of Alabama, June 1986

"George Wallace has made me proud to be an Alabamian."	
Strongly agree	13%
Agree	45
Disagree	25
Strongly disagree	8
Don't know/No answer	9
N	500

"George Wallace has gained respect for Alabama in the nation as a whole."	
Strongly agree	10%
Agree	56
Disagree	22
Strongly disagree	6
Don't know/No answer	5
N	500

"George Wallace has helped show the rest of the country that Alabama and the South as a whole is not a backwards and ignorant region."	
Strongly agree	11%
Agree	58
Disagree	19
Strongly disagree	6
Don't know/No answer	6
N	500

Source: Capstone Poll 178

had shown that Alabama and the South were not "backwards" and "ignorant."

- Blacks, to a greater extent than whites, said they believed Wallace had been their spokesman and had looked out for their interests.
- Only on the question of race relations were blacks somewhat less will-

Table 3.3

Citizens' evaluations of George Wallace as representative of Alabamians, June 1986

"Throughout his career, George Wallace has looked out for the interests of people like me."

Strongly agree	8%
Agree	51
Disagree	29
Strongly disagree	5
Don't know/No answer	6
N	500

"George Wallace has made the national government and national politicians pay attention to what people like me think."

STRONGLY AGREE	7%
AGREE	57
DISAGREE	25
STRONGLY DISAGREE	4
Don't know/No answer	7
N	500

Source: Capstone Poll 178

ing to give Wallace good marks than were whites. The differences, however, are slight. By the end of his career, the man who once stood in the schoolhouse door clearly had the sympathy, support, and good feelings of the blacks in the state.

An even better indicator of the heterogeneity of Wallace's supporters is demonstrated by the results of a question that asked respondents how frequently they had supported Wallace in the past. Table 3.6 shows that while Wallace received more support from some groups than from others, a substantial number of his supporters are found in each sector of the population.

For example, large numbers of both self-described liberals (36 percent)

Table 3.4

Citizens' evaluations of George Wallace's effect on economic development and race relations, June 1986

"George Wallace has hurt the economic development of Alabama."	
Strongly agree	4%
Agree	30
Disagree	49
Strongly disagree	8
Don't know/No answer	10
N	500

"George Wallace has succeeded only in dividing black and white Alabamians from one another."	
Strongly agree	6%
Agree	24
Disagree	53
Strongly disagree	7
Don't know/No answer	10
N	500

Source: Capstone Poll 178

and conservatives (52 percent) said they have supported Wallace "always" or "most of the time." Similarly, about one in three of the state's Republican Party identifiers and those with more education and higher incomes said they have been a consistent supporter of George Wallace's. Finally, survey results showed that Wallace support was about equal among black and white citizens; union and non-union households; males and females; and younger, middle-aged, and older citizens.

The "Central Issue" Disappears

Wallace's ability to hold together a wide assortment of political interests resulted in Wallace himself generally being the central issue in state poli-

Table 3.5

Opinions about George Wallace by race

	White (N = 388)	*Black* (N = 99)
Overall, how would you rate the impact which George Wallace has had on Alabama—has it been very good, good, both good and bad, bad or very bad?		
% Very good/Good	44	50
"Governor Wallace has been the best governor Alabama has ever had."		
% Strongly agree/Agree	46	53
"George Wallace has made me proud to be an Alabamian."		
% Strongly agree/Agree	56	54
"George Wallace has gained respect for Alabama in the nation as a whole."		
% Strongly agree/Agree	63	80
"George Wallace has helped show the rest of the country that Alabama and the South as a whole is not a backwards and ignorant region."		
% Strongly agree/Agree	67	79
"Throughout his career, George Wallace has looked out for the interests of people like me."		
% Strongly agree/Agree	58	66
"George Wallace has made the national government and national politicians pay attention to what people like me think."		
% Strongly agree/Agree	62	72
"George Wallace has hurt the economic development of Alabama."		
% Strongly disagree/Disagree	56	55
"George Wallace has succeeded only in dividing black and white Alabamians from one another."		
% Strongly disagree/Disagree	62	52

Source: Capstone Poll 178

Table 3.6

Socio-demographic characteristics of Wallace supporters

Characteristics*	% support Wallace always, most of time**	N
Self-described ideology		
Liberal	36	64
Middle of the road	41	112
Conservative	52	164
Party identification		
Republican	37	95
Independent	43	120
Democrat	57	227
Union household		
Yes	54	96
No	46	386
Education		
0–12 grades	58	286
More than high school	34	199
Income		
Less than $10,000	61	95
$10–$20,000	52	101
$20–$30,000	45	102
More than $30,000	37	138
Race		
White	46	380
Black	59	98
Sex		
Male	44	209
Female	51	281
Age		
18–40 years	47	223
41–60 years	48	134
61+ years	51	128

*Missing data deleted.

** "In past elections, would you say that you have supported George Wallace always, most of the time, sometimes, or never?"

Source: Capstone Poll 178

tics. Political divisions were rarely defined in any other way, and the differences between factions on issues, ideologies, or programs were of little consequence.

A different situation was created, however, when Wallace retired. When active, he was a unifying force within the state's Democratic Party. Now he was gone. Further, Wallace's longevity and varied appeals had retarded the pace of political change in Alabama. This does not mean, of course, that Alabama, or Wallace himself, had not changed during the previous three decades. Perhaps the 1982 election is the clearest indication of how much the state had changed during the Wallace years. Then the former segregationist's victory was based on a voting coalition that included both black and white supporters.

Still, Wallace's dominating presence in Alabama had, by discouraging the emergence of new political leaders and keeping old issues and coalitions alive, retarded the influence of forces (e.g., urbanization and economic development, the enfranchisement of black voters, party shifts at the national level) producing partisan change in other parts of the South. Wallace's varied appeals reduced the need for a two-party system in Alabama. At least when it came to state politics, Alabamians could either be for George Wallace or against him. Whether they were Republicans or Democrats was not really relevant.

Thus, with Wallace's retirement, both a unifying figure within the state's Democratic Party and the primary force "protecting" the state from partisan changes were removed from Alabama politics. As a result, entering the 1986 gubernatorial campaign, conditions were favorable for political change within Alabama. Whether these changes coming from Wallace's retirement would actually result in intense divisions within Alabama's Democratic Party, or the demise of the state's one-party politics, would depend upon the conduct of the 1986 campaign.

4
The 1986 Primary Election

Like the members of a relay team, Alabama's four leading politicians—the same ones who had been so prominent first in 1978 and later in 1982—did not wait for George Wallace to pass the baton before they began running.[1] Well before Wallace's "fond farewell," Bill Baxley, George McMillan, Charles Graddick, and Fob James had set about the task of winning the Democratic nomination for governor.

Bill Baxley was the first to say publicly that he would be a candidate in 1986. Shortly after the 1982 election, he began telling groups he would be a candidate for governor whether or not Wallace sought reelection. For the next three and a half years, Baxley remained the only announced candidate. As soon as the state's news media began giving serious attention to the 1986 contest, however, the other three candidates let it be known that they also would be contestants.[2]

George McMillan

The first of the other candidates to formally begin his campaign was George McMillan. In October 1985 the former lieutenant governor announced his candidacy and began a series of television ads.[3]

Shortly after McMillan's announcement, the *Birmingham News* commissioned the first of its election surveys. At that time, Wallace was the leading candidate among the possible contenders. The survey also asked voters which candidate they preferred among the four who would eventually compete for the Democratic nomination. According to the results of the survey, Bill Baxley and George McMillan were the leading candidates, each with about 25 percent of the vote. Fob James (17 percent) and Charles Graddick (18 percent) trailed closely behind. (See table 4.1 for voters' candidate preferences during the primary campaign.)

Table 4.1

Voter preferences in Democratic primary

	October 1985	January 1986	April 1986	May 1986
Baxley	25%	26%	26%	28%
Graddick	18	18	25	32
James	17	19	20	21
McMillan	25	18	9	9
Other/Don't know	15	18	20	10

Question wording:

October—"If there was a Democratic Party primary for governor and the candidates were Lieutenant Governor Bill Baxley, Attorney General Charles Graddick, former governor Fob James, and former lieutenant governor George McMillan, for whom would you vote?"

January—"If there was a Democratic Party primary for governor and the candidates were Lieutenant Governor Bill Baxley, former press secretary Billy Joe Camp, Attorney General Charles Graddick, former governor Fob James, and former lieutenant governor George McMillan, for whom would you vote?"

April—"If there was a Democratic Party primary for governor and the candidates were Bill Baxley, Charles Graddick, Fob James, George McMillan, and Barbara Evans O'Neal, for whom would you vote?"

May—"If there was a Democratic Party primary for governor and the candidates were Bill Baxley, Charles Graddick, Fob James, George McMillan, and Barbara Evans O'Neal, for whom would you vote?" (If Undecided, "As of today, do you lean a little more toward Baxley, Graddick James, McMillan, or O'Neal?")

Source: Capstone Poll 148, 160, 169, 175

Despite his strong position, McMillan's campaign already was showing signs of coming apart. In announcing that he would be a candidate for governor, McMillan stressed the need for new leadership in the state. In particular, he made education reform one of the cornerstones of his platform. "I'm tired of an educational system that causes parents to lose faith in their children's ability to reach their potential," he said.[4]

The specific proposal that McMillan pushed the hardest was a call for mandatory testing of teachers' basic skills. In previous statewide contests,

McMillan had received strong support from African-American voters. In 1986, however, he would have competition for this sizable constituency from Baxley, who also had been endorsed in previous campaigns by the state's major black political organizations.

McMillan's teacher testing proposal did not solidify his black support; it had the opposite effect. Teacher testing (and indeed any call for the use of standardized tests) was perceived by many voters in post-civil-rights Alabama politics as a latently racial issue, because standardized testing is thought to discriminate against blacks. It did not take long for African-American leaders to publicly express their reservations about McMillan's stand for teacher competency tests. For example, state senator Hank Sanders from Selma said, "It has raised a serious concern. Testing has been a way of eliminating blacks. We've just had a bad experience with it."[5] Baxley came out against this proposal, saying he "would not let that snake rear its head out of the grass."[6]

The teacher testing issue also generated problems for McMillan with the politically powerful teachers group, the Alabama Education Association (AEA). McMillan later in the campaign admitted that his early television ads concerning the testing issues were probably "unnecessarily abrasive."[7] His strong stand on teacher testing conflicted with his image as a progressive. Yet he had to demonstrate that he was tough enough to be governor, that he could lead by making principled but unpopular decisions. The perception that he was not forceful enough to be governor was a continuing problem for McMillan, who by his own admission had "vocal mannerisms which are less than macho," and this perception had haunted him since the 1982 campaign.[8] McMillan's teacher testing proposal established him as an alternative to Baxley. But the candidacies of the more conservative James and Graddick made it highly unlikely that McMillan could succeed. The disastrous effects of this strategy were obvious. No group rallied to McMillan's cause because of it, and the issue gave black groups and the AEA a reason they needed, and many wanted, to support Baxley.

Charles Graddick and Fob James

As the McMillan campaign was becoming bogged down with these problems, Charles Graddick officially announced his candidacy for governor on January 16.[9] He too called for a new leadership that was not tied to "special interests." He also presented himself as the "newest" of the candidates, despite his two terms as attorney general. He most directly expressed this idea in a statement (which would be repeated with only minor variations often during the primary campaign) in which he said that "after being 'Baxleyed, McMillaned and Fobbed' it's time to change political leadership in Alabama." While his opponents had all been either lieutenant governor or governor, he said, "Nothing had changed."

Fob James, while not formally announcing his candidacy until March, also had made it known that he would be in the race. As early as November 1985, he was quoted as saying that he was gearing up for the 1986 election.[10] James continually cited the accomplishments of his first term and the need to "finish the work he had started."[11] He also stressed the need to reduce government waste, pointing to the increase in the number of state employees and automobiles since he left office and to the high cost of remodeling the state office building—the home of the state legislature, a building he frequently referred to as the "Taj Mahal."[12]

Bill Baxley

Baxley campaigned during this period (and indeed throughout the primary election) on the theme that he was the most qualified candidate for governor. He told a meeting of the Alabama Cattlemen's Association, "I don't think we've ever had a candidate for governor—much less a governor—with the experience I've had."[13] Baxley consistently portrayed himself as the front-runner in the election, saying that his opponents were all running for "second place."[14]

Baxley also stressed a number of issues throughout the campaign, such as promoting economic development, maintaining social service spending, and strengthening the state's education system. He used these issues to present himself as the candidate of the common man. "I can strengthen the state by a combination of compassion and concern for the average citizen along with a new direction for the state and a new image."[15]

While the candidates were busy beginning their campaigns, little change was taking place in their levels of public support. A January public-opinion survey, which showed a decline in support for Wallace, also contained a question concerning whom voters would support if Wallace were not in the race. Baxley was the leading candidate, again with about one-fourth of the vote. The other three candidates (each with 18 or 19 percent of the vote) were tightly bunched behind Baxley. McMillan had fallen from being tied with Baxley in October to being about 8 percent behind. The support for Graddick and James had remained virtually unchanged since October (table 4.1).

That survey also contained a series of questions that asked voters whom they would support in a series of hypothetical runoff elections between each pair of candidates. These results revealed that Baxley could, at that time, beat each of his opponents in a runoff election (table 4.2). Baxley's closest contest was with Graddick, whom he led by a 47 to 37 percent margin. The results also showed that Graddick could defeat both McMillan and James in a runoff and that McMillan would defeat James. The strength that Graddick showed in these hypothetical runoff elections was an indicator of what was to come in the election.

The Campaign Pace Quickens

Throughout the late winter and early spring, the four candidates continued their campaign, each trying to develop within the electorate an image as the one who was the most qualified, the best leader, the most experienced, or the most independent from the existing politics of the state. Little happened during this period to change the activities or strategies of the candidates. In part, nothing changed because of the continued uncertainty concerning whether Wallace would seek reelection.

The pace of the campaign did, however, pick up in late March. The event that changed the campaign was a brief page 2 story in the *Birmingham News* on March 30, which said Bill Baxley had used state cars and his state trooper bodyguards to transport a female Associated Press reporter, Marie Prat, to and from his Montgomery apartment. Baxley denied that he had done anything improper.[16]

The size and placement of the *Birmingham News* story belied the efforts the *News* staff had put into producing it, the controversy that raged within the *News'* office about running, and the way in which it was to color Baxley's campaign and change the tenor of the race.[17] The page 2 placement of the story indicated the caution with which the paper's management dealt with the issue, but it also placed the *News*, its editors, and reporters in uncomfortable positions when the Baxley/state car/female reporter conundrum took on a life of its own during the remainder of the campaign.

All this happened a full year before the story about Gary Hart and Donna Rice broke at the national level.[18] While political scandals of this nature were not unknown, the *News* stumbled into this area and found that it had few precedents to guide its actions. The paper's reporters and editors had

Table 4.2

Support for candidates in hypothetical runoff elections–January 1986 and April 1986

"Suppose that there was a runoff election for governor between each of the following pairs of candidates. For whom you would vote in each election?"

	January 1986	April 1986
Baxley	47%	42%
Graddick	37	44
Neither/Don't know	16	14
Baxley	56%	53%
James	32	34
Neither/Don't know	12	14
Baxley	49%	50%
McMillan	35	30
Neither/Don't know	16	20
Graddick	44%	52%
McMillan	39	29
Neither/Don't know	17	20
Graddick	50%	52%
James	32	33
Neither/Don't know	17	15
James	34%	38%
McMillan	51	44
Neither/Don't know	15	18

Source: Capstone Poll 160, 169

to make decisions about what to report and what to withhold without the instruction that scandals surrounding such people as Gary Hart, Charles Robb, and Bill Clinton have had to offer.

The fact that Baxley was having a relationship with Prat was first brought to the attention of *News* editors in late 1985 or early 1986 by Michele MacDonald, one of the statehouse reporters for the *News*. Because Prat covered the legislature for the Associated Press and because the *News* often used those reports in its own news columns, MacDonald was concerned that Prat, and by extension the *News*, would be compromised in its news coverage. MacDonald was told by state editor Glenn Stephens to watch the situation and to keep him informed about possible conflicts. MacDonald soon discovered that Baxley was using his state vehicle, driven by a state trooper, to transport Prat to and from his apartment in Montgomery.

That information complicated the situation for editors at the *News*. Baxley had made no secret of his desire to run for governor. The fact that this public figure was having a relationship with a woman outside his marriage, while maintaining the public facade of being happily married, was itself a concern. Would the *News* be deceiving its readers if it possessed this information about someone who was asking for the public trust but withheld it from the public? And what about his use of state cars and state troopers? Clearly, that was improper if not illegal. Did the *News* have a duty to tell what it knew? These were questions that vexed the editors of the paper.

While no one could foresee all that would happen if the *News* broke this story, some of the consequences were easily predictable. The *News* would be accused of being anti-Baxley—a charge that, in the public's mind, would be supported by the paper's continued editorial opposition to him. The tone of the gubernatorial campaign would change in ways no would could predict. The *News* itself would become a character in this political drama rather than just an observer. The *News* editors realized that pursuing the story might make the newspaper the target of some expensive litigation.

Added to these arguments was the feeling that Baxley's use of state vehicles did not seem to carry great public weight. Marriage vows are serious, of course, but the public has tolerated adulterers, often by simply looking the other way. The fact that a non-state employee rode in a state car seemed to many to be a minor matter.

Still, the journalists at the *News* would not, or could not, ignore the story, and ultimately they pursued it. During the last week of March, several editors and reporters from the paper went to Montgomery and spent several evenings watching the comings and goings outside Baxley's apartment. They saw Prat entering the apartment early in the evening carrying clothes on a hanger, and they saw her leave the next morning, apparently wearing the clothes she had been carrying. They documented in detail what they saw and noted the times when these events occurred. After watching the apartment and ascertaining what was happening, they called a photographer in to take pictures. On the day the photographer arrived, Prat stopped using a state car and began arriving in a Baxley campaign car.

By the end of the week, they confronted Baxley and Prat separately with the information that they had gathered. Baxley, they said, seemed stunned by what they had found, but he denied that he had done anything wrong. He later denied being surprised by the question. In fact, he said, he knew that it was coming because he knew that the *News* had been watching his apartment. The *News* had it wrong; it had been a car leased to his campaign that had transported Prat, not a state vehicle. But, he noted, that was a point he could not argue at the time.[19] Whatever the case, Prat resigned her position with the Associated Press almost immediately and left town.

The reporters and editors returned at the end of that week and wrote a full story, laying out everything they had seen. Pictures were developed, and on Saturday the package was put together for the Sunday editions. Despite all of this effort, the *News* was taking the situation one step at a time, and the final decision on what to publish—or whether to publish at all—had not been made. Within the *News* offices, the debate still raged over what the newspaper was doing, why it was doing it, and what effect it would have. Wasn't the *News* making too much, asked some within the paper, out of a relatively small incident? Wasn't the business about the state cars simply a subterfuge for getting into print the fact that Baxley was having an affair? And even if it was not, would anyone understand the *News*' motives for pursuing the story? On the other hand, why should the newspaper shield a public official who was openly doing these things?

During the day on Saturday, that debate continued among the publishers and editors of the paper. An attorney for the paper was called in to give advice. Strong opinions were expressed on all sides of the issue. At some point, the managers of the paper decided that the *News* should print the story but should do what it could to play it down. That amounted to a small story on page 2 with no pictures. There would be no details of the comings and goings at Baxley's apartment. The story would contain the basic facts and Baxley's denial of any wrongdoing.

The decision to downplay the story may have provided the *News* some protection from a charge of sensationalism, but the protection was temporary. By withholding much of what they knew, the managers of the paper provided Baxley some room for denial, and it left many outsiders wondering what the real story was. Readers could easily surmise the story meant that Baxley and Prat were having an affair, even though the story never mentioned that directly. The fact that Baxley was giving her rides in his state-owned automobile seemed like a minor infraction.

Baxley's first public reaction after the story came out was to deny that he had done anything wrong. Then he admitted that he had allowed friends and private citizens to use state cars, and he offered to reimburse the state for its expenses. To illustrate his sincerity in this regard, Baxley sent a signed blank check to the State Ethics Commission. (The commission returned the check and announced that it would investigate the situation.) Baxley denied using state cars to transport Prat and said that she had never been at his apartment. He went on to say that his wife was the only constituent to whom he had to answer on this question, and he then refused to discuss it further.[20]

Had Baxley stuck steadfastly to that refusal, he might have been better off. Many could agree both that Baxley had acted incorrectly and that it was nobody's business. The reporters themselves were caught in their own dilemma. Here was a situation that for the most part was a private matter, although there was a public element to it. They did not want to be accused of shirking their duties as journalists or of giving a candidate a break.

The state car/female reporter issue was not the first time Baxley's behavior had come under scrutiny. He previously had been connected to controversies involving his gambling in Las Vegas, his drinking (such as the time he went to a Montgomery bar rather than preside over a "boring" senate debate), and his association with less-than-reputable businessmen.[21] Nor would the state car issue be the last of these types of concerns with which Baxley would be linked in 1986. Other issues arose concerning state prisoners painting campaign signs for Baxley, national guardsmen soliciting campaign contributions for him, and Wallace administration officials openly using their state government positions to encourage businessmen to support Baxley.[22] The state car issue would attract more attention than the others, however. Even though the controversy over Baxley's use of state cars was pushed off the front pages by Wallace's retirement announcement later that week, the issue reemerged numerous times during the campaign and was never far from the surface of campaign discussion. The issue was one that Baxley could never shake or explain away.

His direct denial of what the *News* had printed—that Prat had been to his apartment—infuriated and frustrated the reporters and editors who had seen it happen. That frustration kept the story simmering in their minds, even though the newspaper's managers were unwilling to pursue the story or to print any additional information that they had. Despite the desire on the part of both Baxley and some at the newspaper, the story refused to go away. Although relatively little was said about it during the rest of the primary campaign, it would inevitably resurface when some opponent of Baxley found it useful.

Being Called Ugly by a Frog

With the Wallace announcement, the month of April marked the beginning of the real primary campaign. Each of the four major candidates had waited for this moment for years, and each tried to reap the harvests of support that they had sought to cultivate during their political lives. By the end of April, a Capstone Poll survey showed Baxley and Graddick virtually tied for the lead in the governor's race. Thus since January, Graddick had moved past James and picked up 7 percent on Baxley (table 4.1).

The survey's results also showed that James remained the choice of about 20 percent of the voters, while McMillan's support dropped considerably, to about 9 percent (compared to 18 percent in January and 25 percent in October). The results also indicated that in a hypothetical runoff election, Graddick and Baxley essentially were even (table 4.2). Both Baxley and Graddick, however, had relatively large leads over James and McMillan when matched against them in possible runoff elections. The results indicated that McMillan would defeat James if they were to face each other in a runoff, although these were the two candidates least likely to make the runoff.

These and similar survey results in April had several consequences for the campaign. First, they focused attention on the increased support for Graddick, who, because he was now seen as a likely runoff candidate, became the object of an increasing number of campaign attacks. For example, the day before the April survey was released (but after he and the other candidates were informed of its results by *Birmingham News* reporters), Baxley spoke to a racially mixed audience and said the contest was between himself and "someone trying to turn the clock backwards."[23] He went on to say, "There's a clear choice in direction between going forward into the 21st century or to try and take the clock back on the gains we're so proud of."[24]

James also stepped up his attacks on Graddick. He ran ads countering Graddick's claims concerning the release of state prison inmates during

James's administration. He also criticized Graddick's involvement in the renovation of the state office building. In an attempt to undermine Graddick's claim to be the outsider in the race, both James and McMillan attacked the attorney general for accepting pay raises during his term in office.[25] Later, McMillan would say that "the demagogues in the state would go into ecstasy if they could have Charles Graddick in the governor's office."[26]

Graddick's initial response to these criticisms from McMillan and James was to continue to stress that he was the candidate most likely to bring about change in Alabama's politics. "These guys represent the past. We represent a bright future for Alabama."[27] Graddick campaign officials became increasingly concerned that James's attacks were eroding their candidate's position and threatening his ability to make the runoff. Of particular concern was a James commercial that implied that Graddick did not tell the truth. When campaign polls showed Graddick slipping, they decided to produce a lighthearted but pointed response. They aired a television commercial that showed a frog jumping around the screen while a narrator discussed the differences between what James said he did as governor and what "really" happened. The tag line on the advertisement was, "Being called a liar by Fob James is like being called ugly by a frog."[28]

The candidates also increased their attacks on Baxley, who, because of his position as the incumbent lieutenant governor and his ties to the Wallace administration, was the candidate least able to appeal to the public's desire for political change. In their efforts to project themselves as the representative of the new politics in Alabama, Graddick, James, and McMillan each tried to paint Baxley as part of the old guard. McMillan linked Baxley to the "sleaze of the Wallace administration."[29] Baxley's opponents also attacked Baxley's ties to "special interests" such as the Alabama Education Association, labor unions, trial lawyers, and black political groups. For example, a McMillan television commercial showed a cake with Baxley's face on top. The cake is sliced up as the narrator ticks off the special interests that are supporting Baxley. At the end he asks, "When all the special interests get their piece of Baxley, what will be left for the rest of us?" Graddick, too, joined in this attack against Baxley as the candidate of the "special interests."

Baxley's response was to continue to stress his experience and qualifications and to cite his accomplishments while holding statewide office. He also stated, "I have never been owned by any group."[30] Baxley also tried to deflect his image as the candidate representing the "status quo" in Alabama politics. He did not deny his links to different political groups or his ties to the Wallace administration. Indeed, Baxley said, he was proud of the state and George Wallace, but that did not mean that change was not needed. The issue was how this change would occur. He illustrated his point by telling a story about his son: "Being proud doesn't mean I'm not dissatisfied. I'm proud of my son. When he brought his report card back, I was proud but still dissatisfied. To get him to improve, I did not attack him or be negative. That would tear him down."[31]

Graddick's rise in public support, which appeared to come at McMillan's expense, caused serious problems for the former lieutenant governor. For the remainder of the campaign, McMillan was forced to argue that the surveys were wrong and that he was a credible candidate who would make the runoff. Ironically, he had earlier used the results of public-opinion surveys to demonstrate his strong position in the race.[32]

McMillan adopted the posture of many declining candidates by attacking the public-opinion surveys that showed him losing. He met this opponent as he had others, talking nonstop in what seemed to be an effort to overcome the survey results with words. Toward the end of his campaign, polls became the opponent for McMillan, so much so that during the last weekend of the campaign he said, "Every time I see one of those fly-by-night polls, it's like waving a red flag in front of a bull. It just makes me more determined to go out there and prove them wrong."[33]

McMillan's decline in the polls most clearly hurt him when he tried to obtain the endorsement of the New South Coalition, a new and predominantly black political organization. McMillan had reason to believe he would be supported by this group. One of the New South Coalition's leaders was the mayor of Birmingham, Richard Arrington, the first black elected mayor of that city and someone McMillan had endorsed in his mayoral election campaign. Arrington had earlier said that he would support McMillan if the former lieutenant governor had a chance to win the election.[34]

In seeking the organization's endorsement, McMillan pleaded with the group to ignore the polls and support him rather than Baxley. McMillan said that the group should take this action in order to "rid government of sleazes and cronies who had been enriching their pocketbooks at the expense of everyone in this room."[35] Baxley appealed to the group by telling them that the election was between him and Graddick, a candidate who had given blacks little reason to support him. Indeed, Graddick—the only one of the four candidates who did not speak to the New South Coalition's meeting—was the one candidate who gave the appearance that he did not want the support of black voters.[36]

In the end, the New South Coalition gave a reluctant endorsement to Baxley. The group rationalized that its members were convinced that McMillan could not win the election. As J. L. Chestnut, the chair of the coalition's board of directors, said, "George McMillan is honest, would say the hard things and probably make the best governor. I've been with George McMillan a long time, but I am not about to support a candidate who can't win. I don't think that's what politics is about."[37]

As was his style, McMillan did not accept his failure to win the New South Coalition's endorsement gracefully. He complained that the "back room powerbrokers" were trying to give Alabama "the best governor money can buy." He went on to say that his campaign would continue and he would gain the support of voters because he was the candidate who had "no strings attached."[38]

Later in May, the older, more established black political organization, the Alabama Democratic Conference (ADC), also endorsed Baxley. The ADC had supported Baxley in each of his previous campaigns.[39] During this period, Baxley was also picking up the endorsements of a number of labor unions.[40]

As the campaign entered its final days, the candidates stressed the same ideas that had characterized their candidacies from the beginning. Baxley said he was the most experienced and qualified candidate and tried to demonstrate that he was the most sensitive to the needs of the average citizen. Graddick campaigned as the outsider not tied to special interests. James presented himself as the experienced administrator who was committed to eliminating waste. McMillan portrayed himself as the competent, intelligent, issue-oriented leader.

A Capstone Poll survey conducted just before the June 3 primary found that Graddick and Baxley essentially were even going into the last weekend of the campaign, each with close to 30 percent of the vote. About 20 percent of the respondents said they would support James, while McMillan continued to receive only about 9 percent of the vote (Table 4.1).

On election day, Baxley led the field with 37 percent of the vote, while Graddick received 29 percent. James ran third with 21 percent, and McMillan ran a distant fourth with 13 percent.

The results of the pre-election survey found little difference in candidate support on the basis of age or sex (table 4.3). Higher-income voters were more likely to support James and less likely to support Baxley than were lower-income citizens. More-educated citizens also were more likely to support James (but only very slightly less likely to support Baxley) than were others.

Table 4.3

Socio-demographic characteristics of primary election supporters

"If there was a Democratic Party primary for governor and the candidates were Bill Baxley, Charles Graddick, Fob James, George McMillan, and Barbara Evans O'Neal, for whom would you vote?" (If Undecided, "As of today, do you lean a little more toward Baxley, Graddick James, McMillan, or O'Neal?")

Characteristic*	Baxley	Graddick	James	McMillan	Don't Know/No Answer	N
Age						
18–40 years	30%	32	22	9	7	333
41–60 years	27%	35	21	9	8	254
61+ years	28%	27	20	9	16	207
Gender						
Male	28%	32	26	8	6	314
Female	28%	31	18	10	12	484
Income						
Less than $40,000	33%	32	19	9	8	563
More than $40,000	16%	35	30	12	8	147
Education						
High school or less	30	33	17	8	12	478
More than high school	26	30	27	10	6	315
Race						
White	25%	38	22	8	8	632
Black	43%	8	20	15	14	157
Party						
Republican	15%	32	36	8	9	122
Independent	23%	36	22	10	9	242
Democrat	37%	29	17	9	7	382

*Missing data deleted.

Source: Capstone Poll 175

Graddick's support was about the same among more- or less-educated and higher- or lower-income voters. Black voters preferred Baxley over the other candidates and were least likely to support Graddick.[41]

The Failure of Fob James and George McMillan

Why did James and McMillan fail, particularly in the light of the optimism that surrounded their campaigns at the start of the year?

Fob James emphasized two issues or themes during this campaign. First, he spent considerable time campaigning against government waste. Second, he repeatedly stressed his experience, saying he wanted to finish the work he started during his term as governor, 1978–1982. In the end, neither of these themes worked. Despite James's considerable effort, the issue of government waste attracted little attention from the media. What coverage the issue did receive typically involved detailed and technical discussions of who did what and when with regard to the remodeling of the state office building (the "Taj Mahal")—his prime example of government waste. Not surprisingly, James's major issue never found the spark that ignited public indignation.

The "I want to finish the job" theme also did not generate the type of public response that James wanted. Rather, it became clear that the voters did not want James to finish the job he had started. They thought he had done a less-than-wonderful job the first time. During the last two years of his administration James received an "excellent" or "good" rating from an average of only about 25 percent of the public. At the end of his term in office, almost 40 percent of the public said he was doing a "poor" job.

The public's perceptions of James's performance as governor changed little between 1982 and 1986. In each of the pre-primary election surveys, citizens were asked to evaluate how well James did as governor. The results (presented in table 4.4) clearly show that voters in 1986 did not look back on the James administration as the "good old days." Rather, four years after he had left office, the public was still highly critical of James's performance.

The public-image scores James amassed during the primary campaign are another indication of the critical attitudes that many voters had about the former governor (table 4.5). Questions that asked respondents if they felt "positive, neutral, or negative" about each of the candidates were included in each of the surveys. The answers to these questions are easily summarized by subtracting the number of respondents saying they feel negatively about a candidate from the number saying they evaluate a candidate positively. A resulting score that is greater than zero indicates that voters have an overall

Table 4.4

Citizens' retrospective evaluations of James's term as governor

"How would you evaluate the job Fob James did as governor of Alabama—excellent, good, fair, or poor?"

	October 1985	January 1986	April 1986	May 1986
Excellent	7%	10%	9%	10%
Good	25	23	23	27
Fair	35	40	35	31
Poor	24	21	28	26
Don't know/ No answer	9	6	6	7

Source: Capstone Poll 148, 160, 169, 175

favorable impression of a candidate. The opposite conclusion can be drawn from a score that is less than zero. A score that is exactly zero indicates that a candidate has received an equal number of positive and negative evaluations.[42]

At the beginning of the campaign James was rated slightly more positively than negatively. By the end, however, his "negatives" had outstripped his "positives." Indeed, by the close of his primary election effort, James was rated positively by only two relatively small groups of voters: higher-income respondents and Republicans (table 4.6). James's candidacy failed simply because voters had very critical attitudes about his previous performance as governor. These opinions did not change during the campaign. Consequently, when the former governor said he wanted to go back to Montgomery to do the same things he did before, the state's voters said, "No thanks."

The failure of the McMillan campaign can also be explained by looking at how voters evaluated the candidate. In each of the pre-election surveys, McMillan received an overall positive rating from the respondents. At no time, however, were his ratings very high, and they actually declined somewhat during the campaign. By the end of the primary campaign, McMillan received strong positive ratings only from blacks, higher-income respondents, and Democrats. Each of these groups evaluated other candidates more favorably than they did McMillan.

Table 4.5

Evaluations of primary election candidates

"Do you generally feel positive, neutral, or negative about each of the following people?"

	October 1985	January 1986	April 1986	May 1986
Fob James				
Positive	32%	34%	28%	30%
Neutral/Don't know	38	33	37	30
Negative	30	33	35	40
% Pos. - %Neg.	2	1	-5	-10
George McMillan				
Positive	33%	30%	30%	32%
Neutral/Don't know	50	53	52	45
Negative	16	18	18	23
% Pos. - % Neg.	17	12	12	9
Charles Graddick				
Positive	42%	39%	42%	44%
Neutral/Don't know	42	44	43	35
Negative	16	18	15	21
% Pos. - % Neg.	26	21	27	23
Bill Baxley				
Positive	38%	41%	44%	42%
Neutral/Don't know	41	39	38	30
Negative	21	21	18	28
% Pos. - % Neg.	17	20	26	14

Source: Capstone Poll 148, 160, 169, 175

The failure of McMillan's candidacy was only partially due to his increasingly less positive public image. More important was his failure to generate any public concern or interest in his campaign. In each of the surveys, about half the respondents gave a noncommittal response (i.e., neutral or don't know) when asked to evaluate McMillan. Despite McMillan's record and high level of name recognition, his candidacy failed to "catch on" with voters, and consequently his support fell throughout the election campaign.

Why did the campaign of the former lieutenant governor, former gubernatorial candidate, and leader of a supposedly crack political organization

Table 4.6

Net evaluations of primary candidates by socio-demographic groups, May 1986

Characteristic*	Net evaluations**			
	Fob James	George McMillan	Charles Graddick	Bill Baxley
Age				
18–40 years	-14	9	32	16
41–60 years	-8	10	19	10
61+ years	-6	7	10	13
Race				
White	-13	4	29	4
Black	-3	28	-6	47
Gender				
Male	-6	9	28	11
Female	-12	9	19	16
Education				
High school or less	-15	7	26	22
More than high school	-2	12	18	1
Income				
Less than $40,000	-13	7	44	22
More than $40,000	3	14	20	-16
Party				
Republican	23	-1	27	-13
Independent	-8	6	32	-2
Democrat	-19	14	14	32

*Missing data deleted.
**These scores are figured by subtracting the percentage giving a negative evaluation to a candidate from those giving a positive evaluation.
Source: Capstone Poll 175

generate such a case of the "blahs" among the state's voters? The answer lies in the fact that McMillan never figured out what type of campaign he wanted to run. He started the campaign by taking a conservative position on the teacher testing issue. He told businessmen that if they did not support him, they would end up with Baxley in the governor's mansion.[43] However, the presence of James and Graddick meant that they, not McMillan, would be the candidates supported by business and conservative interests. As this occurred, McMillan adopted an almost populist position, calling James the candidate of the "super rich."[44] At other times in the campaign McMillan stressed the need for new leadership and his opposition to "cronyism and special interests." However, despite McMillan's efforts to convince voters Graddick was not a "fresh face," the attorney general was the one who established himself in the public's eyes as the newest of the candidates.[45]

During the campaign, McMillan also tried to portray himself as the friend of minorities and liberals. His earlier appeals to conservatives and his attacks on special interests, however, meant that as he fell in the polls, groups like the New South Coalition were unwilling to fall on a political sword for McMillan. McMillan's efforts to win the support of liberals or progressives were undercut by the presence of Baxley, a candidate whose record (if not his style) appealed to these groups.

Thus by appealing to almost every group of voters at some time during the campaign, McMillan avoided generating much negative feeling among voters. However, the fact that in each of his attempts to attract voters he found himself "outflanked" by other candidates also meant that McMillan failed to generate much in the way of positive feelings, since the voters had other candidates they liked better. In the end, the inability to position himself in the minds of the electorate, in combination with a style that was ill-suited for the type of campaign that developed in 1986, meant that not that many people cared one way or the other about whether McMillan won or lost.

McMillan was the first and clearest victim of the new realities of an Alabama without George Wallace. In 1982 McMillan had led the anti-Wallace forces, a disparate group whose common purpose was to prevent the election of George Wallace. In 1986 the glue that held this coalition together was gone, and McMillan by himself was not a strong enough force to unite these groups. McMillan found that his central appeal of 1982—that of being the alternative to George Wallace—was no longer relevant, and during the four intervening years he had developed no replacement for it.

The Success of Bill Baxley and Charles Graddick

Just as the public images of McMillan and James help explain why they lost the primary, the perceptions the public had of Baxley and Graddick show why these two candidates moved into the runoff. Unlike McMillan's neutral and James's negative image, the public's views of Baxley and Graddick were largely positive. More importantly, relatively few voters expressed negative attitudes about either candidate. As a result, throughout the primary these two candidates consistently received the largest number of positive ratings and the smallest number of negative ratings from the public. The number of negative responses about both candidates did increase toward the end of the primary campaign, however.

The favorable ratings that Baxley and Graddick enjoyed were in large part the result of their ability to place themselves in positions that appealed to a large number of voters. Baxley talked of his experience and qualifications, citing himself as the one who best represented the interests of those groups that traditionally aligned themselves with the Democratic Party. Throughout the campaign, Graddick presented himself as the outsider who would bring about substantial change in Alabama's state government and politics.

Because they appealed to voters on different but not totally contrasting grounds, Baxley and Graddick had somewhat overlapping coalitions of supporters. Baxley received strong positive ratings from Democrats, blacks, less-educated voters, and lower-income voters. He received net negative ratings from Republicans, Independents, and higher-income citizens. More-educated respondents and whites gave Baxley about an equal number of negative and positive ratings.

Graddick's support was more widespread within the electorate. He was most positively evaluated by younger, white, and male citizens. Republicans and Independents evaluated Graddick somewhat more positively than did Democrats. Graddick's support was about the same among both higher- and lower-income respondents and among more- or less-educated respondents. Only black citizens evaluated Graddick more negatively than positively, and even they were not exceptionally critical in their assessments of the attorney general.

As the last of the primary votes were tabulated, attention turned toward the runoff campaign. What was supposed to be the final step in the selection of the Democratic gubernatorial nominee was expected to be a very close contest fought between two capable and popular candidates. In fact, the contest would actually undermine the favorable images of both candidates, raise questions about their political abilities, and in the end fail to identify the party's nominee.

5

Runoff

The runoff campaign between Bill Baxley and Charles Graddick was the final step for one of them to become governor—or so everyone thought. The prize was just three weeks away, but each man had a very different job to do. Baxley had to reach out to those who had not voted for him the first time to convince them that he was the candidate they were seeking, even though he might be their second choice. Graddick's job was simpler but tougher. A majority of the primary voters had not voted for Baxley, and Graddick had to solidify those voters into an anti-Baxley coalition of those who were seeking a complete break with the Wallace-dominated politics of the past. Part of what made Graddick's job so tough was that his personality and his positions on the issues were not always palatable for those who wanted change. In addition, both candidates had to hold on to the portion of the electorate that had already supported them.

The runoff campaign began without any new accusations, positions, or initiatives by either candidate. Rather, the initial statements and actions of both Baxley and Graddick showed that they intended to campaign on the same basic themes they had emphasized during the primary election.

Four days after the primary, Baxley spoke to the Alabama Associated Press Association stressing his qualifications, saying again that he had the "experience" and "ability" to be governor.[1] He also tried to continue focusing attention on issues as a way of presenting himself as the candidate of the average citizen. For example, on primary election night he said that in the upcoming runoff campaign he wanted the candidates to "talk about issues . . . I want us to talk about the truth."[2] He identified a specific set of social and economic issues that he thought should be discussed—jobs, education, aid to senior citizens, and assistance to disadvantage citizens.

Baxley raised the issue of race, but he did it in a backhanded way, saying that it should not be a concern of the campaign. Early in the runoff campaign he said that Graddick was attempting to pit "race against race."[3] A Graddick television commercial listing "special interest" groups supporting Baxley was one example, Baxley said. Among the groups mentioned was the Alabama Democratic Conference, a black political organization. The leader of this group, Joe Reed, was the only individual mentioned by name in the commercial.

Meanwhile, Graddick continued to stress the need for change in Alabama. The day after the primary he said, "If you look at my opponent and analyze him and find out where he's been and who he's got with him, he represents yesterday. Our campaign really represents tomorrow. We believe there is no choice when you look at the choices for governor."[4]

Graddick also reemphasized his position as an outsider who, unlike Baxley, was not tied to "special interests."[5] Several of the television commercials Graddick used in the runoff tried to focus voter attention on this theme. For example, one ended with the question, "Are you independent enough to be governor, Bill?" Graddick's intention to campaign directly on the link between Baxley and special interests was signaled by an election-night warning for Baxley to "circle his wagons."[6]

The First Debate

The differences between the candidates' campaign themes were clearly visible during the first of their runoff debates.[7] In this June 8 meeting at a Birmingham television station, Baxley repeatedly talked about candidate qualifications by contrasting Graddick's record as attorney general with his own. He argued that the policy proposals made by Graddick were simplistic and unrealistic. Baxley also repeated his claim that Graddick was injecting race into the campaign, pointing to another Graddick television commercial that specifically said Baxley was supported by "black politicians."

Baxley tried to turn the special-interests issue around by claiming that Graddick was tied to the "big boys" while Baxley represented the interests of the average citizen. "His contributions come from the big boys who have the money, have the clout. Mine comes from the little folks who give fifty cents a month." He also pointed out that eight years as attorney general meant Graddick was not really the "new face" he claimed to be.

During the debate, Graddick countered by talking about the need for a change in Alabama politics. He also repeatedly pointed out that Baxley was tied to the "special interests" that had dominated the state for a number of years. He tried to reinforce this linkage in the minds of voters by labeling Baxley a "tax and spend" liberal. Graddick denied that he was using race as an issue.

Baxley's closing remarks consisted of his extemporaneously thanking his supporters and directly appealing to those who previously had voted for McMillan or James, neither of whom up to this point had endorsed either candidate.

Graddick's final remarks were much better prepared. In his clearly focused statement, he said he wanted the state's voters to ask themselves a question, "Are you satisfied with how state government has been run?" He then went on to say, "Ask yourself a further question. Do you want to continue the same ways in the Legislature that you've seen over the past four years? And ask yourself this—are you tired of the special interest big boys calling all the shots to you, the people of Alabama? . . . If you want the possibility of new taxes, if you want someone who represents the old-time special interest bosses in Montgomery, if you want someone who, for whatever reason, stands up for the liberal values in this state, I would suggest to you tonight to vote for my opponent. We've got to make it clear on the 24th of June that we're going to clean up government, and that we're going to throw out the old-time politics as usual. We're going to look to the future."

After the debate it became increasingly clear that Graddick's accusations were having an impact. As a result, Baxley spent much of his time and resources defending himself against Graddick's charges. In a June 13 speech in Birmingham, for example, Baxley repeated his claim that it was Graddick, not he, who was really the candidate of special interests. The lieutenant governor said that the interests he represented were actually those of "average, ordinary people." In contrast, the special interests represented by Graddick were "the same old crowd who think they can buy elections. I don't think the people of Alabama are going to buy that. I think they're going to want a people's man and a people's governor."[8] Baxley also questioned Graddick's allegiance to the Democratic Party by pointing out his opponent's strong support among the state's business interests.

The Second Debate and the Character Issue

The emphasis on the candidates' ties to special interests continued during the second runoff campaign debate, which was held on June 15 at the Alabama Public Television studios in Montgomery.[9] This theme was having such a strong impact on the campaign at this point that Baxley was forced to complain during the debate that his opponent "doesn't want to talk about the issues and our records."

In the debate Graddick said he was an independent leader who would "turn away from the politics of the past." At the same time he said that Bill Baxley "is a puppet of AEA and Paul Hubbard (the head of the Alabama Education Association), of Joe Reed and ADC [Alabama Democratic Conference] and the labor bosses, of the trial lawyers. When a decision is made to take us into the 1990s, he's going to have to go ask them how they feel about it."

Graddick's accusations again forced Baxley to defend himself by saying that he represented the average citizen while the attorney general was the candidate of "big millionaire Republicans. . . . It's hypocritical for him [Graddick] to indicate that mine are special interests groups and his are not," Baxley said.

Baxley also tried to shift attention to the question of the competence of the candidates. He claimed that Graddick was an opportunist who was only interested in "PR" and not real results. Baxley repeated the claim that Graddick was injecting the racial issue into the campaign. "I don't think he's intentionally a racist. But I think he's unleashing forces for political gain, for opportunism, that have caused this state to be held back. It's not the kind of image we need to be projecting to the nation in 1986."

Graddick denied Baxley's claim. "I haven't mentioned anything about race. We look for talent, not the color of somebody's skin. Every time it has been mentioned, it's been by my opponent who says I've been saying something. Not only is it misleading, but it's not true."

What happened at the beginning of the debate, while not affecting the debate itself much, proved to have serious consequences for Baxley and the rest of his campaign. The issue of Baxley's use of state vehicles to transport friends—namely, former Associated Press reporter Marie Prat—had been submerged during the final days of the primary campaign. About two weeks before the debate, the State Ethics Commission had issued an opinion that said using a state vehicle to transport friends was legal as long as state business was involved.[10] Just after this ruling was announced, a *Birmingham News* reporter asked Baxley if he thought his use of the state car fit into the guidelines of this ruling. He said that it did.[11]

That response angered some of the reporters and editors of the *News*, who viewed it as another attempt to evade the issue. Baxley kept denying what the *Birmingham News* reporters thought they knew to be a fact. They had seen Marie Prat riding in a car, driven by state troopers. They had witnessed Prat going in and out of Baxley's apartment. Because of decisions by the *News'* top executives, they had not been able to print all they knew. That inability had given Baxley enough room to maintain his denial, and these denials frustrated *News* reporters and editors.

They decided that if the issue came up during the second debate, they would try to question him more closely about it. Sam Duvall, one of the *News'* statehouse reporters, was selected as one of the panelists for the second debate. Duvall won the toss for which reporter would ask the first question and decided that the other panelists, if they decided to bring up the issue at all, would not press Baxley on it. He led off the debate with a question designed to make Baxley face the issue.

Duvall cited the Ethics Commission opinion, the fact that state cars assigned to Baxley had transported Prat to and from his apartment, and Baxley's statement that his use of state cars was "in line" with the commission's opinion, and then he asked, "Do you consider the transportation of Ms. Prat to be official state business?"

The question caught Baxley off guard, although it should not have. During his debate preparation, the issue had been raised among Baxley's advisers, but the candidate had dismissed it, saying it was not going to be an issue. His lack of preparation showed in his answer.

Baxley challenged what Duvall had stated as a fact—that state troopers had driven Prat to and from his apartment. But he then stammered through a somewhat incoherent response, saying that this allegation had hurt his family and that he never had violated the state ethics law.

Duvall was given a chance to follow up his Baxley's answer with another question. "On a number of occasions," he said, "*Birmingham News* reporters and photographers witnessed troopers assigned to you driving Ms. Prat to your apartment in the evening and driving her away in the morning. Are you saying this is official state business?"

Baxley still denied the charge, saying that "the troopers had denied it, and I have not seen any proof." He then said, "Bear in mind that this is innuendo. The person I have to answer to about innuendo like that is my wife and not you. I have answered that to my wife to her complete satisfaction."

The format of the debate gave Graddick a chance to respond to what Baxley had said at that point, but the attorney general said he did not have anything to say about the issue.

Baxley charged years later that Graddick and Duvall had colluded on the question to set Baxley up.[12] Graddick denied this. Duvall's questions and

Graddick's actions after the debate, however, indicate that both knew things that had not yet been made public. Duvall's second question was much more revealing than Baxley's answer. Duvall disclosed something the *News* had never made known: that the *News* had pictures of something involving the controversy over Baxley, Prat, and the state car.

The next day Graddick zeroed in on the issue of Baxley's character. Despite having nothing to say on the issue the night before, he charged that Baxley had lied about the use of state cars. "Baxley told the people of Alabama he didn't do something he did. The next governor of Alabama shouldn't be somebody who would lie to anyone, much less to the people of Alabama on statewide television."[13]

Graddick also said the *Birmingham News* and the State Ethics Commission should release whatever information they had about the state car issue. The chair of the Ethics Commission refused to comment on the issue (the commission was conducting an investigation of the allegations). The *News* said that it stood by its original story, but went no further.[14] Graddick's press conference was a broad hint that he knew what was behind Duvall's question the night before.

Baxley tried to squelch the "character" issue by again attempting to get voters to focus their attention on the themes of his campaign. "I addressed this matter [the state car issue] repeatedly. The issues in the campaign should be who has the ability to lead the state and our record in office and what we propose to get the state moving forward," he said.[15]

In responding to the state car allegations, Baxley labeled Graddick a "coward" for waiting until after the debate to raise the state car issue. "I don't think the people of this state want a coward to lead them."[16]

Baxley was facing problems on other fronts as well. The day after the second debate, George McMillan publicly endorsed Graddick, saying that if Baxley were elected, "the same special interests which have exploited this state for so long will have a new leader to continue their selfish misrule."[17] (Throughout the runoff campaign, Fob James refused to endorse either Baxley or Graddick.)[18]

McMillan's endorsement of the conservative attorney general caught many observers by surprise, including some of McMillan's own supporters.[19] It also represented a serious problem for the Baxley campaign, which had viewed McMillan primary voters as the most likely source of new support in the runoff.

Baxley's response was to charge that Graddick had bought the endorsement by promising to pay off the former lieutenant governor's campaign debts, a charge that McMillan denied. Baxley backed up his allegation by saying that two of McMillan's aides had earlier approached him with a proposal that involved McMillan's endorsement of Baxley in return for help in paying a $480,000 debt. Both McMillan and Graddick quickly denied Baxley's charges.[20] At the same time, Hinton Mitchem, a defeated candidate for lieutenant governor and a state senator from Albertville, also endorsed Graddick. Baxley said that Graddick had gotten Mitchem's endorsement in return for a promise of a future state government job. Mitchem, like McMillan, heatedly denied the charge.[21]

Sensing that he had Baxley on the defensive, Graddick canceled a third runoff debate. He justified this by saying that he was dissatisfied with the debate's arrangements and added that he really did not think another meeting was needed. In response, Baxley again called Graddick a coward. "Like all cowards, they prefer to do their dirty work behind the scenes. They can't stand the light of day. They want to make allegations and innuendo, but they don't want to do it face-to-face."[22]

The next day, June 18, the *Birmingham News*, saying that the paper's performance had become an issue in the campaign, printed another article about the state car issue. The *News* repeated its story that its reporters had witnessed on numerous occasions Associated Press reporter Marie Prat being taken to and from Baxley's Montgomery apartment in state cars driven by state employees. The *News* also published two pictures of Ms. Prat outside an apartment building getting into a privately owned car (not a state car) while accompanied by Baxley's state trooper bodyguard. The picture did not definitely show Ms. Prat leaving Baxley's apartment. Much of the article, written by the paper's editor, Jim Jacobson, was devoted to an explanation of the *News*' handling of the entire story.[23]

Graddick took the opportunity of the *News*' story to again raise questions about Baxley's character, repeating his claim that Baxley had lied about the state car issue. "I know if a person would intentionally tell a falsehood about one thing he could tell a falsehood about other matters. Truth, veracity, integrity and character (are) at the heart of this campaign right now."[24]

For his part, Baxley said that the *News*' story did not prove anything. "I have yet to see anything connecting me to any wrongdoing."[25] Criticizing both the *News* and Graddick for focusing on this topic, Baxley said that he was going to "talk about the issues in this campaign for the rest of this week. I'm going to turn the other check."[26] As a parting shot and an attempt to gain the sympathy of the state's voters, Baxley said what he most regretted about the entire incident was the harm it had done to his "wife, son and mother."[27]

But Baxley could not quit talking about the issue. He had always been open and free with his comments to reporters, and it was not in his nature to refuse to answer a question. In an interview published in the *Anniston Star* two days later, Baxley again said that he had not done anything "improper. . . . I have not done anything that is unethical or illegal."[28]

Baxley's wife, Lucy, tried to defuse the issue. In a news conference held in the den of their suburban Birmingham home, she said her husband had answered all her questions about the issue to her satisfaction. Then, reasserting the themes of the Baxley campaign, she went on to say, "Charlie Graddick and his friends and *The Birmingham News*, in my opinion, have seen that Bill stands so strong on the issues and on his experience and on his ability to serve as governor of this state that these tactics that I think are just shameful have been put into effect. I'm just so thankful that in this house, Bill and I have a love and a commitment that's strong enough to withstand this. My husband has not violated my trust in him. Nor has he violated the trust the people of the state of Alabama have placed in him."[29]

Even before the state car issue had reached its peak, Graddick was raising another issue related to Baxley's character. This had to do with Baxley's state income-tax returns. The same day the *News* released its photographs, Graddick distributed copies of his income-tax returns for the previous ten years and challenged Baxley to do the same.

Graddick said that he was making this challenge because he had information that Baxley had for several years not paid his state income taxes.[30] When questioned closely about this, Graddick admitted that he had no hard evidence concerning whether Baxley had filed his tax returns and thus was not charging anything, but he added, "I have very good reason to believe he did not (always file his state returns)." Graddick then suggested that the dates of Baxley's return be closely checked, if they were made available.[31] When asked about the source of his information about Baxley's taxes, Graddick said, "I've gotten very good reliable information from a source that declines to be identified." He went on to say that this individual "knows Bill Baxley very well."[32]

Baxley quickly denied Graddick's charges. Baxley did say that in several instances he had asked for an extension and thus had been late in paying his taxes. However, Baxley claimed that he had always "paid every cent of taxes I owe."[33] Baxley's denial did not stop Graddick from repeating his allegation the next day, Thursday, June 19. Graddick again was forced to admit, however, that he had no evidence to back up his claim that Baxley had failed to pay his taxes.[34] Baxley continued to say that he had paid all of his state taxes. He also said he had not yet decided whether to release his tax returns. He did try to take the offensive by saying that by canceling the scheduled third debate, Graddick had not taken the "manly way" to make his accusations.[35]

While at a campaign stop at a Dothan motel, Graddick was asked about Baxley's remarks concerning the canceled third debate. In one of the more bizarre statements of the campaign, Graddick said, "I debated Bill Baxley toe-to-toe. I wouldn't mind going out here by the swimming pool in the grass and getting it on with him—whatever he wanted to do."[36]

Meanwhile, Lucy Baxley was spending the day traveling around Alabama defending her husband on the state car issue. She also appeared in a television commercial in which she responded to the charges against her husband regarding that issue. In Montgomery, again emphasizing the themes of the Baxley campaign, she said that the reemergence of the state car issue was "one more last ditch effort" to attack her husband and to divert attention from the issues and the qualifications of the candidates. "I regret very much that, at a time in Alabama when we're talking about image and we're talking about wanting higher-level things for our state, that a decision of who is to serve as governor is reduced to such as this."[37]

The same day Graddick was saying that Baxley had not paid his taxes and Baxley's wife was defending him against charges that he had used a state car and state employees to transport a female reporter to his apartment, Baxley was being called a liar by George McMillan. The former candidate said Baxley's claim that Graddick had "bought" McMillan's endorsement was incorrect. In fact, McMillan said, "Anything I have read lately that Bill Baxley has said has been a lie." He went on to say, "Perhaps the most important reason of all why I feel so strongly about voting for Charles Graddick is that Charles Graddick is as committed as I was, and I am, to running those sleazy political hangers-on . . . out of that state capital."[38] McMillan did not deny that his campaign had sought help in paying off its debts from Baxley.

On Friday, June 20, Baxley released summaries of his state income-tax returns from 1979 to 1984. This information showed that Baxley had paid all of his state taxes. At the same time, a spokesman for the State Revenue Commission confirmed the lieutenant governor's position, saying that Baxley "had paid all of his taxes. He does not owe the Department of Revenue any taxes at this time."[39] The tax issue died away as Graddick went on to other attacks, but it would resurface later in the general election when a revenue department employee was arrested and charged with the theft of Baxley's tax returns.[40]

As they entered the last days of the runoff campaign, both Baxley and Graddick predicted victory. Graddick spent the last weekend of the campaign encouraging his supporters to vote on election day. He also made a late appeal to black voters, telling a meeting of NAACP leaders that if elected, he would "represent all citizens, regardless of the color of their skin."[41] He also continued to stress his independence from special interests.[42]

Baxley appeared before union and social service organizations. He also held a news conference outside the Montgomery television station where the third candidate debate was supposed to be held. He said that he had met Graddick's challenge regarding his income taxes. At the same time, Graddick's campaign was saying that Baxley had not met the challenge, as he had released information about only six, not ten, taxpaying years. Besides, the Graddick campaign said, the attorney general had never really claimed that Baxley had not paid his taxes. Baxley also said Graddick had done a disservice to the public by refusing to debate. He then went on to discuss his issue proposals regarding jobs, education, services for the elderly and disadvantaged, tourism, and health care. Finally, he said that rather than being a candidate of particular interests, he was one who could bring Alabamians together.[43]

Crossovers

While both candidates were predicting victory, many others were saying that the election was too close to call. Indeed, the last pre-runoff survey conducted by the Capstone Poll found a virtual tie, with Graddick ahead by an exceptionally thin (and statistically insignificant) margin, 48 percent to 45. The closeness of the race suggested that the victor would be the candidate who would have the most success in getting his supporters to the polls. Both candidates were spending resources on the normal "get out the vote" activities of telephone banks and car pools. More than in most elections, however, turnout and who would actually vote was becoming a larger concern, especially to Democratic Party officials.

Democratic Party leaders had taken several actions during the runoff campaign that seemed to benefit Baxley. First, they upheld a challenge to the results of the primary election regarding a seat on the state board of education. In the primary, a black and a white candidate had competed against each other for a school board seat from a section of Alabama that had a predominantly black population. The primary ballot also contained the name of another candidate who earlier had been disqualified by the party. The white candidate won the election by a 357-vote margin, while the disqualified candidate received more than six thousand votes. In supporting the challenge, the party ordered that the two certified candidates face each other again on June 24 (the day of the runoff election). The presence of a black candidate on the runoff day ballot undoubtedly stimulated black turnout in this part of Alabama. Given his strong support among black voters, this decision clearly worked in Baxley's favor.[44]

More importantly, shortly after the primary, party leaders announced that they intended to enforce the rule, adopted following the 1978 election, prohibiting citizens who had voted in the Republican primary from also voting in the Democratic runoff. Alabama is an open primary state that does not require registration with a party to participate in a primary election for a party's nominees. Once a person votes in the Republican primary, however, that disqualifies him or her from voting—or crossing over—in the Democratic runoff election. In a letter to voting officials, Democratic Party chairman John Baker reminded them of the party's anti-crossover rule and recommended that those who came to vote in the runoff election be asked if they had voted in the Republican primary. If a person said yes or refused to answer, the letter said, he or she should not be allowed to vote; if a person refused to answer and still insisted on voting, he or she could vote on a "challenge ballot."

The Democrats worried about Republican influence on the runoff vote for several reasons. On the day before the primary election, Bob Ingram, a longtime political commentator for WSFA-TV in Montgomery, broadcast a commentary saying Republican crossover voting was legal. Baker tried to respond immediately but did not get on the air until the next week.[45]

Most of those who had followed the runoff race recognized that the runoff results would probably be very close. Baxley led Graddick by a substantial margin in the primary, but he had attracted only 36 percent of the vote. While Graddick might have a hard time catching up with Baxley, the lieutenant governor might have an equally hard time attracting more than 50 percent of the vote in the runoff. Party leaders realized that a potential existed for a relatively few votes to decide the outcome, and they did not want those votes to come from Republicans.

Clearly, the Republicans wanted to have such an impact, and they saw their opportunity just as the Democrats did. Graddick had begun his political career as a Republican, and many Democrats believed that he had never really cut his ties with the GOP. Graddick's links to the Republican Party became more apparent when he filed his campaign disclosure forms. Those forms revealed that Graddick had received major contributions from prominent Republicans such as Winton Blount III and Hall Thompson.[46] In addition, Democrats had evidence that Graddick had used a Republican National Committee mailing list to solicit campaign contribution.[47]

That Republicans favored Graddick over Baxley was obvious to anyone familiar with their positions on issues, but it was confirmed when both Graddick and the Republicans began singing the same tune about the legality of crossover voting.[48] On the last weekend before the election, four Republican state senators appeared in a television ad saying that crossover voting was legal. On the Monday before voting began on Tuesday morning, Graddick said the same thing and urged Republican primary voters to show up at the polls and vote, of course, for him. The Democrats tried to counter these moves by going to court. The day before the runoff, the party had a Jackson County judge issue a ruling restating the prohibition against crossover voting.

Baxley made it clear that he supported the anti-crossover voting rule. During the week preceding the runoff he said, "This runoff election is not a new election. This is a continuation of the first election, and the people that made the choice to vote in the Republican primary that first time just by law cannot come back in and participate in any other primary." For his part, Graddick did everything he could do to encourage Republicans to participate in the runoff. "If the people who voted in the Republican primary choose to vote in the Democratic runoff, I bet they'll vote for me. And I hope that they will (cross over). I encourage them to come over and vote for me," he said.

Graddick went beyond merely saying he wanted Republicans to vote in the Democratic runoff. On Monday, his campaign obtained its own day-before-the-election court order, in this case from a Mobile County judge. This order said that it was illegal to prohibit crossover voting.[49] But the actions Graddick and his campaign workers took the day before proved to be even more consequential.

At a Sunday-afternoon meeting at Graddick campaign headquarters in Montgomery, two days before the election, campaign officials discussed crossover voting and how they could prevent the party from challenging voters. Susan McKinney, an assistant attorney general and head of the voting fraud unit of the attorney general's office, was present at the meeting and was asked if there was "anything she could do." She volunteered to write a letter saying that crossover voting was legal, and she then left for the attorney general's office to draft the letter. Graddick later saw and approved the letter, and although it carried McKinney's signature, it had the appearance of an attorney general's official opinion.

The letter cited a 1970 attorney general's opinion that said crossover voting was legal. It ignored the fact that the current anti-crossover rule had been adopted in 1979 and had been approved by the U.S. Department of Justice. The letter also implied that election officials who tried to prevent a registered voter from voting would be subject to civil penalties: "Those who fail to permit any registered voter to vote may subject themselves to civil liability under state and federal law. Any attempt by election officials to require voters to disclose how they voted on June 3 would also be an invasion of the voter's right to privacy." Graddick said the letter was intended to stop election officials from stopping anyone from voting. A person whom election official suspected of voting illegally should be allow to cast a ballot, and then that ballot should be set aside as "challenged" ballot. After its approval by Graddick, the letter was duplicated and delivered to election officials across the state by his campaign workers, an action that Graddick later characterized as a "serious mistake."[50]

Janie Nobles, the press secretary in the attorney general's office, also attended the Sunday-afternoon meeting at Graddick headquarters. While the McKinney letter was being written, Nobles prepared a press release about the letter. That press release was distributed out of the attorney general's office the next morning. On Monday afternoon another press release came out of the attorney general's office that mentioned the order from the Mobile County judge declaring the anti-crossover rule illegal. It did not mention the Jackson County judge's ruling that upheld the party's rules.

Democratic Party chairman John Baker quickly replied that the attorney general office's opinion was flawed because it did not take into account changes in the party's rules and the fact that the U.S. Department of Justice had determined that the anti-crossover voting provision was in compliance with the 1965 Voting Rights Act. The party's move to remind voters of the anti-crossover rule clearly was an action that would benefit Baxley, but the benefits were lost by the assistant attorney general's letter. Once that letter was received, few election officials had the wherewithal to challenge voters who came to the polls on June 24.

As attorney general, Graddick took a final step taken to influence the atmosphere at the polls by requesting that the U.S. Department of Justice deploy poll watchers in the state. Graddick said his request was motivated by a desire to prevent harassment and intimidation of his black supporters. Others suggested, and the Graddick campaign denied, that the request was really an effort to hold down black turnout.[51]

Graddick's "Victory"

The runoff election proved to be as close as expected. Out of approximately 930,000 votes cast, Graddick defeated Baxley by a slim 50.4 to 49.6 percent margin, a difference of 8,756 votes. Graddick's victory was remarkable in that he had gained 70,000 votes on his opponent in three weeks. Figures 5.1 and 5.2 show that Baxley's vote in the runoff election remained static in terms of counties, whereas Graddick's vote in the runoff extended well beyond his vote in the primary.

On election night Baxley admitted he was trailing but said the results were still too close for him to concede. Nothing indicated then that Baxley's hesitancy to concede was anything more than a reasonable desire to check out all possibilities before admitting defeat.

Relatively early on election night, while the vote totals presented by the media showed an extremely close contest, Graddick publicly claimed victory. He went on to thank his supporters and congratulate Baxley for his campaign. Later that night, in a somewhat unprecedented move, he used his position as attorney general to order sheriffs in each county to require that ballot boxes be turned in by a certain time.

The results of the pre-runoff Capstone Poll survey showed that Graddick received strong support from Independents, Republicans, and older citizens, while Baxley was strongly supported by Democrats and younger citizens (table 5.1). Socioeconomic status (as indicated by education or income) was only mildly related to support for Graddick or Baxley. Similarly, little difference in candidate support existed among male and female voters. However, a substantial difference was found in the voting behavior of black and white citizens. A majority of the state's white voters supported Graddick, while Baxley was the overwhelming favorite of black voters.

More importantly, the poll results showed that Graddick had prevented Baxley from getting many of those who had voted for their opponents in the primary election. Both Graddick and Baxley were able to maintain the support of nearly all their primary election voters. Graddick, however, picked up the support of most (about 73 percent) of Fob James's supporters, and Graddick received the support of nearly as many (43 percent) of George McMillan's primary election voters as did Baxley (50 percent).

Why was Graddick able to make up more than 70,000 votes on Baxley in

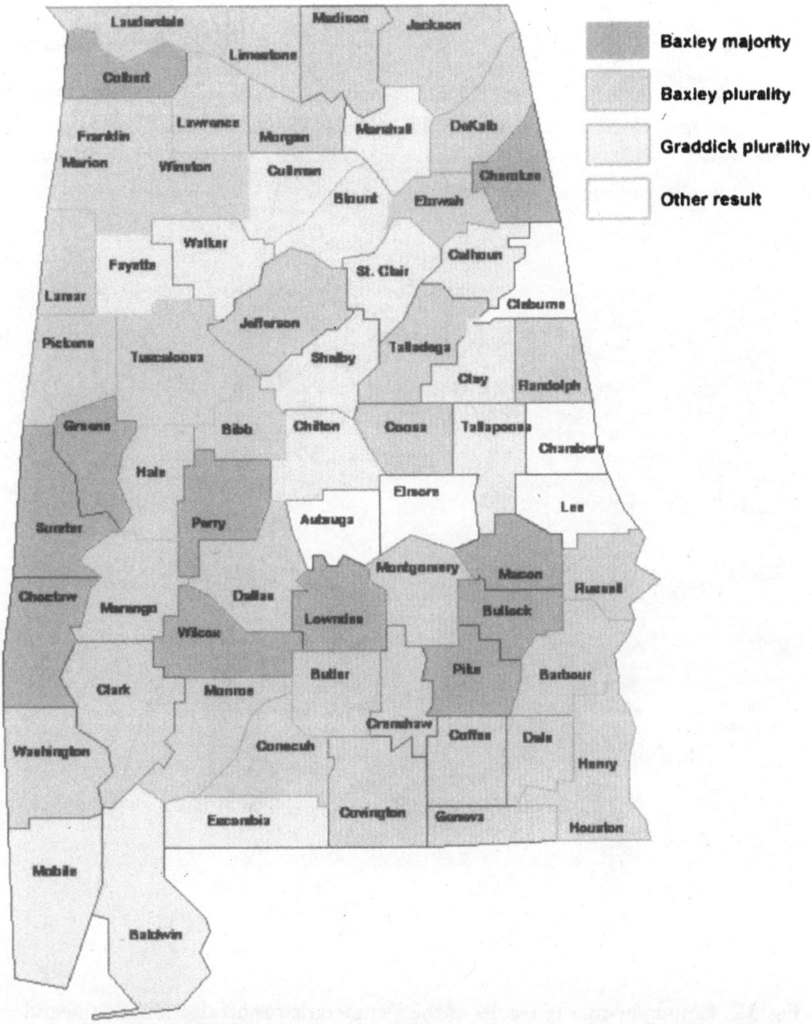

Fig. 5.1. County-by-county results of the Democratic primary election. The results showed that Baxley had won majorities in ten counties and pluralities in many others across the state. Graddick did not win a majority in any county, even his home county of Mobile, where he got 49.4 percent of the vote.

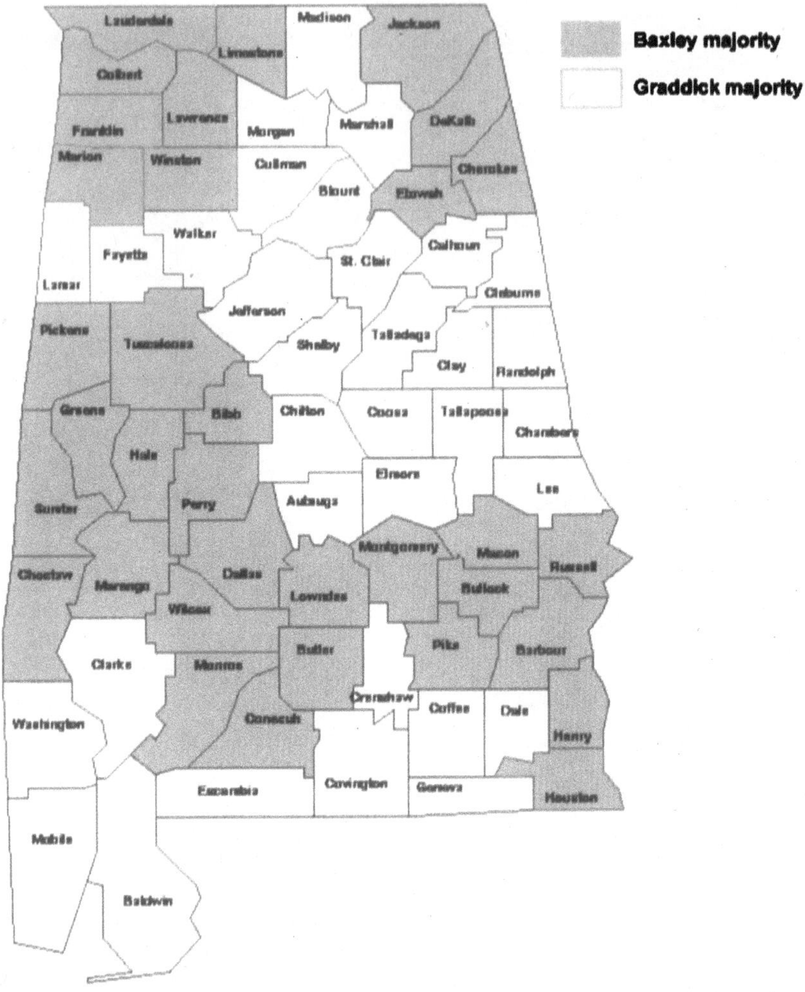

Fig. 5.2. County-by-county results of the Democratic runoff election. By the end of the runoff campaign, Baxley had not been able to turn enough of the counties where he had pluralities in the primary into majorities. Graddick was able to capture enough of the non-Baxley vote to emerge with a bare majority when the results were initially counted.

Table 5.1

Socio-demographic characteristics of runoff election supporters

"If the Democratic runoff election were held today and the candidates were Bill Baxley and Charles Graddick, for whom would you vote?" (If Undecided—"As of today, do you lean a little more toward Baxley or Graddick?")

Characteristics*	Baxley	Graddick	DK/NA	N
Age				
18–40 yrs	52%	45%	3%	397
41–60 yrs	40	53	8	294
61+ yrs	40	46	14	233
Race				
White	35	58	7	705
Black	78	13	9	204
Gender				
Male	42	49	8	379
Female	47	47	7	555
Education				
High School or less	44	48	8	537
More than high school	46	48	6	383
Income				
Under $40,000	49	46	6	654
More than $40,000	39	58	3	136
Party				
Republican	29	63	8	119
Independent	29	66	5	265
Democrat	60	33	7	483
Vote in primary				
Baxley	94	4	1	247
Graddick	4	94	2	194
James	24	73	3	93
McMillan	50	43	7	72

* Missing data deleted

Source: Capstone Poll 176

the three-week runoff campaign? The most critical part of the answer to this question was that Graddick was able to control the agenda for the campaign. As they entered the runoff campaign, both candidates were faced with the problem of identifying the issues or themes they needed to have on the campaign's agenda so that they could maintain their existing base of support. They also needed to attract a sufficient number of new supporters from the ranks of those who had voted for either James or McMillan in the primary.

From the very beginning of the campaign, Baxley wanted voters to base their decisions on three different issues: competence, representing the "average" voter, and race. He repeatedly discussed his position on a set of socioeconomic issues, such as jobs, education, and support for the elderly and the disadvantaged. His competence theme helped maintain his already strong support among traditional Democratic voters. Baxley hoped that by focusing attention on the "representative" theme, he would attract the liberal supporters of McMillan. His continued emphasis on the themes of candidate experience and qualifications would help him attract some of James's supporters.

Baxley raised the racial issue out of a genuine concern about the possibility of a return to racial politics. His initial motivation for getting into politics, he said later, was civil rights.[52] He wanted to change Alabama, and as attorney general he had certainly changed the direction of the law enforcement arm of the state government. During the campaign he undoubtedly saw the race issue as a way to mobilize his black supporters and possibly as a way to "challenge" the state's white voters to support him in order to show that they were not prejudiced. The risk for Baxley in raising the race issue was that it could result in an even higher level of support for Graddick among whites.

The issues that Graddick's campaign initially stressed during the runoff were also ones he used during the primary: the need for a change and Baxley's ties to "special interests." The continued focus on these issues obviously helped Graddick maintain his existing core of supporters. However, these themes also gave the Graddick campaign a potentially effective way to attract the former supporters of both James and McMillan. Both of these candidates, who had many different ideas regarding specific policy issues, had campaigned during the primary on the need for reform. The supporters of both defeated candidates, while differing in their opinions on many other issues, probably were also interested in changing the politics of the state.

This area of similarity between the James and McMillan camps meant that if Graddick could focus voter attention on the related themes of change and special interests (which primarily involved questions concerning the "style" of governing) rather than on the competency and economics themes (which involved the "substance" of government) being raised by his opponent, then he stood a good chance of constructing a winning, though an ideologically diverse, coalition.

With the reemergence of the state car issue later in the campaign, Graddick added the issue of Baxley's character to the agenda. It stayed on the agenda when Graddick created the controversy concerning Baxley's tax returns and when Baxley, McMillan, and Mitchem got into a long-distance shouting match about who was lying and who was telling the truth. Baxley's calling his opponent a "coward" may also have unintentionally kept the character issue on the agenda.

Overall, Graddick was more successful than Baxley in controlling the agenda. Much more media attention was given to questions about special interests and the character of the candidates than to the issues or the records of the candidate. Baxley and his allies (including his wife) continually tried to reassert the themes of his campaign, but these attempts were consistently pushed aside by the different twists and turns in the state car controversy or by a series of character-related (and often unsubstantiated) charges by Graddick or someone associated with his campaign. What happened concerning the agenda for the runoff is best summarized by this headline in the *Montgomery Advertiser* on June 20: "Issues Fading as Candidates Repeat 'Dirty' Accusations."

Perhaps it was inevitable that Graddick would control the agenda for the runoff. With the end of the Wallace era, Alabama voters were especially interested in the possibility of a change in the state's politics and government, subjects about which they were extremely unhappy. Baxley's long involvement in state government and his image (warranted or not) as the inheritor of Wallace's core coalition meant that he was seen as the candidate of the status quo.

Baxley's inability to control the agenda was also the result of a surprising lack of aggressiveness on his part. This behavior may have stemmed from a number of sources. Baxley's position as the front-runner may have made him cautious and defensive. His aggressive, but losing, campaign in 1978 may have made him hesitant to follow the same course in 1986. Graddick, however, had none of these inhibitions. His previous campaigns had shown him to be an aggressive campaigner, and his status as an underdog in 1986 made an aggressive strategy appropriate.

Baxley's behavior and his campaign style made his character a relatively

Table 5.2

Evaluations of runoff election candidates

"Do you generally feel positive, neutral, or negative about each of the following people?"

	October 1985	January 1986	April 1986	May 1986	June 1986
Charles Graddick					
Positive	42%	39%	42%	44%	41%
Neutral/Don't know	42	44	43	35	29
Negative	16	18	15	21	30
% Pos. - % Neg.	26	21	27	23	11
Bill Baxley					
Positive	38%	41%	44%	42%	35%
Neutral/Don't know	41	39	38	30	34
Negative	21	21	18	28	31
% Pos. - % Neg.	17	20	26	14	4

Source: Capstone Poll 148, 160, 169, 175, 176

easy target for Graddick. Baxley's public record is littered with stories about gambling, drinking, shady associations, and other dubious actions. The state car issue that the *Birmingham News* raised was only the most recent of these "scandals." As a result, Graddick merely had to raise the issue of Baxley's character. He didn't have to convince the public there were problems in this area.

Toward the General Election—Guy Who?

The harshness of the campaign took its toll on the public perceptions of both Baxley and Graddick. The number of "positive" evaluations received by both candidates declined, while the number of "negative" assessments rose (table 5.2).

Some shifts also occurred in the types of voters giving Baxley and Graddick positive or negative ratings. By the end of the runoff, Baxley continued to be favorably evaluated by the groups traditionally aligned with the Democratic Party (i.e., Democratic identifiers, less-educated, lower-income, and black citizens). However, during the runoff campaign his support shifted so that he received strongly negative ratings from Republicans and Indepen-

Table 5.3

Net evaluations of runoff candidates by socio-demographic groups, June 1986

Characteristic*	Net evaluations**	
	Charles Graddick	Bill Baxley
Age		
18–40 years	0	15
41–60 years	15	0
61+ years	24	-6
Race		
White	24	-10
Black	-32	54
Gender		
Male	13	0
Female	10	7
Education		
High school or less	17	4
More than high school	3	5
Income		
Less than $40,000	8	9
More than $40,000	18	-14
Party		
Republican	44	-29
Independent	29	-22
Democrat	-9	29

*Missing data deleted.
**These scores are figured by subtracting the percentage giving a negative evaluation to a candidate from those giving a positive evaluation.

Source: Capstone Poll 176

dents. He also was more negatively than positively rated by white citizens (table 5.3).

Graddick's image remained stable or improved during the runoff campaign among Republicans and Independents, while it became substantially more negative among Democrats. Graddick continued to be more favorably evaluated by higher-income and more-educated citizens. He also received strong positive ratings from whites, while his image among blacks became strongly negative.

Overall, as the runoff ended and attention shifted toward the general election, little importance was given to the increasingly less positive images of Graddick and Baxley. After all, no Republican had been elected governor in more than one hundred years, and the winner of the generally ignored Republican gubernatorial primary was the almost invisible Guy Hunt, the same person who had lost so decisively in 1978.[53]

But Charles Graddick had a problem, and it wasn't Guy Hunt. Many Democrats were yet not ready to let the runoff election go.

6
Challenge

On the morning of June 24, 1986, Ed Patridge went to vote in the Democratic runoff election. A native of Bibb County, Patridge had been president of the Brent Bank since 1956. Three weeks before, he had been at his local polling place voting in the Republican primary. As chairman of the Bibb County Republican Party, Patridge had been obliged to help his party select the best people for the few offices it was contesting.

On this morning, however, Patridge was not acting as the chairman of the Republican Party but as a citizen of Alabama. Like others in his state, he knew that for most offices, nomination for a statewide office by the Democrats was virtual assurance of election. Alabama had not elected a Republican governor in more than a century. At that point during the twentieth century it had sent only one Republican U.S. senator to Washington.

Patridge said he wanted to have a voice in selecting the next governor of the state. "I wanted the best person we could get to be the governor," he said later. Patridge had heard the warnings of Democratic Party officials who said Republicans—that is, those who had voted in the Republican primary on June 3—would not be allowed to vote in the Democratic runoff.[1] He had also heard one of the Democratic candidates for governor, Attorney General Charles Graddick, openly solicit votes from Republicans. He had read about opinions of two different judges in the state, one saying crossover voting—the term given to what Patridge was trying to do—was legal and another saying it was not. He knew the tradition of voting in Alabama—that whenever an election is held, any registered voter could vote.

Patridge knew all of these things and had made up his own mind. "I thought it was legal, so I did it," he said. The bank president also had armed himself with a letter from a Montgomery law firm stating a former attorney general had ruled "crossover" voting was legal. Patridge had planned to show this letter to any polling official who challenged his right to vote.

But Patridge was not challenged. He signed in and was given a ballot.

He marked Charles Graddick as his choice for governor. He returned to his bank to conduct the day's business, satisfied that he had participated in the democratic process once again.[2]

What Ed Patridge did that day also was done by between 10,000 and 20,000 other people, possibly as many as 30,000 (the exact numbers have never been determined). Their actions, though honest and well intentioned, created a firestorm of controversy that played itself out over the next four months and helped change the shape of Alabama's politics.

The day after the election, Charles Graddick, aglow from his victory the day before, told reporters that he had been asleep the night before for about three hours but that he had "never touched the mattress."[3] Graddick had pulled off a stunning upset. More than 70,000 votes behind only three weeks before in the primary, he had marshaled his forces and picked up enough support to edge out Baxley, the man who long had been expected to succeed George Wallace. Graddick's supporters were understandably elated, and Graddick himself struck the pose of a humble and magnanimous winner.

Graddick began tying the final knots on his victory. He went to see Wallace and reported that the governor had told him things that were "very inspirational."[4] He called Baxley and reported that in their conversation, Baxley "congratulated me and [said he] knew that I would make a very good governor." Graddick added, "He [Baxley] did, however, say that he was not going to make any official statement with regards to the outcome of this race until the official count is made." Still, Graddick stated that Baxley "indicated that he wouldn't enter a challenge into this contest."[5]

On other fronts, however, hints of a possible challenge to the election results were present. On election night, Baxley's campaign manager alluded to a need to investigate "legal issues."[6] The day after the election, a number of supporters urged Baxley to challenge Graddick's apparent victory.[7]

Graddick continued to act as the Democratic nominee. On the Thursday after the election he met with some members of the state legislature, trying to build some goodwill for his future administration. No black legislators were invited to the meeting—a telling omission in the minds of many people.[8]

While he continued to act like a winner, Graddick found victory itself might be more elusive. Before the week was out, a series of events had begun that would keep the election outcome in doubt for more than three months and would turn 1986 into a most unusual election year. Graddick, who had been so masterful in controlling the agenda of the runoff campaign, would find himself continually outmaneuvered and outgunned in his fight to retain the nomination.

Who Won?

A tradition in modern American politics is that you have not won an election until your opponent concedes. During the first few days after the runoff election, Bill Baxley refused to concede. Even though he apparently had decided against contesting the election at that point, Baxley had not given Graddick his concession because of the extreme closeness of the vote. Instead, Baxley and his family went to Gulf Shores and remained hidden away from the media.

Baxley's lack of a concession and his refusal to speak to the news media fueled talk of a challenge. Many Democrats were incensed by the idea that Republican votes had provided Graddick with a margin of victory, and their mood was not helped when Jean Sullivan, a Republican National Committee member from Selma, bragged that as many as 20,000 of the 33,000 who voted in the Republican primary had crossed over to vote in the Democratic runoff. "I don't think there is any doubt that the Republicans nominated Charlie Graddick," she said. When it was pointed out to her that one Republican runoff race drew less than one hundred votes, she said, "That's because all the Republicans were voting in the Democratic primary."[9] Graddick openly acknowledged that this was the case and even thanked the Republicans for their help.[10]

Democrats were also seething at Graddick's high-handed use of the attorney general's office in preventing them from enforcing the anti-crossover rule and his ordering sheriffs to seize ballot boxes in each county—an action that was called "unprecedented" by party leaders.[11]

On top of all these events was the fact that Graddick had not publicly endorsed the party's nominee to the U.S. Senate, Richard Shelby, or committed to making any public appearances with him. Already suspicious of Graddick as a former Republican, Democrats began to see evidence of an understanding between Graddick and the Republicans.

John Baker, chairman of the Democratic Party, had left town right after the election to attend a pilot certification program in Pensacola, Florida. No sooner had he gotten there, however, than his phone began to ring. People were calling to ask about rumors they were hearing about a challenge to the election. One of the callers was Graddick, who insisted on meeting with Baker. The chairman cut his program short and returned to Montgomery, where he had Graddick and several campaign aides over to his house for dinner. Baker also invited some party officials and Richard Shelby.[12]

During this same time, Baxley had been getting many phone calls and some visits from people who wanted him to challenge the results of the election. One of those, he said, was from Fob James, who had never gotten over the frog commercial that Graddick had run during the primary election campaign. By Thursday Baxley had decided to mount a challenge, but he was not ready to say so publicly. Baxley, in an interview years later, said he knew at the time that a challenge would probably end his political career.[13]

At the dinner at Baker's home on Thursday evening, Graddick expressed concern about a possible challenge and received little comfort from Baker, who said he knew little about any such moves. Shelby pressed Graddick on an endorsement of his candidacy, but Graddick made no commitment. In the midst of all this, Baker received a call and left the room. The call was from Baxley, who wanted to discuss a possible challenge to the election. The evening ended inconclusively for all concerned, but word spread about Graddick's reluctance to commit to Shelby, confirming the suspicions of many Democrats.[14]

An official count of Tuesday's returns came on Saturday and showed that out of more than 900,000 votes, Graddick had received 8,756 more than Baxley. An accounting firm had overseen the count, and no one disputed the numbers. Just before the official vote count began on Saturday, two Madison County residents, Kennith and Nellie Pike, handed Baker a petition stating that they were officially contesting the election results. The Pikes had originally supported Fob James in the primary and had switched to Baxley in the runoff. Their contest petition claimed that Graddick's margin of victory was due to the illegal votes of Republicans who had voted in the Republican primary on June 3 and then crossed over to vote in the Democratic runoff on June 24. The petition cited National Republican Committee member Jean Sullivan, who said that she and "thousands" of other Republicans had voted in the Democratic runoff; it also said the Republican chairman of Madison County voted in the Democratic runoff after voting in the Republican primary.[15]

The Pikes said then and later maintained that they were not part of any Baxley plan to take the nomination from Graddick. "Nobody promised me anything, and nobody gave me any money," Kennith Pike said.[16] Pike described himself as a "semi-retired" farmer who sold crop insurance; he had been appointed to fill out an unexpired term on the Madison County Commission in 1984 and had lost a bid to be elected to a full term. Nellie Pike was a recreation instructor for the city of Huntsville and a member of the Madison County Democratic Executive Committee.

Graddick publicly called on Baxley to concede and indicated that he expected him to do so. "Based on my conversations with Bill Baxley the morning after the election," Graddick said," I fully expect him now to concede the race." A Graddick spokesman dismissed the Pikes' challenge as "frivolous."[17]

Graddick and his supporters had some reason for optimism. After all, he did have the most votes; the challenge had been undertaken by two obscure people; Baxley had indicated to him earlier in the week that he was not interested in contesting the election if the final vote count showed him behind; finally, proving the contentions of the Pikes' challenge—that thousands of Republicans had not only crossed over but also had voted for Graddick—would be, in the words of party chairman Baker, "mind-boggling."[18]

Within twenty-four hours, however, Graddick realized that his reasons for optimism were not as strong as they had appeared. He had been engaged in a serious of meetings and telephone calls that had convinced him the challenge to his election was a serious threat. One of the most significant of these meetings was with Paul Hubbert, executive director of the Alabama Education Association and a strong supporter of Baxley.[19] The meeting took place in the home of Jim Solomon, a Graddick aide, but accounts of what was said differ widely. According to Graddick, Hubbert came in with a list of "demands" for the next governor. When Graddick would not agree to them, according to this version, Hubbert ended the meeting with a vow that Graddick would never be governor.

Hubbert said the two discussed some concerns that the AEA had. Graddick had been quoted telling a group of state legislators earlier in the week that when he was governor, the AEA "wouldn't be able to get in the door."[20] But the main point of the meeting, Hubbert said, was Graddick's request that Hubbert advise Baxley against joining in the challenge to his election. Hubbert said he would think about that request, but he later told Graddick that he would not advise Baxley to stay out of the challenge.[21]

Party chair Baker appointed a five-man committee to consider the challenge, and the membership of the committee was a clear signal that Graddick would have little influence among the party's leaders. Baker named himself as chairman, and committee members were Pat Lindsey, Baxley's Choctaw County campaign coordinator (who later was replaced by Franklin Kellett of DeKalb County); John Knight, chairman of the Montgomery chapter of the Alabama Democratic Council, a black organization that had supported Baxley; Bill Blount, the Democratic Party's state treasurer; and Jack Boggan, a Gardendale real estate agent. No one who supported Graddick was named to the committee.

The composition of the committee should have come as no real surprise to Graddick. Relatively few people among the party's leadership had ever supported Graddick, and Graddick had never paid much attention to the party. While Baxley had served on the party's executive committee in years past and had regularly attended its functions, Graddick had largely ignored those activities, preferring to fill his political organization's ranks with his own people, loyal only to him and not to the party structure. This preference for outsiders lent some legitimacy to Graddick's claim of being the "new face" in Alabama politics, but it left him without the resources to conduct the intraparty battle he was facing. Graddick's lack of supporters within the party structure made him unable to lay any claim to the party's machinery.

Another indication that things were not going well for Graddick was the fact that not only had Baxley refused to concede, but his campaign aides were, in a sense, claiming victory. Tom Fletcher, Baxley campaign chairman, said on Saturday, the day of the official vote count, that Baxley agreed with the challenge though he had not yet joined in it. "Our position is that Baxley really is the Democratic Party nominee," Fletcher added.[22] Graddick supporters tried to dismiss that proposition as absurd, citing again and again the fact that Graddick had won the election, but it was becoming clear that simply having more votes was not enough to give Graddick the nomination.

On Sunday, Graddick blasted party officials for "preparing to rig the election results." Clearly, he could see what was coming, and he began his appeal to the public to help him prevent it. He complained about the composition of the committee that would hear the challenge and tried to put some distance between them and the rest of the party. "Thousands of honest Democrats, Baxley and Graddick supporters alike, are about to be defrauded by a handful of those very same special interests I campaigned against. This fraud, proposed on a major scale, will not succeed," he told reporters.[23] It was an appeal that Graddick would make again and again during the next tumultuous weeks.

The silence from Baxley himself had been deafening. For five days after the election he had refused to make any public statements. He would not concede; he would not comment on the vote count; and he would neither support nor call off the challenge. He had taken his family to Gulf Shores, and although he stayed in close touch with his campaign officials, he made no contact with news reporters. His silence left Graddick dangling, unable to lay effective claim on the nomination and unsure about what moves he should be making.

Finally, on Monday, June 30, Baxley came out of exile and at a press conference declared he would not concede and that he felt the nomination should be his. Graddick had openly encouraged Republicans to cast illegal votes, he said, and those votes had provided Graddick with his margin of victory. Flanked by more than fifty supporters, Baxley said the laws against crossover votes are "crystal clear."[24] Graddick spokesmen immediately labeled Baxley "a spoiled child" and a "sore loser," but the party had already begun to gather evidence about the challenge.[25]

Although state officials conduct the elections, state law in Alabama grants to political parties the power to enforce their own rules about how elections are run. When the petition contesting the vote was filed, the party became a quasi-judicial body with the power of a court to investigate the circumstances surrounding the contest and to make a ruling on its finding. The power to investigate included issuing subpoenas, impounding evidence, and swearing in witnesses who are compelled to give evidence truthfully under a threat of perjury if they do not.

The responsibility for handling this procedure fell to John Baker, chairman of the party. Baker had been a state senator from northeast Alabama in the 1970s and was one of a small band in the legislature who had formed an opposition clique to George Wallace. The group, while never really successful in stopping much of Wallace's proposed legislation, was occasionally able to slow it down. Baker ran unsuccessfully for the U.S. Senate in 1978 and became party chair in 1985. The events of 1986 thrust him into a position of power and influence that few party chairs have ever known.

Inevitably, the controversy over the Democratic gubernatorial nomination would find its way into the courtroom. From the moment a challenge to Graddick's victory was filed, there were few who doubted that the courts, either at the state or the federal level, would be asked to decide or confirm a final result. At that point, though, no one could have anticipated the dizzying array of judicial battles, involving a half-dozen courts and nearly a score of judges, that were to occur during the next three months. Even those close to the controversy had trouble keeping up with the three-ring judicial circus that sprang up during the month of July, and those who were following the events from a distance found them baffling. (A chronology of these events is presented in table 6.1.)

Essentially, three judicial battles took place during July and August:

1. Baxley had to secure Republican primary voter lists so he could compare names on those lists with names on the Democratic runoff lists to determine the number of crossover voters.

Table 6.1

Chronology of legal system events, June 4–August 15

June 3
Democratic and Republican primary elections are held.

June 4
Democratic Party state chair John Baker sends a letter to each of party's county chairs reminding them about the party's anti-crossover voting rule.

June 9
Baker sends a letter to each county circuit court about anti-crossover voting rule.

June 17
Baker again reminds county chairs about the party's anti-crossover voting rule.

June 22
Graddick says Republicans should be allowed to vote in Democratic runoff. A letter is sent from the state attorney general's office to election officials saying any registered voter is allowed to vote in runoff.

June 23
A Jackson County judge issues an order saying crossover voting is illegal.

June 23
A Mobile County judge issues an order upholding the legality of crossover voting.

June 24
Runoff election held. Efforts are made in some locations to prohibit crossover voting. Graddick claims victory. Baxley does not concede. As attorney general, Graddick sends orders to voting officials in thirty-six counties ordering ballots impounded.

June 25
Graddick meets with Governor George Wallace.

June 26
Graddick meets with about 50 state legislators.

June 28
Democrats hold an official vote count from runoff election. The results show Graddick leads Baxley by 8,756 votes. Kennith and Nellie Pike file an official challenge to runoff results. The challenge claims that Graddick's victory is the result of "illegal" crossover votes.

June 30
The Democratic Party State Executive Committee forms subcommittee to hear election challenge. John Baker chairs that committee.

July 1
Baxley files challenge to runoff election.

July 2
Democratic Party asks Jefferson County Circuit Court to issue subpoenas to Republican officials in order to obtain GOP's primary election voting lists.

July 10
Huntsville lawyer Thomas K. Jefferson files federal lawsuit alleging voting fraud by Graddick.

July 11
Black voters allege Graddick violated the Voting Rights Act.

July 14
The Democratic committee begins hearings on Baxley's challenge but adjourns until July 21.

July 15
Jefferson County circuit judge Jack Carl issues order allowing Baxley to see Republican voter lists, but in each county separately.

July 17
A meeting of the Democratic committee is delayed until July 28 because Republican officials refuse to release needed information.

July 18
Alabama Supreme Court rules that the circuit court lacks the power to interfere with political parties' subpoenas and that Republican voter lists must be turned over to Democrats.

July 21
John Baker orders that members of Attorney General Graddick's state and election staff must answer questions about their roles in the gubernatorial election contest issue.

July 23
The Alabama Supreme Court refuses to reconsider an earlier decision letting Democratic Party carry out subpoenas for Republican voting records.

July 24
Jefferson County circuit judge Carl orders a halt to the Democratic Party hearings, ignoring the state supreme court ruling.

July 25
A federal court ruling orders Republican officials to release election information.

Continued on the next page

Table 6.1. *Continued*

July 29
Judge Carl lifts a ban on the hearings and the questioning of Graddick's staff but says Democratic Party cannot hear testimony until it provides Graddick with list of individuals who cast crossover votes, whom these individuals supported, and where vote was cast.

July 29
The Alabama Supreme Court gives control over election contests to state Democratic Party and orders Judge Carl to refrain from issuing additional orders in the case.

July 30
A federal court panel in Montgomery hears testimony on the Voting Rights case.

July 31
Judge Carl rules Democratic Party lost jurisdiction because it has not followed legal guidelines.

July 31
Bill Baxley and the state Democratic Party ask the Alabama Supreme Court to overturn Judge Carl's ruling delaying hearings into election contest.

August 1
A federal court panel in Montgomery rules that Graddick violated the Voting Rights Act and orders the Democratic Party to either have new runoff election or declare Baxley its nominee.

August 11
The Democratic Party hearings on Baxley's challenge begin.

August 15
A Democratic Party panel rules that Baxley is the party's nominee for governor.

2. Two black citizens from Pike County (not to be confused with the Pikes from Madison County, who had filed the original challenge) filed suit against Graddick in federal court, charging that his actions before the runoff violated the 1965 Voting Rights Act.[26]
3. The status of the Democratic committee was challenged and confirmed during other court battles, and eventually the hearings held by the committee became the focal point of the controversy and the center of most of the attention given to it.

In these disputes, Baxley's legal strategies focused on proving three things: that there were a large number of Republicans who voted illegally; that most of these illegal votes went to Graddick, thus providing his margin of victory; and that Graddick was guilty of "misconduct" because he encouraged Republicans to vote illegally and because he obstructed party officials from properly enforcing the laws.

Graddick's defense against Baxley's thrusts seemed less defined and more reactive. In particular, Graddick's attorneys argued that the challenge should be dismissed since Baxley had not followed proper procedures regarding when a challenge had to be filed and the type of evidence that was needed to support a challenge. Additionally, the legality of crossover voting was "an open question," they said, because the Democratic Party had not consistently enforced the rule against crossovers. Finally, the evidence that was being presented regarding the number and behavior of crossover voters did not support a conclusion that Graddick's runoff victory was the result of these votes.[27]

The Fight for Public Opinion

During these initial legal maneuverings, Graddick moved ahead on the public relations front. Two days before the Fourth of July, he issued a press release voicing his concern over the proceedings and saying that Alabama was confronting a "crisis of democracy." The special interests that he had battled during the primary and runoff were now, Graddick argued, conspiring to take away his nomination. Indeed, these same interests were behind the rule against crossover voting itself. During the late 1970s, he stated, "certain special interests in Alabama began to exert undue influence on party leaders." These interests, he added, were the reason the party adopted the "anti-crossover rule."[28]

George McMillan, who had endorsed Graddick in the runoff, called on Baxley to end his challenge. So did former governor Albert Brewer. Brewer called Baxley's challenge "frivolous," but McMillan used much harsher language: "Apparently, Bill Baxley and his friends have forgotten that Russia is the place where party officials choose the government and the United States is the place where the people decide."[29] Graddick also hired Joseph Califano, a former aide to President Lyndon Johnson and former secretary of Health, Education and Welfare under President Jimmy Carter, to help him in fending off the challenge. Some of the more conservative members of the legislature made their concerns about the challenge public, saying that failure to certify Graddick would do long-term damage to the Democratic Party.[30]

During the second week of July, three days before the Democratic committee was set to begin its hearings, Graddick arranged a meeting with two undisputed Democratic nominees, Jim Folsom Jr. (lieutenant governor) and Richard Shelby (U.S. Senate). Part of the arrangements called for a picture and question-and-answer session with the press afterward, and Graddick managed to place himself between the lieutenant governor and senatorial nominees for the pictures. While making his point visually, Graddick's answers to the questions underscored the awkwardness of his position. As a former Republican, his ties to the Democratic Party were tenuous at best, and he had difficulty explaining that away. "I want to lay to rest the perception that Charlie Graddick is not a Democrat," he said.[31]

Graddick's high-handedness toward the party had been evident on election night, when he dismissed the suggestion that he campaign for Shelby against the incumbent, Senator Jeremiah Denton. He would be too busy with his own race, Graddick said then. Now, with Shelby at his side, Graddick backpedaled. "I am personally endorsing the ticket from top to bottom," he said, "particularly Dick Shelby. He's got a tough race." When asked about his previous statements about not campaigning for Shelby, Graddick said lamely, "What I should have said was I am going to support the ticket. The fact is, I am going to help Richard Shelby." Adding to Graddick's difficulties that day was the fact that neither Folsom nor Shelby called on Baxley to withdraw his challenge. All they said was that the committee should move quickly to resolve the matter. Folsom, in fact, referred to Graddick as the party's "possible nominee."

Baxley made his own moves to secure favorable public opinion. Like Graddick, he also a saw conspiracy in the election. In this case it was a conspiracy that "existed at the national and state level of the Republican party and with Graddick to encourage crossover voting."[32] Additionally, Jere Beasley, a former lieutenant governor and bitter foe of Baxley in the 1978 primary, endorsed Baxley's challenge, and Baxley himself sent letters to about fourteen hundred party officials outlining his reasons for contesting the results.[33]

Baker's committee held its initial hearing on July 14 in Montgomery's Civic Center, and some five hundred people, supporters for both sides, showed up for the first day's proceedings. Except for some of the rhetoric, it turned out to be a dull affair. Baxley was there, having just finished his National Guard duty, but Graddick did not attend, working instead at his attorney general's office a few blocks away. After a bit of rhetoric and legal maneuvering on both sides, Baxley's attorneys asked for a delay and received it. The committee scheduled its next meeting for a week from that day.[34]

The Voting Rights Case

While the Graddick and Baxley camps were firing public salvos at each other, two Tuscaloosa attorneys filed a suit in federal court in Montgomery charging that Graddick had violated the 1965 Voting Rights Act by using the attorney general's office to encourage Republicans to vote illegally. The lawyers were Jack Drake and Ralph Knowles. They were supporters of Bill Baxley and later were instrumental in Baxley's presentation before the committee. At the same time, Huntsville attorney Thomas K. Jefferson filed a suit in federal court in Birmingham asking that Graddick be disqualified from being the Democratic nominee because he had committed "monumental and colossal election fraud" during the runoff campaign. Neither suit gained much attention from reporters, but the rulings they produced were to have a massive effect on the outcome of the challenge—and on the public's perception of Charles Graddick. (The suits were later combined and heard by the federal panel in Montgomery.)

The suit filed by Drake and Knowles listed Jerry and Dejerilyn Henderson as the plaintiffs. Jerry Henderson was a county commissioner in Pike County and had been active in the Alabama Democratic Conference. The suit argued that the rights of all black citizens had been violated when Graddick had issued the letter during the runoff telling polling officials not to prevent possible crossover voters. That action, along with Graddick's open solicitation of Republican voters in the runoff campaign, constituted a change in the voting laws of the state—a change that, according to the suit, was illegal because all voting laws in Alabama must be cleared by the U.S. Department of Justice under the 1965 Voting Rights Act. The lawyers also argued that there had been enough crossover votes cast to give Graddick his margin of victory.

Graddick's lawyers, including Washington, D.C., attorney Hamilton Fox, made the point that the rule against crossover voting had never been enforced, even though it had been in place since 1979. No one had ever been challenged because of it, they said, and the party's decision to enforce it this year was due to the possibility that Graddick might win. The party had made only minimal efforts to publicize the fact that crossovers would be challenged, they said.

How many crossover voters were there, and for whom did they vote? Neither of those questions was ever answered precisely, either in the federal court hearing or later in the committee's hearings. When the Hendersons' lawyers announced that they wanted to introduce polling data as evidence, Fox objected, saying that it was "hearsay." Judge Frank Johnson agreed but said it would be allowed "for whatever it is worth, which is very little." Natalie Davis, co-owner of the Davis-Penfield survey research unit in Birmingham, then testified that among more than 5,000 people questioned during the runoff campaign, her interviewers found 90 who said they had voted in the Republican primary and were planning to vote in the Democratic runoff. About 84 percent of these were planning to vote for Graddick and 16 percent for Baxley, she said. Projecting these figures onto the actual number of votes cast, she estimated that there were about 16,000 crossover votes. If these votes were subtracted from the totals, she said, Baxley would win by about 2,000 votes.

Davis's testimony was disputed by James Larry Powell, a survey researcher from Mississippi State University, who was called to testify by Graddick's lawyers. Powell said that the sample of 90 voters that Davis had used was too small to make the kind of projections that Davis was making. A much larger number of voters would have to be surveyed in order to come up with more precise voting totals, he said. The issue of using polling data to determine the outcome of the election was not resolved in the federal court hearing and would arise again when the committee met.

Before the hearing ended, the court heard some confusing testimony and arguments about how many crossover voters the Baxley forces had found during their examination of the Republican and Democratic voter lists. Baxley's campaign manager, Tom Fletcher, testified that his supporters had found nearly 10,000 probable crossover voters. A Graddick campaign worker, Pat Robinson, disagreed, saying he counted only about 7,000 from the list supplied by the Baxley campaign; many of the names on the Baxley list, he said, were duplicates. Just how many names there were was another point that came to no resolution during the hearing.[35]

On July 31, two days after the hearing concluded, the three-judge panel, which included Frank Johnson, Truman Hobbs, and Myron Thompson, issued a ruling that shook the political landscape.[36] The panel ordered that the Democratic committee, which was set to begin its hearings the next week, to do one of two things: either name Baxley as the nominee or hold a new runoff election. The thing it must not do, the ruling said, is give the nomination to Graddick. The judges made several points in their ruling:

1. The rule against crossover voting had pre-clearance from the U.S. Department of Justice and could not be changed.

2. The fact that crossover voting could have affected the outcome of the election—not whether it actually did—was enough to support their ruling that Graddick not be certified as the nominee.
3. As attorney general, Graddick had violated the law. "The June 24 runoff was so close, the number of illegal crossover votes so great, and Mr. Graddick's violation so flagrant, this court cannot take the chance that Mr. Graddick received the Democratic nomination as a result of his illegal actions."
4. Graddick should not benefit from his illegal actions. "Mr. Graddick stood to benefit directly from his violation. Accordingly, this court will not indulge the possibility that Mr. Graddick would have won the runoff even had he not prohibited the Democratic Party from enforcing its rule."

The harsh tone of the ruling was aimed squarely at Graddick, and it hurt him badly with the public. Graddick, who had been in Mississippi on National Guard duty that week, tried to explain the ruling as merely a difference of opinion about the law, but it was more than that. A federal court had ruled that as attorney general he had acted illegally, and that gave his opponents damaging material to use against him. No matter what else Graddick did or said during the campaign, his opponents could always cite the court ruling that Graddick had committed a "flagrant" violation of the law in order to get himself elected governor.

The ruling also deprived Graddick of the one thing he had called for during the previous six weeks: immediate certification as the Democratic gubernatorial nominee. He could no longer lay claim to that prize, and he could no longer use effectively the argument that he had received more votes than Baxley. The court ruling gave Graddick only one way out of this untenable situation—calling for a new election. The Graddick camp, stunned by the federal court, did just that. Saying the party needed to set up another election, Graddick said, "All I can tell Bill Baxley is he'd better circle up his wagons, because we're coming to get him again."[37]

Baxley, meanwhile, was confident that he could both show that he was the true winner of the election and that he could gain the public's support and understanding. "People are fair minded," he said. "When they see exactly how he [Graddick] misused his office and how he did things you would think [former president Ferdinand] Marcos in the Philippines would do, then people will come back to our side."[38]

Similarly, Pike County commissioner Jerry Henderson, who, with his wife, Dejerilyn, had brought the federal suit against Graddick, made it clear that he did not think another election should be held. "Morally, we should have rules against cheating, and Mr. Graddick was caught cheating," Henderson said. "I would not want our state's chief executive to be one who had been found guilty of violating the citizens' rights." He went on to say that "a new election would, in essence, give the person caught cheating another chance."[39]

The committee had another option, however. According to the court's ruling, if it found that Baxley had received the majority of the "legal" votes in the runoff, it could certify him as the nominee without an election. The court charged the committee to do this "pursuant to its procedures and the stringent rules under Alabama law for an election contest." The wording of the court's opinion left the door open for just how the committee would make that determination. Graddick's forces argued that "stringent rules" meant Baxley would have to specifically identify crossover voters and the candidates for whom they voted. They were confident that the Baxley campaign could not do this under the present circumstances. They felt, then, that the committee's only choice would be to have another election.

The committee also had another option, one that had not been mentioned in the court's ruling and had not until now been openly discussed—the option of disqualifying Graddick as a candidate altogether. Under its own rules, the committee could find that Graddick was not a fit nominee for the party. The case for disqualification was much stronger now that a federal court had ruled that Graddick was guilty of violating the law.

On the day after the ruling, party chairman Baker said that none of the options the court gave the committee was "very attractive." Calling a new election might in the end saddle the party "with a nominee who the federal court has accused of flagrantly violating the law of the land." Clearly, the option of disqualification was one that was on the minds and tongues of many Democrats that weekend.

Public Opinion and the Controversy

The federal court's ruling had thus shifted the nature of the dispute dramatically in a single stroke. No longer could Graddick claim to be the party's lawful nominee. Instead, the man who had gotten the most votes in the election was now in imminent danger of having his victory taken from him. The decision about who was to be the party's official nominee, or how this person was selected, now rested with the party's committee, a group unlikely to be sympathetic to Graddick's cause.

The legal maneuverings and courtroom hearings had placed the public in a spectator role concerning the outcome of the runoff election. The results of a Capstone Poll survey conducted during the week before the committee met and published the second day of the hearings showed that citizens were paying close attention to the dispute, did not like what they were seeing, and had definite ideas about how the controversy should be resolved.

About 59 percent of the respondents in the statewide survey said they had paid a "great deal" of attention to the dispute, while an additional 27 percent said they had paid "some" attention. Watching Democrats fight one another over the outcome of the runoff election had done little for the image of the party or its two principal candidates. About 60 percent of the public said they disapproved of how the party had handled the election controversy. About 29 percent said the runoff election controversy had made them more likely to vote Republican in the future (table 6.2).

The survey results also showed that the number of people who said they felt negatively about both Baxley and Graddick had risen dramatically (table 6.3). In fact, for the first time, the overall public image of both candidates was more negative than positive. The percentage of people who said they felt negatively about Baxley was up to 47 percent, compared to 31 percent in both a July survey and in the pre-runoff study. Graddick suffered a similar fate. Some 41 percent now said they felt negatively about him, while 34 percent said that they felt positively toward him. In July about 40 percent gave Graddick a positive evaluation and 25 percent rated him negatively. In the pre-runoff survey he received a 41 percent positive and a 30 percent negative rating.

Most surprisingly, the survey's results showed that the public's disgust with the lingering controversy suddenly had given Republican Guy Hunt a realistic chance of being elected. When matched against Graddick, Hunt trailed by a 46 to 32 percent margin (table 6.4). Hunt looked even better against Baxley. The survey's results showed that Hunt and Baxley were essentially tied, with the GOP candidate leading by a 44 to 42 percent margin.

When asked which of the two options identified by the federal court the Democratic Party should select in order to resolve the controversy, the public clearly said that it wanted a new runoff election (table 6.5). About 70 percent said that the party should hold a new election, while only 18 percent wanted Baxley declared the nominee.

In a later, October, survey (Capstone Poll 191), citizens who said the Democratic Party should have held a new runoff ($N = 323$) were asked why they believed this. About 63 percent of these respondents said they wanted a new runoff because they believed that voters should select the party's nominees. In contrast, only 23 percent of these respondents wanted a new run-

Table 6.2

Effects of the Democratic Party controversy on public opinion, August 1986

"How much attention have you paid to the controversy surrounding the outcome of the Democratic runoff for governor—a great deal, some, not very much, or none at all?"	
Great deal	59%
Some	27
Not much	11
None	3
Don't know/ No answer	1

"Do you approve or disapprove of the way in which the Democratic Party has handled the challenge to the outcome of the runoff election?"	
Approve	29%
Disapprove	60
Don't know/ No answer	12

"Has the controversy about the runoff election made you more or less likely to vote for the Republican Party in the future, or has it no effect on you?"	
More likely	29%
No effect	54
Less likely	12
Don't know/ No answer	5

Source: Capstone Poll 185

off because they believed that Graddick had fairly won the original contest. The public's support for resolving the election controversy by holding a new runoff is not surprising in a state with a strong populist tradition. Belief in democratic government and the idea that citizens should choose their leaders through elections is an important component of this tradition.

When asked about their preferences if a new runoff were held, respondents in the August survey were evenly split between Baxley and Graddick (as they had been in the original contest). Some 42 percent said they would

Table 6.3

Evaluations of runoff election candidates, August 1986

"Do you generally feel positive, neutral or negative about each of the following people?"

	October 1985	January 1986	April 1986	May 1986	June 1986	July 1986	August 1986
Charles Graddick							
Positive	42%	39%	42%	44%	41%	40%	34%
Neutral/Don't know	42	44	43	35	29	35	25
Negative	16	18	15	21	30	25	41
% Pos. -% Neg.	26	21	27	23	11	15	-7
Bill Baxley							
Positive	38%	41%	44%	42%	35%	35%	32%
Neutral/Don't know	41	39	38	30	34	34	21
Negative	21	21	18	28	31	31	47
% Pos. - % Neg.	17	20	26	14	4	4	-15

Source: Capstone Poll 148, 160, 169, 175, 176, 181, 185

Table 6.4

General election candidate preferences, August 1986

"Suppose that a general election for governor were held today and the candidates were Democrat Charles Graddick and Republican Guy Hunt, for whom would you vote?"

Graddick	46%
Hunt	32
Neither/Don't know	22

"Suppose that a general election for governor were held today and the candidates were Democrat Bill Baxley and Republican Guy Hunt, for whom would you vote?"

Baxley	42%
Hunt	44
Neither/Don't know	14

Source: Capstone Poll 185

Table 6.5

Outcome of a new runoff election

"What do you think the Democratic Party should do regarding the runoff election? Should it declare Bill Baxley the winner, or should it hold a new election?"	
Declare Baxley the winner	18%
Hold a new election	70
Neither/Don't know	12

"Now, if a new Democratic runoff election for governor were held today and the candidates were Bill Baxley and Charles Graddick, for whom would you vote?" (If Undecided, "As of today, do you lean a little more toward Baxley or Graddick?")	
Baxley	42%
Graddick	45
Neither/Don't know	13

Source: Capstone Poll 185

vote for Baxley in a new runoff, while 45 percent said they favored Graddick (table 6.5).

The good news for Baxley in these poll results was that Graddick was not viewed as blameless and Baxley was not seen as a sore loser (table 6.6). About 50 percent of the state's citizens thought Graddick had acted unfairly when he encouraged Republicans to vote for him in the Democratic runoff election. A plurality of respondents also said they believed that crossover voters provided Graddick with his margin of victory. At the same time, by a slim 47 to 44 percent margin, the public said Baxley was justified in protesting the outcome of the runoff election.

Clearly, the public was paying attention. How the Democratic Party's committee resolved the contest would have a major influence on the outcome of the 1986 contest, as well as future elections in the state.

The Democratic Party Hearings

The committee resumed its hearings on August 4 in a large meeting room in a downtown Birmingham hotel. Television cameras lined the sides of the

Table 6.6

Opinions about responsibility for runoff controversy, August 1986

"Do you think that Charles Graddick acted unfairly when he encouraged Republicans to vote in the Democratic runoff election?"	
Yes	50%
No	37
Neither/Don't know	13
"Do you think that Republican crossover voters provided Graddick with his margin of victory?"	
Yes	45%
No	32
Neither/Don't know	23
"Do you think that Bill Baxley is justified in protesting the outcome of the runoff election?"	
Yes	47%
No	44
Neither/Don't know	9

Source: Capstone Poll 185

room, recording each action and word of the committee members, witnesses, and growing number of lawyers representing the two sides of the controversy. Crowds of spectators attended the hearings. Symbolically, Graddick's supporters tended to sit on the committee's right, while Baxley's partisans generally were found on the committee's left.

On the first day of the hearings, Baxley's attorneys called Natalie Davis, the Birmingham pollster who had testified for them in the federal court hearing. She gave the same information to the committee that she had given to the court, concluding that Graddick received about 85 percent of the election's crossover votes. Jerry Ingram, a public-opinion survey researcher for Auburn University at Montgomery, backed up some of Davis's contentions, although Ingram had done no polling during the runoff and had no figures of his own to present.[40] They were followed by Gordon Henderson, an Indiana political consultant whose statistical analysis of 850 precincts in sixteen counties showed that Graddick received almost 100 percent of the crossover vote.[41] "I know 100 percent is kind of hard to believe, and I have been trying to disprove my findings since last Thursday—I can't," he said.[42] Henderson's testimony was ridiculed by Graddick's lawyers, who later that week called polling experts, including Larry Powell of Mississippi State University and Jim Stovall, then co-director of a research unit at the University of Alabama (and a coauthor of this book), both of whom testified that the sample of ninety presented by Davis was too small to make valid judgments on vote totals or preferences.[43]

All of the controversy and testimony on voter lists, polling results, and regression analysis were ultimately confusing to the public and did not provide definitive evidence of what happened in the election. From Baxley's and the Democratic Party's point of view, it may have been unnecessary and even destructive. A number of people within the party and within Baxley's campaign argued that the federal court's ruling had given the party everything it needed to disqualify Graddick. It was not necessary to prove that crossover votes had provided Graddick with the margin of victory. The party committee could simply cite the court's ruling as its reason for taking the nomination away from Graddick. That point of view did not prevail, however, and the party engaged in a confusing battle over statistics.[44]

The hearings shifted on Tuesday, August 12, to the question of Graddick's actions immediately before the runoff election. Baxley's lawyers moved to disqualify Graddick as a candidate, and the committee said it would hold a separate hearing on that question later, but it allowed Baxley to go ahead and present evidence about it. Baxley's attorneys called Susan McKinney, the assistant attorney general who wrote the letter that was sent to election officials saying that any registered voter was eligible to vote in the runoff. McKinney said the letter had not been designed to help Graddick's campaign. On Wednesday, Baxley's lawyers called Janie Nobles, the attorney general's press secretary, who testified she had written a press release based on the letter that McKinney had written.[45]

In an effort to discredit the list of Republican crossover voters that Baxley had presented to the committee, Graddick's attorneys called four Shelby County Republicans whose names had appeared on Baxley's list. All of them testified that they had not voted in the Democratic runoff election on June 24. Instead, they had voted in the Republican runoff in their districts.[46]

By the middle of Thursday morning, the testimony had been concluded and the committee retired to make its decision. It had become apparent to most observers that the hearings had gone in Baxley's way. Many Graddick supporters held out the hope that the committee would call for a new election rather than naming Baxley as the nominee, but hanging over them was the fact that the motion to disqualify their candidate had not been acted upon. Even if a new election were called, Graddick would still have to fight off the disqualification motion. Graddick's lawyers had felt they had presented their case well, but even so, they already were planning an appeal of a decision they were fairly certain would be unfavorable. In fact, Graddick's campaign workers were so certain about the decision that they showed up at the Hyatt on Friday morning with bumper stickers that read, "I'm mad, too, Charlie!"

Inside the committee, there was no doubt about the first action. The federal court had said Graddick could not be the nominee, and no one on the committee was inclined to challenge the court on that decision. The debate centered on the question of awarding the nomination to Baxley or calling for a new runoff election. Most of the committee members saw problems with another election. It would be expensive for the state—one estimate was that it would cost one million dollars—and would only continue the conflicts of the Democrats, quite possibly driving people into the ranks of the Republicans. The general feeling among the committee was that Graddick would be an easy winner in another election. (This feeling prevailed despite the fact that a poll published earlier in the week showed that a new election was what people wanted and that Graddick was anything but a sure winner.) These possibilities and speculation were discussed into the evening until the committee reached a consensus decision.[47]

What surprised many outside the committee was how long the decision was in coming. At 1 p.m. on Friday, August 15, some twenty-seven hours after the hearings had adjourned, John Baker read the unanimous decision of the committee: Bill Baxley had received the majority of the legal votes cast in the runoff and was therefore to be the gubernatorial nominee of the Democratic Party. Baxley partisans cheered, and Baxley hugged his wife and shook hands with his attorneys. Graddick stared straight ahead.[48]

The committee's written opinion said that Graddick had been guilty of misconduct because of the letter McKinney had written immediately before the runoff election. The question of Graddick's disqualification, however, had been set aside until another time when it might be necessary to take it up. As it turned out, that time never came. The evidence about the number of illegal votes was "conflicting," the opinion said, but "we are satisfied that a sufficient number of illegal votes did alter the results of the election and that was due, in larger part, to the illegal actions and misrepresentation made by the Attorney General and members of his staff at the highest level."

The committee had done what a few weeks before had appeared unthinkable. Although Baxley immediately made statements about "Democratic unity" and "getting on with the campaign," the fight for the nomination was by no means over.

Bill Baxley shakes hands with a voter at an airport rally on the day before the Democratic runoff election. Roy McAuley, Courtesy of the *Press-Register*

Bill Baxley speaks to a small audience from the top of a table during the Democratic primary campaign. Mary Hattler, Courtesy of the *Press-Register* © Reprinted with permission.

Bill Baxley and his wife, Lucy (*right*), were often on the campaign trail together. Roy McAuley, Courtesy of the *Press Register* © All rights reserved. Reprinted with permission.

Attorney General Charles Graddick presses his campaign as an Independent candidate during the general election campaign. Jay Ferchaud, Courtesy of the *Press Register*

Small-town rallies such as this one for Charles Graddick in Evergreen during the primary election were a staple of the 1986 election. Mike Casey, Courtesy of the *Press Register* © All rights reserved. Reprinted with permission.

During the primary campaign, Guy Hunt drew small crowds of supporters, few of whom believed he would have a chance to be elected governor. Victor Calhoun, Courtesy of the *Press Register* © All rights reserved. Reprinted with permission.

The 1986 campaign saw former governor Fob James, who had been out of office for four years, try to make a political comeback. Frances Coleman, Courtesy of the *Press Register* © All rights reserved. Reprinted with permission.

Near the end of the primary campaign, former governor Fob James was doing battle with Charles Graddick, trying to get into the Democratic runoff election. Mike Casey, Courtesy of the *Press Register* © All rights reserved. Reprinted with permission.

George McMillan entered the 1986 campaign hopeful that his near upset of George Wallace in 1982 would propel him to the top of the crowded campaign field. Mike Casey, Courtesy of the *Press Register* © All rights reserved. Reprinted with permission.

George McMillan showered his audiences with words during the primary campaign, but his candidacy failed to gain any traction with Democratic voters. Jay Ferchaud, Courtesy of the *Press Register* © All rights reserved. Reprinted with permission.

7
Democratic Aftermath

The decision by the Democratic Party committee set off a storm of protest among the state's citizens. The Democratic Party headquarters was inundated with irate calls, while the Republican headquarters was swamped with calls from individuals volunteering to help in the general election. Republican officials declared that the Democratic decision had given them the governorship. The state's news media scrambled to find Guy Hunt and get his reaction to the decision.[1]

This firestorm was highly predictable in the light of the public preference for a new runoff (a preference about which the party's leaders had been fully informed). By choosing an option that clearly violated the principle that voters should select their leaders, the party and its candidate, Bill Baxley, had angered a large segment of the electorate. Their obvious task now was to try to dissipate that anger and shift the public's attention away from the controversy. That proved to be much more difficult than anyone imagined.

The major cause of the difficulty was that the committee's ruling naming Baxley the nominee did not end the legal and political struggle over the outcome of the runoff election. Rather, the controversy continued through the summer and into the fall and kept reminding voters of how Baxley had gained his nomination.

New Directions for Graddick

The day after the committee decided that Baxley would be the Democratic gubernatorial nominee, the lieutenant governor called a news conference at which he said, "I sincerely hope this bitterness and divisiveness is pretty much behind us and we can now move forward to the general election united."[2] Baxley's hopes might have been sincere, but any expectations along these lines were totally misplaced. The "bitterness and divisiveness" that had ruled the party for six weeks would continue, and the prospects of a united Democratic Party were nonexistent.

Baxley could have taken no comfort in the combative nature of his opponent, and that nature manifested itself fully in the next two weeks. Graddick had two battles to fight, a legal one and a political one, and he began the legal fight immediately. On the afternoon of the committee's decision, his lawyers filed an appeal with the same federal court that had ruled against him on August 1. They argued that the committee had not followed the court's guidelines because it had not "purged" any votes—that is, it had not disqualified a single vote—and had not heard from anyone who had cast an illegal vote. The polling data presented to the committee about possible crossover votes, his lawyers said, were not sufficient evidence to declare that Baxley had received the majority of legal votes cast in the runoff election. Consequently, the court should order the committee to hold a new election.[3]

While Graddick initially expressed some optimism that the court would see it his way, the expressions themselves were hollow and short-lived. It was obvious that Graddick's standing with the court had been badly damaged by his actions before the runoff election and that the court was unlikely to reverse what the committee had done.[4]

During the next week, after the choice of Baxley had been affirmed by the full Alabama Democratic Executive Committee, Graddick filed a motion before the Alabama Supreme Court asking that the committee's decision be set aside.[5] In doing this, Graddick was bypassing the normal procedure of filing an appeal with the full executive committee, but his attorneys said that such an appeal would be useless. Consequently, they went straight to the supreme court, but again the prospects of winning were remote.

These two suits served legal notice on the Democratic Party and Bill Baxley that Graddick planned to remain in the fight for the nomination. Graddick's best hope remained in the court of public opinion, and the attorney general wasted no time in beginning that battle either.

On August 22, one week after the committee's decision, Graddick, in a loud and emotional speech to a large audience in Montgomery, vowed that one way or another he would be on the ballot in November. Covered with sweat during the outdoor rally, Graddick said the state needed to rid itself of the special interests that had supported Baxley, and he used the term "sleazebags" to describe those associated with Baxley. (Earlier in the campaign, McMillan had used the term "sleaze" in referring to those associated with the Wallace administration.) If the courts would not order a new election or allow him a place on the ballot, he said, he would run a write-in campaign.[6]

Baxley reacted calmly to Graddick's statements, saying that his opponent's words were "bordering on hysteria. I hope he has not lost his equilibrium."[7]

Educating the Public

Graddick's mental state should have been a minor concern for Baxley at this point. He had much more pressing problems to deal with. They were twofold: uniting the Democratic Party and convincing voters that his nomination was legitimate. He also had to fend off Graddick's legal challenges, a task that proved to be somewhat more difficult than Baxley's lawyers had first anticipated.

Baxley, of course, had few worries about the Democratic Party structure. The state executive committee had stood solidly—almost unanimously—behind him ever since his runoff campaign with Graddick. Baxley had to worry about those people who considered themselves Democrats but who were not within the party structure. Many of them had voted for Graddick, and if Baxley had any chance at victory in November, he had to convince these people that they had to unite behind him to defeat the Republicans.

He sounded this theme soon after his selection by the committee. In a speech to the state executive committee the next week, Baxley blasted the Republican candidate and his policies. He also lumped Graddick in with the Republicans, saying that Graddick would end his write-in campaign because Republicans would buy him off. "The Republicans' money will come in and they're going to do everything they can—not so much to elect their candidate—but to defeat me and defeat our party," he said.[8]

The job of uniting Democrats went hand-in-hand with Baxley's more difficult task—persuading people that the party did the right thing in declaring him the nominee. It was clear that most people in Alabama did not believe the committee should have given him the nomination. As we have seen, a Capstone Poll survey conducted shortly before the August Democratic Party hearing found that while members of the electorate supported Baxley's right to protest the election, they also wanted the party to hold a new runoff election. Less than 20 percent said that Baxley should be named as the nominee.

Immediately after the August Capstone Poll was published, Baxley said that he had an "education job" in front of him in explaining his position to the voters. He decided to do this "education job" through a television advertisement that used a football analogy to demonstrate that Graddick had acted unfairly. The ad compared Graddick's runoff victory to a football team that had scored a touchdown because the team had too many players on the field.[9]

The advertisement was a weak and ill-considered response to a massive problem that was confronting Baxley and the Democrats. The analogy itself was flawed, since, depending upon the situation, the football violation referred to in the ad could have resulted in running the play again, not in a victory for the other team. If the analogy were carried through, it could be used to argue that the Democrats should have held another election. The ad was quickly withdrawn, and the "education job" that Baxley had promised faded into the routine of campaigning that Baxley began. He still argued that it was the Republicans, who had illegally crossed over, and Graddick, who had encouraged them to do so, who were responsible for the situation in August, but that reasoning was never accepted by the public.

In fact, the public continued to believe—even up to a week before the general election in November—that the Democrats should have held a new election. Three Capstone Polls during the general election campaign asked what the Democrats should have done in August, and each of the three showed that more than 60 percent of the voters still believed that a new runoff would have been the proper choice for the Democrats. In August and throughout the fall, many of the top Democrats felt that by November the public would have either forgotten about the controversy or that the electorate's desire for a new runoff would have waned. Neither of these things happened. The events of September and October kept the controversy under discussion, and the public's basic belief that an election is the proper way to select political leaders was unshaken.

Graddick's Legal Battles

As the summer waned, Graddick hoped that some court somewhere would weigh in on his side. He did everything possible to make that happen. In addition to the appeals to the federal court and state supreme court, Graddick took on a third legal battle. Two Jefferson County men filed a suit in federal court in Birmingham asking that the Democratic Party be forced to hold a new runoff; Graddick joined in that suit once it was filed.[10]

The court where Graddick had the least hope of a sympathetic hearing was the Montgomery federal court. That court was primarily concerned with the Voting Rights Act and in making sure that Graddick did not benefit from his violation of it. While it had outlined the options that the Democratic committee could take, those options were designed more to keep Graddick from getting the nomination than to ensure that he received a fair hearing from the Democrats. Consequently, Graddick's appeal to this court was not undertaken with much optimism by him or his attorneys. His attorneys did argue that the committee had not complied with the court's August 1 ruling, but not surprisingly, those arguments fell on deaf ears. In fact, within a week after the case was heard, the court denied the appeal and issued another stinging reproach to Graddick. In an unusually personal rebuke, the court called Graddick by name (rather than referring to him as the "plaintiff" or "petitioner") and said that he "evidences a complete misunderstanding of the controlling legal principles and the application of those principles to the evidence presented in this case." Graddick's next move was in the state court system.[11]

State law provides that the Democratic committee's ruling could be appealed to the full Alabama Democratic Executive Committee within ten days after it was issued. Once the appeal was heard by the executive committee, it could then go to the state supreme court. The Graddick camp decided to bypass an appeal to the full committee, believing it would be useless and time-consuming to appeal to a group that had so many Baxley backers in it. This decision to bypass the legitimate channel of appeal provided the lawyers for Baxley and the Democratic Party a technical point to argue against Graddick's appeal. Graddick's lawyers said the Democratic Party had not followed its own rules for hearing election challenges in that the committee heard no testimony from those who had supposedly voted illegally.

The court did not hear oral arguments but accepted only written briefs from the lawyers, and on September 3 it issued its ruling. By a vote of six to two, the court agreed with Baxley and the Democratic Party, saying that Graddick did not have the right to appeal directly to the state supreme court. He should have gone to the Alabama Democratic Executive Committee within the ten days allowed by law, and since he had not done that, no state court had the power to intervene. The two justices who agreed with Graddick—Hugh Maddox and Gorman Houston—dealt with the issue itself rather than the procedure and argued that the Democratic committee should not have named Baxley the nominee. Rather, it should have called for a new election, they said, because Alabama law "does not allow polling evidence to be used to declare winners of contested political elections."[12]

Baxley's attorneys were quick to say that the supreme court ruling was the end for Graddick's appeals, but they had more work ahead of them—more than they expected. Two Jefferson County men, J. F. Curry and Daniel Farnell, filed a suit in federal court in Birmingham during the first week in September that would extend the legal battles of all those concerned. They argued that the Democratic Party had violated their civil rights by giving the nomination to Baxley. Their lawyer, Tuscaloosa attorney David Ellis, said his clients had voted in the Democratic primary on June 3 and the Democratic runoff on June 24.

The suit was filed in the court of federal judge Foy Guin, a man who had a long history of participation in Republican affairs in the state. He had run for the U.S. Senate in 1954 as a Republican (thus becoming that year's sacrificial lamb to the reelection of John Sparkman) and had served on the Alabama Republican Executive Committee and on the Committee to Reelect the President, Richard Nixon's campaign committee in 1972. Guin was rewarded with a federal judgeship by Nixon in 1973.

Guin was a new face in the legal controversy, and Graddick had reason to hope for a sympathetic hearing. When he joined in the suit, Graddick finally found himself in a court where he was raising the issues he wanted considered, such as the evidence the Democratic committee had used to decide against him. There was also the larger issue of whether a committee of the Democratic Party could set aside an election and designate the nominee without a new election. The judge scheduled a hearing quickly and then took more than two weeks to issue a ruling.

Guin's thirty-five-page ruling came on September 17 and surprised Baxley and the Democratic Party like a lightning bolt from an unclouded sky. He ordered that, if Graddick would agree to drop his write-in campaign, the Democrats should hold a new runoff to determine the nominee. The Democrats had disenfranchised voters by their actions, he wrote, and they did it by using insufficient polling data. Guin was critical not only of the small numbers used by Baxley's witnesses during the Democratic hearing but also of the regression analysis that an out-of-state expert had presented. Conclusions based on this evidence, he said, are "totally absurd" and "not worthy of credence in any court." "Regardless of how many polls or analyses were run, the incontrovertible conclusion is that no one knows to a certainty how the voters cast their ballots," he said. "Not one voter testified as to his or her actual vote, and no one used investigative polling techniques to inquire into votes actually cast."

Guin was also critical of the Democratic Party for using this evidence as an excuse to avoid a new runoff. "This court is unwilling to let the SDEC [State Democratic Executive Committee], any Democratic candidate or any pollster opine how Republicans voted in the June elections, and to let their will thus be substituted for that of the voters." Guin said the idea that the Democratic committee could do what it wanted to without having to answer to anyone "shocks the conscience."[13]

Reaction from Baxley and the Democratic Party was oddly mixed. The Democrats immediately announced an appeal, asking that Guin stay his order until an appeal could be filed. Baxley, on the other hand, said that he would not object to a new runoff election. His statements turned out to be nothing more than words, however. At the very time he was making them, his Tuscaloosa attorneys, Jack Drake and Ralph Knowles, were preparing to go to Atlanta to file an appeal with the Eleventh Circuit Court. Faced with the possibility of a new runoff, Democratic Party officials began to revive the issue of disqualifying Graddick as a candidate.

The reaction of the Graddick campaign was exactly the opposite—unified and joyous. Finally, the state's attorney general had won a court battle, and while the victory had not yet been sealed, it provided him with some legal ammunition to fire back at his opponents. Campaigning in Tuscaloosa, Graddick announced that he would drop his write-in campaign in the light of the judge's ruling. He berated the Democrats for using "guesswork, surmise and polling data" and substituting that for the election, and he repeated what Guin had said about it, that it was "not worthy of belief."[14]

Graddick's victory had an unreal quality to it, however. Judge Guin's ruling, even though extensive and tightly reasoned, was pitted solidly against the flow of legal and political events to that point. So far, of all the judges who had heard the case, only two others had viewed the issues in the case as Guin had, and it seemed unlikely that Guin's ruling would ultimately prevail. In addition, it was getting past the time when another runoff election could reasonably be held before the general election. Indeed, the general election campaign with candidates from each major party had begun, and even Graddick with all of his legal battles was acting like a candidate, not a litigant. Most observers felt that Guin's order for a new runoff would interrupt this process.

Once they had recovered their balance from the shock of Guin's ruling, Baxley and the Democrats expressed confidence about their ability to have it overturned. They had even more reason to feel confident three days later when the three-judge panel to hear the appeal was announced.[15] The panel, they found, would consist of Frank Johnson, Robert Vance, and John Godbold. Johnson had headed the three-judge panel that had found Graddick in violation of the Voting Rights Act in August; that panel had delivered stinging and personal rebukes to Graddick at the time of the initial ruling and at the time of his appeal. There was little doubt that Johnson had a major hand in writing both of those opinions. Having had the opportunity to deal with the issues raised in Guin's ruling before, Johnson had not taken it, and it did not appear likely that he would take it now. Vance had been the chairman of the Democratic Party in Alabama, but he had resigned that position in 1977, two years before the party had adopted its no-crossover rule. Still, many believed that if he had any sympathies in the case, it would be toward the party's establishment forces.

Baxley's lawyers were openly delighted with the makeup of the panel, while Graddick's attorneys were dismayed that they had to face Frank Johnson once again. In fact, the makeup of the judicial panel brought an almost immediate challenge from the Graddick campaign, but instead of asking Johnson to recuse himself, Graddick's lawyers asked Vance to step down. They argued that Vance's previous connections with the Democratic Party hierarchy presented an apparent bias in Baxley's favor. Vance refused, and the Graddick forces could sense their impending defeat.[16] The court issued its ruling on October 1, and as many on both sides expected, it said that Baxley was the legal nominee of the Democratic Party.

In fact, the court's ruling was as bad as anything the Graddick forces had feared, because it again made references to Graddick's actions in encouraging crossover votes. "Mr. Graddick and those working with him orchestrated the casting of thousands of illegal votes. The precise number cannot be ascertained. . . . [T]he principal actors who caused the confusion, and did so in violation of the law, were Mr. Graddick and those aligned with him. They are in no position to seek substantive advantage for this confusion." The court did not directly refute the reasoning offered by the Guin ruling; it simply said that the Democratic committee had acted reasonably in considering polling and statistical evidence in ruling that Baxley had received the majority of the legal votes cast.[17]

Having begun the court battles, the Graddick campaign felt compelled to continue them to their conclusion, even though the chances for a victory were extremely slim. Within a week, Graddick had submitted an emergency request to U.S. Supreme Court justice Lewis Powell to set aside the ruling and order a new runoff. Powell turned the request down, noting that Graddick had not presented sufficient evidence to warrant granting his petition. He also noted that such a stay would only be permitted when it was likely that the entire court would take up the matter, and, he said, the Supreme Court was not likely to take this case. Despite Powell's opinion, Graddick asked the entire court to hear the matter on an emergency basis, a request that was unanimously denied by the court on October 14.

The three-month legal battle was finally at an end. It had, in fact, become a secondary battle as the general election campaign had gotten under way. Even after the Guin ruling, few people expected that Graddick would be the Democratic nominee in November. The original federal court ruling of August 1 had remained intact and had its desired effect—to keep Graddick from being the Democratic nominee. The continuing legal battles had another effect, however. They kept the issue of what the Democratic Party had done before the electorate long after Baxley and the Democratic leaders had hoped to set it aside. While the Alabama electorate thought less and less of Graddick during these days, the public had never approved of the way the Democrats had set aside the outcome of an election and appointed one of their own as the nominee. Every time Graddick went to court, the issue made the headlines again, and the legitimacy of the Baxley nomination was called into question. Ultimately, Baxley won the legal question, but that victory was to prove costly to him in the court of public opinion.

8

The General Election

The Democratic Party controversy and the continuing legal battles and political questions it spawned blurred the start of the general election campaign. Labor Day, the traditional kickoff date that politicians use to begin the fall vote-hunting season, was virtually ignored by both politicians and the press in Alabama in 1986. In fact, there was a sense by the politicians and the media in late August that the Alabama electorate had had enough of politics and politicians.

Still, the general election campaign had to be conducted, and when it did begin, it continued to be the three-ring circus that had characterized politics so far during the year. The campaign began with questions about who the gubernatorial nominees of each of the major parties would be and continued with a special session of the legislature, a write-in campaign, the theft of tax returns, and a variety of other sideshows. The business of electing a governor and the consideration of how that governor would lead the state during the next four years were often lost as the press and politicians focused on the political subplots of this unusual year.

The Emergence of Guy Hunt

At first glance, Guy Hunt seemed to be the unlikeliest of gubernatorial candidates.[1] Tall and neatly tailored, he sported a friendly manner and twangy speech, but he was not the type to electrify large crowds or dominate small groups. Instead, he seemed like a man bound for obscurity—the perfect sacrificial lamb for a political party with no hope or intention of winning a race.

In stark contrast to the Democratic candidates, little was known about Hunt's background or private life. He had been born on June 17, 1933, in the midst of the Depression on a farm in Cullman County, near the small community of Holly Pond. At the time he ran for governor, he still lived in that same community. At sixteen, he graduated from high school and was offered a scholarship by the University of Alabama, but America's involvement in the Korean War led him instead into the military. After his tour of duty, he returned to Cullman County to take up farming and business.

In 1962 he ran unsuccessfully for state senator, and two years later he was elected probate judge for Cullman County. He was reelected to this post in 1970. He was an early supporter of Ronald Reagan's presidential candidacy in 1976 and was chosen by Reagan to head his campaign in Alabama. He attended both the 1976 and 1980 Republican conventions as a Reagan delegate. In 1978 he was the Republican gubernatorial nominee, and predictably he lost by more than 400,000 votes to Fob James. He did not run in 1982 when Montgomery mayor Emory Folmar won the Republican gubernatorial nomination. From 1981 to 1985 he was the state executive director of the U.S. Department of Agriculture's Agriculture Stabilization and Conservation Service, appointed to that post by Reagan.

In June Hunt won the 33,000-vote Republican primary handily and seemed to be on his way to a resounding defeat in November. Even in July, when the Democrats were in a full free-for-all over the gubernatorial nomination, Hunt trailed both Graddick and Baxley in one-on-one races. Then, before both the court ruling overturning the results of the runoff and the Democratic Party hearings naming Baxley as the gubernatorial nominee, Graddick led Hunt in a two-way race by 57 to 18 percent (Capstone Poll 181). Hunt did better against Baxley but was still far behind, 48 to 28 percent. Hunt did little to seize the moment. While the Democrats continued to squabble, Hunt traveled around the state speaking to relatively small audiences and deftly fending off questions about the possibility of his stepping aside for a stronger candidate.

Talk of the Republicans switching candidates persisted through the month, however, so that by the end of July Republicans were issuing official statements of their support for Hunt. Republican chairman Emory Folmar said the party's backing for Hunt was strong and unchanged.[2] The August 1 ruling by a federal court that Graddick had violated the Voting Rights Act changed not only the fortunes of the Democrats but also those of the Republicans. A number of prominent Republicans—including some members of the executive committee—had contributed to Graddick's campaign, and some began to talk openly of Graddick becoming the Republican gubernatorial nominee. Hunt and others dismissed any discussion of getting out of the race. Instead, he continued his low-profile activities and allowed the Democrats to continue their squabbles.[3]

Hunt's strategy—if it can be called that—worked. By mid-August, when the

Democratic committee was meeting to decide the challenge, Hunt's stock had risen dramatically among the electorate. As shown in chapter 6, in a survey published on Wednesday of the week of the Democratic committee's hearings, the 30-point lead that Graddick had over Hunt in July had been cut in half and Hunt was evenly matched against Baxley. Suddenly, Guy Hunt was something the state had rarely seen in more than a century—a Republican with a serious chance of being elected governor.

Could Guy Hunt really be elected governor? In mid-August, the November election was two and a half months away, and whether or not Hunt could maintain these numbers against the Democratic nominee was still an open question. The Democrats themselves were still unsure of who the nominee would be.

Switching Candidates

Soon after Graddick had been tossed off the Democratic ticket, talk began to surface that he might run as the Republican gubernatorial nominee. Graddick had once been a Republican, had received substantial Republican support in the primary, and, it was now apparent, had few friends within the Democratic Party structure. Ideologically, his ties to the Democratic Party were tenuous at best. And, in this year of the unexpected and unthinkable, the thought of Graddick at the head of the Republican ticket did not seem so outlandish after all. Still, GOP leaders continued to insist that Hunt would be the party's nominee. "The notion of anyone replacing Guy Hunt on the ticket is ridiculous," party chair Emory Folmar declared.[4]

The rumblings of a Graddick GOP candidacy were fueled by the man who would benefit most from it—Bill Baxley. On September 4, Baxley announced at a news conference that he knew of a "plot" involving people in Graddick's campaign, industrialists Winton Blount and Winton Blount III, Republican chairman Emory Folmar, and former state GOP chairman Perry Hooper. The plot, he said, would "force poor old Guy Hunt off that ticket and replace him with either Graddick or Emory Folmar or some other Republican."[5] Baxley did not reveal a source for his information, but his reasons for talking about a "plot" were obvious. One was to keep it from happening. Baxley knew that he was better off running against two candidates than one. His base of support did not constitute a majority of the voters, and if he could divide his opposition he had a better chance at winning in November. Baxley also wanted to deflect some of the charges that he was the "hand-picked" candidate of the Democrats. He tried to demonstrate that people in the other party were not above overriding an electoral decision either. At his news conference he said of the "plot" that it was the "ultimate hand-picking because Guy ran his race fair and square, and he won."

Ironically, the Republicans almost took the bait that Baxley had offered them. Even if there had been talk in some Republican circles of replacing Hunt, the difficulties were obvious, and the talk probably never amounted to much. But two days after Baxley's accusation, state representative Spencer Bachus, Hunt's campaign chairman, said that people from Graddick's campaign, including a prominent Republican, had met with him to ask that Hunt step aside and allow Graddick to assume the GOP mantle. Graddick's campaign denied the meeting took place, and later that day Bachus issued an ultimatum: either the Graddick people would admit that it happened or he would be forced to reveal the place of the meeting, the time it occurred, and the people who were involved. "I am not going to be portrayed as making up meetings that did not occur," he said. "If the Charlie Graddick campaign does not come clean and admit the meetings occurred, I will release the names, the times and the places." He said the Graddick camp had until Monday, September 8, to do so.

That weekend, however, Hunt spoke with Bachus and told him to stop talking about this matter. Hunt met with the press on Monday and told them he was in the race to stay. "Guy Hunt cannot be bought, but I am not going to embarrass people by naming names." Hunt said he had instructed Bachus to let the matter drop and that he was not going to comment any further about it. He promised, instead, to run a "positive campaign." That quickly and simply punctured the boomlet of Charlie Graddick's Republican candidacy.[6]

Hunt had reason to feel secure in his candidacy. Not only was removing him an unseemly option for the Republican hierarchy, but his standing with the public was growing.[7] A September Capstone Poll survey showed that the number of people who thought positively of Guy Hunt had risen since August. At that time 23 percent of those interviewed said they thought positively of Hunt; in September that figure had increased to 31 percent. The number of people who thought negatively of him had remained at about 21 percent in both surveys (table 8.1).

How Do You Spell G-R-A-D-D-I-C-K?

In 1980 Pickens County probate judge Robert Kirksey asked Attorney General Charles Graddick for a legal opinion concerning write-in votes in Ala-

Table 8.1

Evaluations of general election candidates

"Do you generally feel positive, neutral, or negative about each of the following people?"

	Oct. 1985	Jan. 1986	April 1986	May 1986	June 1986	July 1986	Aug. 1986	Sept. 1986	Oct. 1986	Nov. 1986
Charles Graddick*										
Positive	42%	39%	42%	44%	41%	40%	34%	28%	25%	20%
Neutral/Don't know	42	44	43	35	29	35	25	32	28	28
Negative	16	18	15	21	30	25	41	40	47	52
% Pos. – % Neg.	26	21	27	23	11	15	-7	-12	-22	-32
Bill Baxley										
Positive	38%	41%	44%	42%	35%	35%	32%	32%	30%	30%
Neutral/Don't know	41	39	38	30	34	34	21	21	21	18
Negative	21	21	18	28	31	31	47	46	49	52
% Pos. – % Neg.	17	20	26	14	4	4	-15	-14	-19	-22

Guy Hunt				
Positive	23%	31%	37%	37%
Neutral/Don't know	55	47	39	31
Negative	22	21	24	32
% Pos – % Neg	1	10	13	5

*The candidate evaluation question was asked about Guy Hunt beginning with the August 1986 survey. The evaluation question about Charles Graddick was deleted from the November 1986 survey (Capstone Poll 193) when he withdrew from the race. Results in this table are based on 447 interviews conducted before that occurred.

Source: Capstone Poll 148, 160, 169, 175, 176, 181, 185, 188, 191, 193

bama elections. Could a candidate or campaign issue print stickers or rubber stamps that voters could use in the voting booth? Was the last name of the candidate sufficient for a write-in vote to be counted? Did the name have to be spelled correctly?

Graddick answered the inquiry by concurring with the opinion of a previous attorney general, Richmond Flowers. "The Attorney General has ruled in a prior opinion that stickers or rubber stamps may not be used, and that the name must actually be written," Graddick's office wrote. Graddick also agreed with Flowers on the requirement that a last name alone was insufficient for a write-in ballot. The correct spelling was not required, both attorneys general said, "if it can be determined from the spelling on the ballot the person for whom the elector intended to vote."

It was one of the small ironies of an ironic year that during the last week in August the Graddick campaign was considering going to court to overturn a ruling that Graddick himself had made when acting as attorney general. Palmer Hamilton, one of Graddick's chief strategists, said that the opinion on write-in voting that Graddick had approved represented a "very narrow" view of the election laws.[8]

The dilemma that Graddick posed for himself was not the first and certainly not the last of the campaign. Graddick had been declared ineligible for the Democratic nomination by a federal court because he had issued what appeared to be an attorney general's ruling saying that crossover voting was illegal. He had found himself in trouble with the Democratic Party because of his open courting of Republican votes, his history as a Republican, and his failure to cultivate friends within the party's establishment. He allowed the state supreme court to turn down his appeal of the party's decision on a technicality rather than on the issues because he had not followed the proper appeals channel.

Now he was in a write-in campaign that offered him only very long odds on success. It would stretch his campaign and its resources to the limit. Graddick was in danger of losing any of the public's sympathy he had left by being branded a sore loser and spoiler, terms he had used against Baxley just a month before. A write-in campaign was the surest way to burn his bridges completely with the Democratic Party, and if that campaign destroyed the Republican chances for victory in November, he would undoubtedly become Alabama's politician without a party.

Perhaps the bitterest pill of all for Graddick's palate was the position that he had put himself in relative to his nemesis, Bill Baxley. By rushing headlong into a write-in campaign and by positioning himself as a tough guy who would stick it out, Graddick had inadvertently helped rather than hurt Baxley's campaign, and he had given Baxley yet another weapon to use against him. Baxley was quick to recognize and use it. Soon after Graddick indicated that he was going to mount a write-in campaign, Baxley predicted that he would drop it. Graddick would be bought off by the Republicans, Baxley told the Alabama Democratic Executive Committee a week after his nomination, and the campaign would come down to a two-man race between him and Guy Hunt. He also he predicted that Graddick would be offered "employment in a law firm" to drop his write-in plans.[9]

Baxley's ploy was simple and obvious, and it worked. Graddick was boxed in. He now had to go through with his write-in plans, no matter how difficult, or leave himself open to the charge that Baxley was indeed right—that he had dropped out because of Republican pressures or offers. But he would also have to suffer Baxley's taunts throughout the campaign and would have to live with the knowledge that his candidacy might be the key to a Baxley victory.

Graddick's position was difficult but not impossible. There were some things in early September from which he could take some hope. Graddick kept bringing up the fact that nearly half a million people had voted for him in the June 24 runoff. Many of those people were still with him in early September, despite the beating his public image had taken during August. Graddick produced the results of his Florida-based pollster that showed close to 30 percent of the electorate was willing to write in his name in November.[10]

The September Capstone Poll survey, conducted during the second week of the month, showed the same thing. In a three-way race, with people knowing that they would have to write in Graddick's name, Baxley was slightly ahead of Graddick, 33 to 29 percent, and Hunt was slightly behind (28 percent) (table 8.2). This silver lining surrounded plenty of clouds for Graddick, however. The number of people who said they thought negatively of Graddick had remained at about 40 percent, the same level as in the August survey, but the number of people who said they thought positively of him had declined, from 34 to 28 percent.

While the Alabama electorate still did not approve of what the Democratic Party had done in August (60 percent said that the party should have held another runoff election), that disapproval had not translated itself into sympathy for Graddick (table 8.3). In fact, many people held him partly responsible for the situation. Nearly half of those interviewed (46 percent) said the controversy over the Democratic nomination had made them feel

Table 8.2

Voter preferences in three-candidate race for governor

"Suppose that a general election for governor was held today and the candidates were Democrat Bill Baxley, Republican Guy Hunt, and Charles Graddick as a write-in candidate. For whom would you vote?"*

	September	October	Late October
Baxley	33%	36%	34%
Hunt	28	32	37
Graddick	29	21	17
Don't know/Undecided	10	11	13

*The findings for the late-October survey reflect the results collected before Graddick withdrew from the campaign (N = 437).

Source: Capstone Poll 188, 191, 193

less favorable toward Graddick. That figure was up from the August survey, in which 38 percent said they felt less favorable toward Graddick. Nearly 48 percent of those interviewed—about the same as in August—said they felt that Graddick had acted unfairly in encouraging Republican crossover votes during the runoff (table 8.4).

Respondents in the September survey were also asked about write-in voting. Less than 10 percent said they had "ever cast a write-in vote," and less than a third said they knew "how to cast a write-in vote." About half (53 percent) said they thought it was "easy" to cast a write-in vote in Alabama.

Such results could not have been heartening to the Graddick campaign as it faced the daunting task of educating the state's voters on the six different ways to cast a write-in vote in Alabama. Any sympathy that might have accrued to Graddick because of the way the nomination had been taken from him in August was not converting itself into voter strength; in fact, Graddick was showing signs of substantial slippage in the public's mind. Sustaining such a campaign, and raising the money to keep it going, would not be an easy task for the Graddick camp.

Adding to Graddick's troubles was the fact that his friends were beginning to desert him, particularly in the press, and newspapers all over the state were beginning to take him to task for continuing his fight for the nomination. The *Anniston Star,* never a supporter of Graddick's but will-

Table 8.3

Opinions about election controversy

"What do you think the Democratic Party should do (have done) regarding the run-off election? Should it declare (have declared) Bill Baxley the winner (its nominee), or should it hold (have held) a new election?"

	August 1986	September 1986	October 1986	November 1986
Declare Baxley the winner	18%	23%	28%	24%
Have a new election	70	64	60	64
Don't know/No answer	13	13	12	12

Source: Capstone Poll 185, 188, 191, 193

Table 8.4

Opinions about election controversy and Charles Graddick

"Have the events since the runoff election made you feel more favorable or less favorable about Charles Graddick, or have they made no difference in your opinion about him?"

	August 1986	September 1986
More favorable	15%	15%
No difference	43	33
Less favorable	38	46
Don't know/No answer	4	6

"Do you think that Charles Graddick acted unfairly when he encouraged Republicans to vote in the Democratic runoff election?"

	August 1986	September 1986
Yes	50%	48%
No	37	38
Don't know/No answer	12	13

Source: Capstone Poll 188, 191

ing to live with him as the nominee, in June, compared him to Aaron Burr, an "excruciatingly ambitious man" who had a hard time accepting defeat. "Give it up, Charlie," the paper said. "You're making yourself obnoxious."[11] The *Montgomery Advertiser* was also critical, though more even-handed, calling the actions of both Graddick and Baxley "disgusting."[12] And the *Birmingham News*, a paper that had stuck with Graddick through the runoff and had called repeatedly for a new election, echoed the same sentiment. "Graddick says he is the only person who can beat Baxley, but polls taken since the Democrats anointed their man have suggested otherwise. In fact, they show voters are almost as fed up with the attorney general as they are with the lieutenant governor."[13]

Despite the many problems involved with a write-in campaign and the difficulties raining down on the Graddick candidacy, the Graddick camp felt it had no choice but to soldier on. After all, there was a possibility that a legal miracle could occur and that they would find themselves in a new runoff election. And there was also the possibility that they could maintain enough support through the next two months to capture a victory in November. As tough as the fight would be, it was preferable, at this point at least, to giving up. In early September the campaign office ordered a million pencils with Graddick's name on them; they were to become the symbol of his fight.[14]

The Baxley Dilemma

Baxley may have cleverly outmaneuvered Graddick and may have relished seeing Graddick squirm, but he had his own difficulties to deal with. By the end of August, Baxley had in hand what he had sought for so many years—the Democratic nomination for governor. Only now that nomination had been seriously devalued. Unlike almost all other Democratic nominees during the past century, he was by no means a certain winner in November. He could count neither on the traditional tendency of Alabamians to vote Democratic in a governor's election nor on any deep reservoir of personal popularity to sustain him through the fall campaign. His hope was that he could explain the Democratic Party's decision so that it would be acceptable to a substantial number of voters and that he could focus attention on the weaknesses of his opponent.

The seriousness of Baxley's situation was demonstrated by the results of surveys in August and September. In August, before the Democrats had decided to appoint him as the nominee, Baxley and Hunt had been even in a two-way race for the governorship; by September, Hunt had pulled ahead

Table 8.5

Voter preferences in two-candidate race for governor

"Suppose that a general election for governor was held today and the candidates were Democrat Bill Baxley and Republican Guy Hunt. For whom would you vote?"

(November only, if Undecided, "As of today do you lean a little more toward Baxley or Hunt?")

	August 1986	September 1986	October 1986	November 1986
Baxley	42%	39%	39%	40%
Hunt	44	51	50	52
Don't know/No answer	14	10	11	8

Source: Capstone Poll 185, 188, 191, 193

and was leading 51 to 39 percent (table 8.5). Many believed that to be a temporary phenomenon, that it would be difficult for Hunt to sustain a lead like that one over the nominee of the traditionally dominant party. People were angry, but they would get over it—or so Baxley's supporters hoped.

Baxley's problems with the electorate went deeper than that, however. As noted before (see table 8.3), most Alabamians believed that the Democrats should have called for another runoff election. Despite the attempts by Baxley and others to explain the Democratic Party's position, more than 60 percent of the voters still believed in September that a new election should have been held, while 23 percent said the party was justified in naming Baxley as its nominee. The fact that the party did not call for another election made Baxley appear to be what his opponents had been claiming he was all along—the hand-picked candidate of the special interests and old-line bosses of the party. The alienation that many felt from the Democrats was real and substantial.

The focus of the alienation was on Bill Baxley, however. Nearly half of those in the September survey said they felt less favorable toward Baxley because of the controversy, about the same as was found in the August survey. The number feeling that Baxley was justified in his contest of the nomination remained stable (table 8.6). And even though Graddick was getting his share of the blame for the situation, Baxley was the focus of much of the public's anger, frustration, and disaffection. Many people believed that the

Table 8.6

Opinions about election controversy and Bill Baxley

"Have the events since the runoff election made you feel more favorable or less favorable about Bill Baxley, or have they made no difference in your opinion about him?"

	August 1986	September 1986
More favorable	17%	14%
No difference	35	34
Less favorable	44	46
Don't know/No answer	4	5

"Do you think that Bill Baxley is (was) justified in protesting the outcome of the runoff election?"

	August 1986	September 1986
Yes	47%	48%
No	44	40
Don't know/No answer	9	11

Source: Capstone Poll 188, 191

Democrats had taken their votes away and that they had justified it with the flimsiest of evidence. Baxley was the clear beneficiary of this action, and they were willing at this point to vote for anyone but him. This anger translated into another high negative rating for Baxley, much like the one he had received in August. Nearly half of the public (46 percent) said they felt negatively about him, and only 32 percent said they felt positively toward him.

Baxley was faced with a number of options at the beginning of the general election campaign. He could try to explain the rightness of the Democratic Party's decision in hopes that the voters' anger would dissipate. At first, this is what he tried to do, and as the results of the September poll showed (with 64 percent calling for a new runoff), it had little effect. In fact, Baxley's explanations seemed to do little more than keep the attention of the electorate focused on this event—something that Baxley could not afford. Another option for Baxley was to try to redirect the public's attention to his opponent, a man of limited experience and qualifications. This tactic was filled with dangers because it could easily backfire, bringing even more wrath on Baxley's head. Finally, Baxley could try to take advantage of whatever opportunities presented themselves to demonstrate his leadership experience and qualities. Such an opportunity seemed to be in the making in mid-September.

Special Session Heroics

By September the state of Alabama was running out of money. The education budget had been prorated (reduced) by 5 percent for the 1985–86 year, and Governor Wallace was predicting that the new year's budget, beginning October 1, would exceed revenues by 6 to 10 percent. The state's general fund was almost out of money because of declining oil and investment revenues. The state desperately needed some new and immediate sources of income to continue providing services for its citizens.

The dilemma for the governor and the state legislature was obvious. How could state legislators raise taxes while many of them were running for reelection? And how could they fail to respond to the state's need for more money? Seeing no way out of this vise, Wallace called the legislators back to Montgomery for a special session. Many of them openly expressed doubts that Wallace would be able to get any new tax proposals passed, and some even doubted publicly that there was any crisis at all. Wallace set before them a cafeteria line of tax proposals, which included a variety of "sin" taxes on beer, cigarettes, and racetracks, a tax on municipal utility companies, and repeal of a sales tax law that the state supreme court had recently found the state to be overcollecting on. Wallace later added to that list a proposed tax of five cents per can on soft drinks. Wallace justified all of these proposals by saying that if the state did not find some new money, the Department of Health and Human Services would have to close its day-care centers on October 1 and the Department of Mental Health would have to stop serving some of its patients. Medicaid services would also be cut. Wallace was committed only to the idea of taxing racetracks. He invited the legislators to submit other ideas for raising money if they did not like his.

The legislators' reluctance to raise taxes, even during a financial crisis in the state, was an echo of public sentiment about the issue. There was clearly no consensus for raising taxes, although the opposition to it was not overwhelming either. As part of the September Capstone Poll survey, respondents were asked if they favored or opposed "the state government raising taxes in order to help reduce the financial problems it is currently facing." About 59 percent said they were opposed to a tax increase, while 33 percent were in favor of it. They were then asked if they would "most like the state government to solve its financial problems by cutting services or by raising taxes." About 34 percent said they would cut services, while 37 percent said they would raise taxes. These results parallel results from previous surveys that indicate that people are not against taxes per se, but they need to be convinced about their necessity.

Because of the speed with which Wallace had called the special session, the leadership channels that he had previously depended on had not developed, and his proposals had no strong advocates. Neither were there alternate tax proposals placed before the legislators. Finally, a proposal was made to move money from the State Insurance Fund and the Revenue Sharing Fund to cover the immediate needs facing the state government. Republican legislators claimed to have proposed the idea originally, but it was quickly taken over by Baxley and pushed in the senate. Wallace said he would go along with the idea if its legality could be assured, leading some Republicans to charge that the whole special session was staged to boost Baxley's candidacy.

Whatever the source of the idea, it seemed the only way to get the legislators out of a tight situation, and it soon was being supported by most of the lawmakers. Republican lawmakers seemed bemused but not terribly upset by Baxley's co-opting of their proposals, and the plan was quickly passed by the legislature. Graddick, who had taken no part in the special session, dismissed it as meaningless to the campaign. "I think the people of Alabama have pretty much made up their minds whether they're going to vote for Bill Baxley or not, and what he does in the legislature really doesn't matter," he said.[15]

Baxley's forces tried to make it matter, however. One Baxley partisan called Baxley's actions a "bold stroke of leadership," and the campaign quickly produced a television advertisement that told how Baxley had rescued the state from its financial crisis. That ad was aired repeatedly during October to support what would become the chief emphasis of Baxley's campaign—leadership and experience.[16]

Tax Returns

The question of Baxley's tax returns—raised briefly during the runoff campaign by Graddick—revived itself when James White, the state revenue commissioner, announced on September 22 that one of his employees had been arrested for "divulging confidential income tax information."[17] (That employee was Harry Michael Yeomans, a file clerk in the income tax division and brother of a Graddick campaign official.) The tax returns he was accused of stealing were those of Bill Baxley.

In making his announcement, White said that Yeomans had given a statement saying that a reporter from the *Birmingham News* had requested the returns. "He also admitted duplicating the returns and giving the copies to the reporter," White said. From that point, the story of Baxley's tax returns—their content and the way in which they were made public—went in a number of directions. First, there was Yeomans himself. His brother, Andy Yeomans, was a private investigator and a campaign worker for Graddick in Jefferson County. Andy Yeomans denied having any knowledge of the theft of the returns and said that he had never spoken to Graddick about them.

Then there was Sam Duvall (the same person who raised the state car issue in the second runoff debate), a reporter for the *Birmingham News*, and the man to whom Yeomans supposedly gave the returns at a meeting behind the Cracker Barrel restaurant in Montgomery. Duvall and other journalists of the *News* denied getting the returns from Yeomans. A number of other news organizations also said that the returns had been sent to them in the same manner. None of these organizations, including the *News*, had published information about the returns, however. Another person who said he had received the returns anonymously was Pat Robinson, a member of the Graddick campaign and an assistant attorney general in the White Collar Crimes Division. "I received a call from someone who said there was a package for me at the front desk. . . . I opened it up, and it was Baxley's tax returns," he said.[18] Robinson, unlike the news organizations, did not keep them to himself. He made several copies of them and delivered them to four television stations, the ALANET radio news network, and United Press International. Robinson added that, as far as he knew, Graddick did not know about any of this.[19]

Apparently, Graddick knew something about Baxley's taxes as early as June, when, about a week before the runoff election, he called a press conference in Birmingham and gave out copies of his own income-tax returns (see chapter 5). He challenged Baxley to do the same, saying that he had heard from a reliable source that Baxley had not paid his taxes. Writing about this incident three months later, Ted Bryant of the *Birmingham Post-Herald* said, "We have two basic problems here. One, the failure to pay taxes is an indictable offense. Why was the chief law enforcement officer of the state making such accusations instead of pressing charges? Two, as a law enforcement officer, Graddick has access to income tax records should he choose to pursue the proper route to obtain them. Why was he quoting a reliable source instead of offering proof? Reporters pressed him for answers but received none."[20]

Graddick was again pressed for answers about how he had known about Baxley's income-tax returns. By late September his "reliable source" had changed into an "anonymous" source. A Graddick spokesman said the attorney general had received "anonymous phone calls from more than one individual" about the tax returns. He ignored them at first but finally decided to challenge Baxley on them, the spokesman said. Graddick tried to deflect the questions about his own role in this controversy by calling attention to the contents of those returns. "It appears to me . . . that the real issue is what does his income taxes show," he said.[21]

It was a full two days after White's press conference before information about what the tax returns contained was published. That information came in a front-page story in the *Birmingham News* and revealed that Baxley was chronically late in paying his taxes. Baxley had also paid a price for his tardiness. In 1981 he owed the state $4,769 in taxes; when those taxes were finally paid in 1986, however, Baxley had paid a total of $7,734 because of interest and penalties. The returns showed that Baxley had paid lesser interest and penalties on his 1982, 1983, and 1984 taxes.[22]

A week after Yeomans had been arrested, Baxley released copies of his federal and state income records for 1979 through 1984 to news reporters. They showed that Baxley was also consistently late in paying his federal taxes, an action that can be taken legally if the proper forms are filed (something that Baxley always did). They also showed that Baxley had earned nearly $800,000 during that six-year period and had paid more that $20,000 in state income taxes. Later in the campaign, Baxley released his 1985 tax returns, which he was also late in filing. Baxley and his wife, Lucy, had paid $40,000 in federal income tax and nearly $6,000 in state income tax on their combined $194,000 income. Baxley had also made $10,000 in late payments to the federal government for previous years' returns.[23]

The issue of who took Baxley's tax returns—and who knew about it—wound up in the hands of a Montgomery grand jury, which continued its investigation, without resolution, through the end of November.[24] The contents of Baxley's returns revealed little other than that Baxley was a fairly wealthy man and that he, like many others in his income class, had not promptly paid his taxes. He had, however, paid substantial penalties for his lateness. There was nothing illegal in any of this, but it was understandable that Baxley was reluctant to talk about his taxes.[25]

Baxley and the *Birmingham News*

When Baxley released his 1985 income tax records in late October, he did so with a challenge that Guy Hunt do the same thing.[26] After all, he told reporters, he had revealed himself and had been asked some tough questions. Now he called on them to "ask Mr. Hunt the same questions about his taxes as you are mine. I know some of you will. I doubt if the *News* will," he said. Baxley's shots at the *Birmingham News* had become an integral part of his campaign routine.

The income-tax controversy was a good example of the animosity that had grown between the lieutenant governor and the state's largest newspaper, and the dynamics of that split. Baxley laid the blame for the tax-return theft at the feet of the *News*. "My gut feeling is that it was a combination of the Graddick campaign and the *Birmingham News* working hand-in-hand," he said. "It did not, it absolutely did not, hatch in the mind of that guy who has been charged."[27] For Baxley, the case of his stolen returns was yet another example of the way in which the *News*' editorial policy and its news coverage worked in concert with one another.

Baxley was convinced that someone on the *News* staff participated in the theft of his tax returns, and from his point of view, such conclusions were logical. He had been the target of the *News*' most aggressive reporting during the campaign. On the issue of his tax returns, the *News*' editors and reporters had shown more concern about what the returns contained than how they were obtained. In fact, Tom Bailey, managing editor of the *News*, was quoted in one of the *News*' own stories about the returns as saying, "The fact is that we received the returns anonymously in the mail. However, the returns stand for themselves, regardless of where they came from. It seemed to us that whoever mailed the returns was no friend of Bill Baxley. At the same time, Bill Baxley and Charles Graddick made taxes an issue early in the campaign; we intended to check them out and publish anything we found of significance."[28]

Two days after the theft of the returns was announced by the state revenue commissioner, the *News* became the first news organization to publish information about their contents, even though the returns had been in the hands of other journalists for as much as three months. The *News* managed to look past the fact that the returns had been illegally obtained and reasoned that they were "news" and thus warranted publication. Other news organizations made different decisions. For example, Montgomery television station WSFA-TV announced that when it received the returns, it contacted the state revenue department and then destroyed the copies without broadcasting any information about them.[29]

Two days later, an editorial in the *News* took Baxley to task about his late payments and the fact that he had apparently received preferential treatment from the Department of Revenue in having some of his penalties waived. "For lawyers and other self-employed people to ask for extensions on filing their returns is not unusual. But Baxley has gone far beyond what is normal and acceptable. He has abused a taxation system that relies heavily on voluntary compliance, and he has gotten away with it." The *News* ended its editorial by saying that the public should remember what the returns showed about Baxley. It dismissed the fact that they had been revealed illegally as "bickering over how they came to light."[30]

From Baxley's viewpoint, particularly in this case, he had not done anything illegal—he had not, in the *News*' terms, "gotten away with it"—and he should have been accorded the right of any citizen to keep tax returns confidential. Other politicians, including Hunt, had chosen not to reveal their tax records, and they had not been forced to do so. The *News*, however, saw Baxley as a politician seeking the state's highest office. His tax returns, according to editors and reporters at the newspaper, were a legitimate subject of concern to the public, and the *News* had performed a service in publishing them.

The fact that it was the *Birmingham News*, however, colored the entire episode. The editorial animosity that the paper had shown toward Baxley, especially in the 1986 campaign, was no secret, and at times that animosity seemed—particularly to Baxley partisans—to spill over into the news columns. Baxley supporters, and many more neutral observers, had a long list of indictments against the paper's treatment of the lieutenant governor. That list included the *News*' exposure of Baxley's relationship with Associated Press reporter Marie Prat in March;[31] its publication of pictures related to that issue just before the runoff election; the paper's "anybody-but-Baxley" editorial stance, which led it to endorse three different people for governor during 1986; the repeated hammering of the Democratic Party and its decision not to hold another runoff; the dismissal of Graddick's actions in the runoff campaign that were later ruled illegal by a federal court. All of these items added up to a simple set of facts for Baxley supporters: the *Birmingham News* did not like him and would use whatever means it had—be it news columns or editorials—to defeat him.

Years later, the *News*' editorial attitude remained a mystery to Baxley. "It was the one thing about the campaign I never figured out," he said. The *News* had endorsed Baxley during his 1970 campaign for attorney general, an endorsement he felt had been a major boost to his victorious campus. "I also felt like I had good relations with all the people at the *Birmingham News*," he said. Baxley did not blame the publisher or editors but instead said that someone in the newsroom had something against him. But he was at a loss to say who or what.[32]

When Will the Campaign Begin?

With all of the court cases, the special legislative session, and the controversy over Baxley's taxes, many observers were prompted by late September to ask, "When will the campaign begin?" The seemingly endless judicial battles that Graddick had faced and the heated exchanges between the two Democrats had obscured the fact that Hunt was the Republican nominee. The Hunt campaign was happy to see that the Democrats were still clawing at one another. As long as Hunt did not get drawn into the fray—and he made sure that he did not—their squabbles kept alive the image of a disunited party and the fact that they had nullified the runoff election without calling for another one.

Only one thing might have made Hunt happier—Graddick dropping out of the race. Hunt said that his poll results were the same as everyone else's—that he and Graddick were splitting the anti-Baxley vote and that the vote in September constituted a majority of the voters. Hunt publicly called on Graddick to give up his write-in campaign. "If he really wants to defeat Baxley, as he contends, he would drop out of the race," he said.[33] But Hunt's calls were muted. The longer Graddick stayed in—providing he eventually dropped out—the better off Hunt was.

In fact, Hunt did not say much about anything at all. His low-profile campaign seemed to suit him personally, and it turned out to be a highly effective strategy. The Hunt campaign sensed that people were already angry enough at the Democrats; the Republicans did not have to stoke the fires. The Democrats were doing well enough on their own.

By the end of September, Baxley could finally turn his attention toward Hunt, and he immediately accepted the League of Women Voters' invitation to debate. Hunt was more reluctant. He said he would participate in a debate under certain conditions. One was that Graddick be allowed to participate; another was that there be provisions to prevent "mudslinging." Baxley had accepted the invitation unconditionally, but Hunt hung back. Then he began to ease away from it. People had watched the debate during the primary and runoff, he said, and they had been turned off. He said he would consider a debate after the Graddick litigation had ended so he would know who the real Democratic nominee was. That litigation did not end until the middle of October, and by that time Hunt realized that he did not need to debate Bill Baxley or anyone else.[34]

Baxley did not have time to linger or consider. He had to get his campaign moving, and moving quickly. He desperately tried to find an alternate issue that he could use to divert attention away from himself and the troubles of the Democratic Party. He talked about education, about the needs of the poor, the elderly, and the handicapped, the problem of illicit drugs, and industrial development. He had promised a "positive campaign" against Hunt, but that kind of campaign was not capturing the attention of the voters. Voters had to be made to either dislike Hunt or feel that he was so incompetent that they would not vote for him despite what the Democrats had done. That was the only strategy left to Baxley during the first weeks of October.

Baxley had pointed out the fact that Hunt did not have a college education and that he had worked as a salesman. Baxley was trying to make the point that a governor had to know a great deal and would have to compete with other well-educated men. This was dangerous ground, however, because there were many voters who were or had been salespersons and many more who had never attended college. But Baxley, the self-declared candidate of the average citizen, had little choice. There was no time to allow voters to find out what they needed to know about Hunt. Baxley had to tell them. There was not time enough left in the campaign for Baxley to hope that Hunt would demonstrate his incompetence. Baxley had to plant the idea and try to make it grow. The Baxley campaign and the Democratic Party prepared a set of television ads that raised questions about Hunt's experience and abilities. One had a narrator saying, "Who do you want to hire as your next governor? Let's take a look at the Republican candidate, Guy Hunt. Here's his job application. Higher education: none. Work record: Hoover vacuum cleaner salesman, Amway salesman and probate judge. State government experience: none. Remember, on November 4, we're not sending a message, we're electing a governor." Another showed an actor resembling Hunt as a door-to-door salesman and said in part, "The Republicans are selling a pretty package with no substance. On November 4, let the buyer beware." By the middle of October, Baxley had stopped showing that ad because, he said, it was "demeaning."[35]

Hunt, however, proved to be an elusive target for that kind of attack. He laughed off the ads and Baxley's other attacks. "I've never been a vacuum cleaner salesman," he said, "but I believe that surveys show that vacuum cleaner salesmen are much more highly regarded than both lawyers and politicians."[36] He refused to be defensive about his background or to be drawn into a discussion about his qualifications.

The October Surprise

In August officials of the Democratic Party had been confident that as the general election campaign ran its course, a state of normalcy would return; that is, most people would look at Guy Hunt and not like what they saw, that they would forget their anger at the Democratic Party, and that they would return to their lifelong habit of voting for the Democratic candidate for governor. Many could not believe that there would be any set of circumstances under which a half million Alabama voters would walk into a polling booth and vote for a Republican, particularly Guy Hunt. People might not like Bill Baxley, but he was more experienced than Hunt, and he was the Democratic nominee.

When the September Capstone Poll survey showed that Hunt remained a strong candidate—and, in fact, had increased his strength against Baxley in a two-way race—the belief that it would be only a matter of time before people saw through Hunt and the Republicans continued to dominate the thinking of many Democrats. "It's not a time to panic. People will get over being mad," said John Baker, chairman of the party and head of the committee that gave the nomination to Baxley.[37] After all, by mid-September the campaign had hardly started, the legal war between Baxley and Graddick continued to distract politicians and journalists alike, and Hunt had been successful in staying away from it all. In another month, many believed, the Democrats would be in much better shape.

The Capstone Poll survey, a poll of 537 registered voters conducted in early October, delivered what was for many Democrats the October surprise of the campaign. Among the things it showed were:

- Guy Hunt, despite a lack of experience and education and despite the fact that he was a Republican, was still a viable candidate for governor. In a three-way race, Baxley (36 percent) and Hunt (32 percent) were close, with Baxley having a slight lead but one well within the poll's margin of error (see table 8.2). In a two-way race, however, Hunt held a substantial lead over Baxley, 50 to 39 (see table 8.5).

- Many voters were losing interest in Graddick's write-in campaign. Graddick was getting only 21 percent of the vote in a three-way race, a drop from his September percentage of 29 percent. Graddick's demise had many explanations. Judge Guin's ruling ordering a new runoff election had been quickly overturned, and the U.S. Supreme Court refused to see enough merit in Graddick's case to hear it. Graddick's campaign to persuade voters that it was not hard to cast a write-in vote might have had exactly the opposite result—persuading them that it was too hard to do. In addition, Graddick's negative ratings continued to rise, from 40 percent in September to 47 percent in October (see table 8.1). In the final analysis, however, it may have been that Graddick was suffering from the fate traditionally reserved for third-party candidates: a feeling among the electorate that a vote should not be wasted on someone who cannot win. Graddick's whole write-in campaign had been conducted under a cloud of uncertainty, and it was beginning to tell in his standing in the polls.
- People were still angry with the Democratic Party in general and Bill Baxley in particular. Baxley's negative rating continued to be as high as ever (49 percent compared to 46 percent in September). Some 60 percent continued to believe that the Democrats should have held a new election instead of naming Baxley the nominee in August. As discussed in chapter 6, when these respondents were asked why, more than 60 percent (or about 40 percent of the entire sample) said that the people had a right to choose the nominee (table 8.5). In contrast, Guy Hunt's image improved somewhat. The number of registered voters giving him a positive rating increased from 31 to 37 percent, and he was rated negatively by 24 percent, compared to 21 percent in September.

These results began to shed some light on how much trouble the Democratic Party was in with the electorate and how little their gubernatorial nominee was helping them out of it. While the public's anger apparently did not extend to all Democrats (other nominees for state offices were in fairly good shape, and Richard Shelby was closing the gap on Jeremiah Denton in the U.S. Senate race), it was apparent that the return to traditional voting habits would not be as easy or as quick as many had thought in August.[38]

A Series of Charges

So far during the campaign, Guy Hunt had demonstrated that he could absorb, with some good humor, most of what the Democrats had thrown at him and that he could maintain his status as a legitimate candidate for the office of governor. His lack of a college education and his career as a farmer and salesman, and even the $200,000 he owed from his 1978 campaign, had not provided for the Democrats the kinds of targets they needed to reduce his standing with the public.

Baxley found a more substantial target, though, when he looked at Hunt's record as a politician and public servant. The day after the results of the October survey were published, Baxley held a press conference and charged that Hunt had resigned under a cloud as the state director of the U.S. Agricultural Stabilization and Conservation Service (ASCS).[39] Although at least two newspapers were investigating the matter, Baxley jumped the gun on them by saying that Hunt had resigned from his position while undergoing an investigation into "serious improprieties." Hunt had supposedly used his position to ask employees to help him pay off his 1978 campaign debt. Baxley offered few details or proof, and consequently his charges sounded hollow. In fact, the next day a spokesman for the ASCS in Washington said that the investigation into Hunt's activities had been a routine one and that it had turned up nothing.

Two days later, however, both the *Birmingham Post-Herald* and the *Birmingham News* printed detailed stories substantiating much of what Baxley had implied. The *Post-Herald* story carried details of a report on the investigation, a report that Hunt said he had never seen. The report said that there was evidence that Hunt might have engaged in illegal activities, but the investigation was dropped when Hunt resigned. The report cited evidence that Hunt had ordered ASCS employees to prepare political mailing lists and correspondence, that he had asked for reimbursement for political expenses, and that he had interfered with the investigation by asking his employees not to cooperate. The *News* story said that Hunt's Washington boss in the ASCS had urged him to resign after the report was submitted. (A week later, the *News* quoted the official as saying that Hunt had done a good job as ASCS director and that he had not meant to imply that Hunt was guilty of anything.) The report itself had recommended that Hunt be fired.

For the first time in the campaign, Hunt was on the defensive. He denied that he had broken the law or acted improperly, and he said the investigator was "strictly interpreting things the way he wanted to and adding fabrication to it." Hunt went on to give his explanation of each of the charges against him, labeling them either untruths or misunderstandings. He then refused to let it dominate his campaign, saying that the Democrats were harping on it because they were desperate.[40]

The Democrats weren't finished with Hunt. During the next week, Baxley charged that Hunt had formed a public service group in 1978 and then had pocketed the money it raised and used it to pay off his political debts. The organization, Baxley said, was the Coalition of People Power and was formed a few weeks after Hunt had lost the gubernatorial race to Fob James. Baxley declined to reveal the source of his information but said he would make affidavits available supporting the charge unless Hunt explained how the money was used. Baxley also said he did not know how much money was involved. Hunt again denied the allegations, saying the organization was short-lived and never raised enough money to pay even its printing costs. The balance of the expenses, he said, were "paid out of my own pocket." Others who were members of the organization's board of directors backed up Hunt.[41]

The Democrats were hoping that these charges—and others, if they could find them—would raise enough questions about Hunt to begin swinging voters back into Baxley's camp. They prepared another set of television ads, again emphasizing Hunt's lack of experience but also saying that he had been forced to resign from his ASCS job.[42] There were two problems with the allegations against Hunt. One was that the Democrats lacked the "smoking gun," the clear proof of wrongdoing that it would take to topple Hunt from his lofty perch in the public's mind. The report on Hunt's activities in the ASCS was damaging, but Baxley had made the charges without having the report, thus lessening the impact of both the charges and the report. The second problem was that the charges were coming from Bill Baxley, a man whom the public was already rejecting. Baxley's September promise of a "positive campaign" seemed to give way to the expediency of getting elected, confirming what many people already believed about him. Consequently, the charges might be hurting Hunt, but they were not helping Baxley.

Baxley produced one final charge. A week before the election he said that the Alabama legislature had passed, at Hunt's request, a special law requiring the Cullman County Commission to reimburse Hunt for monetary mistakes made by the probate judge's office if those mistakes were made in "good faith." Hunt was probate judge at the time, and Baxley said this law was an example of the preferential treatment that Hunt has sought while a public official. The charge was a flimsy one because Baxley never produced any evidence that county funds were misused, and the sponsor of the law was Tom Drake, an ardent Baxley supporter.[43]

That final charge was lost in the week's speculation about the fate of Charles Graddick. With just a week left to go in the campaign, Graddick was said to be running out of money, time, and support. On Monday the *Birmingham Post-Herald* published a poll showing Graddick running a distant third to Baxley and Hunt.[44] Hunt would beat Baxley, the poll results said, if Graddick were not in the race. Could—or should—Graddick continue his efforts if they would mean giving a victory to Baxley? Graddick canceled his television ads and his campaign appearances and went into seclusion to consider his next move.[45]

Graddick Drops Out

From the very beginning the Graddick campaign faced long odds, and in September, playing the role of the underdog seemed like the way to gain sympathy and support. Graddick pictured himself as the people's choice whose nomination had been snatched away by the power bosses. His extended court battles eroded that image, and the unsavoriness of the controversy over Baxley's stolen tax returns washed back onto his campaign.

The campaign had started out jauntily, ordering a million pencils bearing his name. But that attitude turned defensive as the campaign learned the difficulties of mounting a write-in campaign. Graddick decided to go on a teaching campaign, and at many stops he would spend time instructing listeners about how to cast a write-in vote in their area. September's headlines were dominated by his court battles, not his campaign efforts, and when the U.S. Supreme Court turned down his final plea, Graddick had few resources left.

One of the major problems, of course, was money.[46] Graddick had raised nearly $3 million for his primary and runoff campaigns, at some points bringing in $350,000 or more each week. During the general election campaign, however, Graddick was barely able to scrape together $500,000. Heavy individual and organizational contributors, such as the Alabama Farm Bureau and the Business Council of Alabama, either sat out the general election or switched their support to Hunt. Graddick's campaign debt was mounting, and if he was to continue to be viable he would have to spend a great deal more in the final days before the election.

Baxley had predicted all along that Graddick would drop out of the race, and Baxley had done what he could to ensure that Graddick stayed in. He persistently goaded Graddick, saying that he was a tool of the Republicans and that he would stay in until close to the election and then pull out. It would all be timed to give the Republicans the maximum advantage, he said. On the Friday before Graddick canceled his Monday campaign appearances, Baxley promised to give $10,000 to Graddick's favorite charity if he would stay in the race through election day.[47] All through the campaign, Graddick had insisted that he was in the race to the finish.

Whether Graddick was in or out of the race concerned the Hunt campaign, too. During the same week that Baxley made his offer, Hunt's supporters began a set of commercials aimed directly at those thinking about voting for Graddick. "Voting for Charles Graddick can only accomplish one thing," one of them said, "and that's electing Bill Baxley." The message was clear, simple, and direct, and given the perception that Graddick was losing ground, it had a good chance of working.

Graddick spent Monday, Tuesday, and Wednesday of the last week of the campaign out of sight. He had canceled all of his public appearances, and he stopped distribution of his final television commercials. For three days his staff fended off inquiries into his whereabouts and his activities, but it was soon apparent that he was closing down his campaign.

One of the people Graddick met with during that time was Tom Coker, a well-known Montgomery lobbyist with close ties to business groups and Republicans. Coker said his friends in the business community had supported Graddick and were concerned that he would end the campaign not only losing but with a large debt. He told Graddick that if he dropped out, he could count on something like $250,000 to help pay off those debts. Although he did not say so directly, Coker was acting with an understanding that the Hunt campaign would underwrite this pledge. He would not have made it otherwise. After the election, however, Hunt officials refused to honor that understanding, and Coker was left out on his own, having to raise substantial amounts of money and having to pay off a good portion of that debt himself. When Hunt ran for governor in 1990, Coker was a high-profile volunteer for his Democratic opponent, Paul Hubbert.[48]

Early Thursday afternoon in Montgomery, Graddick appeared before the press and announced that he was dropping out of the race. "Continuing to run might only serve to give the election to the candidate of the present old-time power structure I have sworn to fight," he said. "I cannot and will not risk giving them a victory." Graddick did not endorse Hunt, as many had expected him to do, but he urged his supporters to "vote your conscience."[49]

Baxley immediately charged that Graddick had made a deal with the Republicans, but the *Birmingham News* quoted an anonymous Graddick aide as saying it was Graddick's supporters, not Republicans, who had persuaded him to quit the race. The *News* quoted the aide as saying, "A group of Charlie Graddick's concrete supporters who've been with him all the way through this thing have told him, 'Look, we hate Bill Baxley's guts. If we will commit to you to raise the money to take care of the campaign debts, will you get out so there won't be any risk of Bill Baxley being governor?' And Charlie said, 'Yes, I'll do that.'"[50] Still, stories continued about whether Graddick did receive any money to end his campaign.[51]

The results of a Capstone Poll survey conducted when Graddick was considering discontinuing his campaign showed that the decision to withdraw made good political sense. Graddick had fallen further behind in the three-man race. Only 17 percent of the public said that they would vote for the attorney general (see table 8.2). Indeed, Graddick's strength had eroded to such a point that he was no longer even playing the "spoiler" role: Hunt (37 percent) rather than Baxley (34 percent) was now the leading candidate.

The survey also found that Graddick's public image had continued its decline (see table 8.1). More than half (52 percent) of the state's citizens now gave Graddick a negative rating. Only one in five Alabamians rated Graddick positively. None of the population groups studied gave the attorney general a net positive rating. It is safe to say that outside the circle of hard-core Graddick supporters, not many voters were upset when the attorney general's campaign ended.

Trouble for Baxley

Baxley was one of the relatively few people in Alabama who was sorry to see Graddick withdraw. Baxley could expect to gain votes from only a few of Graddick's supporters, while Hunt would reap a bountiful harvest.[52] Graddick had remained in the race just long enough to do him the maximum amount of damage, keeping the actions of the Democratic Party in August as one of the chief campaign issues. His dropping out five days before the election gave Baxley little chance to woo his supporters or to redirect the focus of the campaign.

On the Sunday and Monday nights before the election, Baxley gave one final pitch to the voters. He bought a half hour of airtime on a number of television stations and spoke extemporaneously about his qualifications and those of Guy Hunt. Baxley mentioned the long and exhausting campaign and the troubles his family had been through. He mentioned those who had opposed him, including the *Birmingham News*. Near the end, he used a line he had used previously at a press conference. He told the voters to remember that this was an election for governor, "not an audition for the Andy Griffith show."[53]

The Election

On Tuesday, November 4, more than 1.2 million voters cast ballots in the governor's race; 56 percent of them voted for Guy Hunt to succeed George Wallace as governor of Alabama. That evening, at 9:35 p.m., Bill Baxley conceded, telling his supporters that this would probably be his last time to run for public office. He said he had no regrets about his decision to challenge the results of the runoff election, and he attributed his loss to the fact that people did not understand the Democratic Party's decision. In a carefully prepared victory speech, Hunt obliquely disagreed: "The people of Alabama have spoken, and the message is loud and clear—the people of Alabama elect the governor of Alabama."[54]

The results of the Capstone Poll's pre-election survey (which showed Hunt leading Baxley by a 52 to 40 percent margin) revealed that Hunt's strongest support came from younger, more-educated, and higher-income voters (table 8.7). Not surprisingly, Hunt had strong support among Independents and Republicans. Among white voters, Hunt led Baxley by a 61 to 32 percent margin, while among blacks Baxley received 84 percent of the vote compared to Hunt's 6 percent. A majority of the citizens who had supported either Graddick (77 percent), James (70 percent), or McMillan (53 percent) in the Democratic primary voted for Hunt in the general election.

The survey also showed that Baxley's campaign efforts had some effect on how people felt about Hunt. By the end of the campaign about 37 percent of the public gave him a positive rating, the same number as found in the October survey. However, Hunt's negative ratings had grown to 32 percent from 24 percent in early October. Hunt was evaluated most favorably by Republicans, Independents, and higher-income respondents (table 8.8). He was negatively rated by blacks and Democrats. By the end of the campaign, citizens had become less confident about Hunt's competence and honesty.

Baxley's campaign efforts did not, however, improve his own image. Indeed, if his final campaign activities had any effect it was to further tarnish his already negative image. The lieutenant governor finished his campaign with a majority (52 percent) of the state's citizens saying that they felt nega-

Table 8.7

Socio-demographic characteristics of general election supporters

"Suppose a general election for governor was held today and the candidates were Democrat Bill Baxley and Republican Guy Hunt. For whom would you vote?"

(If Undecided, "As of today do you lean a little more toward Baxley or Hunt?")

Characteristics*	Baxley	Hunt	Don't know/ No answer	N
Age				
18–40 yrs	37%	59	4	411
41–60 yrs	39%	51	10	338
61+ yrs	47%	41	12	215
Race				
White	32%	61	7	800
Black	84%	6	10	151
Gender				
Male	37%	56	7	427
Female	42%	50	8	546
Education				
High school or less	44%	49	8	560
More than high school	34%	58	7	404
Income				
Under $40,000	45%	49	6	644
More than $40,000	25%	70	5	165
Party				
Republican	12%	85	3	157
Independent	24%	68	7	336
Democrat	67%	24	4	386
Vote in primary				
Baxley	91%	8	1	205
Graddick	15%	77	8	226
James	19%	70	10	78
McMillan	36%	53	11	53

* Missing data deleted.

Source: Capstone Poll 193

Table 8.8

Net evaluations of general election candidates by socio-demographic groups, late October, November 1986

Characteristic*	Net evaluations**		
	Charles Graddick	Bill Baxley	Guy Hunt
Age			
18–40 years	-28	-29	7
41–60 years	-34	-26	2
61+ years	-36	- 3	3
Race			
White	-28	-36	14
Black	-59	52	-42
Gender			
Male	-32	-32	9
Female	-32	-16	1
Education			
High school or less	-31	-12	1
More than high school	-34	-38	9
Income			
Less than $40,000	-35	-17	- 2
More than $40,000	-35	-53	26
Party			
Republican	-23	-61	53
Independent	-23	-55	26
Democrat	-44	23	-36

*Missing data deleted.

**These scores are figured by subtracting the percentage giving a negative evaluation to a candidate from those giving a positive evaluation. The results for Graddick are based upon interviews (N = 437) completed prior to this withdrawal from the campaign.

Source: Capstone Poll 193

tively about him. Only about three in ten citizens gave him a positive rating. Of the groups examined, Baxley received overall positive ratings from only Democrats and black citizens. He received strongly negative ratings from Republicans, Independents, higher-income respondents, more-educated citizens, whites, males, and those under sixty years of age.

The Impact of the Controversy

Clearly, the major factor resulting in Baxley's negative image and election defeat was the public's unhappiness with the resolution of the runoff election controversy. Several pieces of evidence demonstrate the effect of the controversy.

First, after the runoff election but before the Democratic Party committee's decision, Baxley was no worse than tied with Hunt. In each survey conducted after the committee hearings, however, Hunt led Baxley by a relatively unchanging 50 to 40 percent.

Second, Baxley failed to change public opinion concerning the runoff controversy. The final pre-election survey showed what had been the case in August—that roughly two-thirds of Alabamians thought the party should have held a new runoff election (see table 8.3). About 67 percent of those who said that the Democrats should have held a new election rated Baxley negatively, compared to 12 percent of those who said that the party did the right thing in declaring Baxley its nominee. Similarly, only 22 percent of those who wanted a new election said they were going to vote for Baxley over Hunt, compared to 78 percent of those who said the party was right in selecting Baxley. Among Democratic Party identifiers who wanted a new runoff, Baxley received a small plurality but less than a majority of the votes (42 percent). However, only 42 percent of the Democratic identifiers agreed with the party's decision not to hold a second runoff election.

Third, the Democratic Party controversy during the summer did not hurt Baxley because citizens believed that he was wrong in protesting the outcome of the runoff or because they believed that Graddick did nothing improper. (Indeed, the results of the surveys consistently showed that the public's reaction to the controversy hurt Graddick's image and electoral prospects as much as, if not more than, Baxley's.) Rather, the controversy led to Baxley's defeat because the party's decision to name him as its nominee was perceived as violating the principle—well grounded in the populist tradition of the state—that citizens should select their leaders through elections.

Fourth, the controversy also hurt Baxley by keeping the issue of "change" on the political agenda. As we have stated, Wallace's retirement, Graddick's efforts, and the public's dissatisfaction with the quality of the state's government made change a major item on the political agenda during 1986. What was meant by "change" was never clearly defined in the campaign. To some it meant a shift in the style of government from cronyism to a more merit-oriented form of personnel selection and decision making. To others it meant a shift in the content of state politics. To still others it meant simply changing the current set of politicians who were reaping the personal benefits of holding state office and replacing them with another set of politicians who would do the same thing.

However it was defined, the way in which Baxley was selected kept the issue of change sharply in focus during the general election. It also made Baxley appear to be the hand-picked candidate of the special interests who were currently in control of state government (something Graddick had claimed all along) and consequently one of the incumbent rascals who had to be thrown out of office. Thus, the controversy gave Baxley what amounted to a double kiss of death in Alabama politics: he was seen as a violator of the state's populist principles and as part of the disliked state government.

9
Consequences

The 1986 gubernatorial election has had a lasting and significant impact on both its immediate participants and Alabama as a whole. For some of the candidates the conclusion of the 1986 campaign marked the end of their political careers. For others, election day began an extended professional lull or detour. For still another, the end of the 1986 contest signaled the start of a new, and for a time successful, stage of political life. For Alabama as a whole, the 1986 election hastened the emergence of a more competitive partisan politics.

Among the participants, 1986 most clearly marked the end—finally—of George Wallace's political career. Seeing his support eroding because of the public's increasing concern about his health, Wallace withdrew as a candidate early in the campaign. As he wryly reported after the general election, his retirement announcement made him "a lame, lame duck."[1] After leaving office, Wallace remained largely off the state's political stage. Yet, his career and political legacy continued to attract attention in the form of biographies, documentaries, and docudramas.[2] One of Wallace's last public appearances came late in the 1996 presidential election campaign when Bob Dole, the GOP's nominee, held a rally in Montgomery. After the event Wallace met with Dole. There, the former Democratic governor and presidential candidate told Dole, "I already voted for you. I voted absentee yesterday."[3] Wallace died in September 1998.

George McMillan entered the campaign with an image of a progressive, competent, and intelligent public servant. By the end he was seen as a politically inept, embittered, and in some ways unprincipled man. McMillan's endorsement of Graddick—and his continued and enthusiastic campaigning for him—cut him off from many of his supporters without bringing him any visible gain. Since 1986, McMillan has left the state's political scene. He is now heading McMillan Associates, a marketing and consulting company involved in producing events such as City Stages, a music festival in Birmingham.[4]

Fob James, despite a well-financed campaign, never overcame the public's negative perceptions of his previous term in office. His neutrality during the 1986 runoff and his silence during the subsequent controversy did mean that of all the Democratic candidates, James was the least damaged by the Democrats' election contest. Still, his poor showing in the primary, the firmness of his negative public image, and his background as a Republican suggested that James's political career was effectively over, especially within the Democratic Party.

This expectation was confirmed in 1990 when James again sought the Democratic gubernatorial nomination. As was the case four years earlier, he ran a well-financed, serious campaign focusing on familiar themes such as competence and ending waste in state government. Once again, however, these efforts failed. In the 1990 Democratic primary, James again finished third, receiving about the same percentage of the vote (21.6) as he had in 1986 (20.8).

In 1994 James adopted a different approach, and as a result his political career was revived. Shortly before the candidate filing deadline for the 1994 election, James switched back to the Republican Party. Running as the best-known and most-experienced candidate, James won the GOP's nomination for governor relatively easily. Then, riding the tide of the 1994 national Republican landslide, he narrowly (with 50.4 percent of the vote) won a second term as governor.

The second James administration was as controversial as the first. For four years, news reports about the state government were filled with stories about disputes over education funding, the use of chain gangs in state prisons, tort reform, appointments to the Auburn University Board of Trustees, school prayer, and James's continuing, almost quixotic, battle with the federal courts. These and other controversies, plus a more than the normal amount of administrative infighting, multiplied the number of James's opponents and fed the impression that the governor was politically vulnerable.

As a result, James faced a crowded field of candidates in the 1994 Republican primary. After a bitter campaign he finally won the GOP's nomination, defeating Montgomery businessman Winton Blount in a runoff by a 56 to 44 percent margin. Ironically, one source of James's victory was the support he received from Democratic primary voters who crossed over and voted in the GOP runoff.[5] Unlike in 1986, the presence of these crossover voters did not result in electoral challenges or judicial hearings. The Alabama Republican Party had no rule prohibiting Democratic primary voters from participating in the party's runoff elections.[6]

James's political problems did not end with the Republican runoff. In the general election he faced a unified Democratic Party and its candidate, Lieutenant Governor Don Siegelman.[7] In his campaign, Siegelman promised to rectify the problems of the James administration and to address the state's many social and economic needs. In particular he promoted a state lottery as a means to increased financial support for education. For his part, James ran a low-key, almost disheartened, campaign. Thus on election day it was not a surprise when James lost to Siegelman by a 58 to 42 percent margin. With this defeat, James retired from state politics, though his son, Tim, was an unsuccessful candidate for the GOP's 2002 gubernatorial nomination.

Charles Graddick was for a brief time the big winner in 1986. However, his actions regarding the largely unenforceable crossover voting rule and his lack of support among Democratic Party leaders soon cost Graddick his victory. By the end of the campaign, his public record was filled with court rulings documenting his illegal activities. Large segments of the state's electorate were alienated by his campaign style. His post-runoff behavior further separated him from the Democratic Party and made him vulnerable to future challenges regarding his fitness to be the party's nominee for any office.

Despite talk during the election campaign of his becoming the GOP's nominee, the Republican Party has shown little interest in Graddick since 1986. In 1989 he formally switched to the Republican Party and then, during the 1990 campaign, briefly appeared as a Guy Hunt supporter.[8] In this role Graddick revived his aggressive and negative campaign style. In particular he tried to link Hunt's Democratic opponent, Alabama Education Association director Paul Hubbert, to the disputed 1986 race. "Paul Hubbert was the architect of the dog-and-pony show in Birmingham," he declared. Graddick also continued to portray Democrats as the party of "special interests." By doing this he also managed, despite his denials, to introduce the race issue into the campaign. Graddick zeroed in on the relationship between Hubbert and Joe Reed, also an official with the AEA and, more importantly, head of a major black political organization, the Alabama Democratic Conference. Of Reed, Graddick said, "I guess he'll be chief of staff in a Hubbert administration. Joe Reed will be on the floor in an important position in the Hubbert cabinet. Instead of in the balcony, he'll be on the floor telling people what to do."[9] For its part, the Hunt campaign tried to maintain some distance from Graddick, though it did not disown his remarks. After the election, Governor Hunt appointed Graddick to fill a vacancy as the Montgomery County district attorney. He left this position and moved into a private law practice in 1992.

Graddick's one post-1986 venture into statewide politics was a notable failure. In 1994 he ran as a Republican for lieutenant governor. In a year in which GOP candidates were winning in unprecedented numbers both in Alabama and nationwide, Graddick decisively lost this race to Don Siegelman by a 62 to 38 percent margin. In 2004 Graddick was appointed to fill a vacant Mobile County Circuit Court judgeship.[10]

Bill Baxley was also for a brief time a winner during the 1986 campaign. He was the leading vote getter in the primary, and by his own reckoning, and that of his supporters, he was the "real" winner of the runoff. He successfully challenged the results of the runoff and won a string of court decisions upholding the party's decision. However, his failure to convince the public that he was the party's legitimate nominee resulted in his becoming the first Democratic gubernatorial candidate to lose a general election in more than one hundred years.

Following his defeat, Baxley left public life and started a successful private law practice. His cases often put him in the public eye, but he has avoided any visible involvement with the state's electoral politics.[11]

Shortly after the 1986 election, Baxley and his wife, Lucy, were divorced. Lucy Baxley has gone on to have a successful political career. She won a very close election to state treasurer in 1994 and then was easily reelected in 1998. In 2002 she became the state's first female lieutenant governor. She ran for governor as the Democratic nominee in 2006 but lost to Republican incumbent Bob Riley. Meanwhile, Bill Baxley married Marie Prat, the former Associated Press reporter who generated the first of the many controversies surrounding the 1986 campaign. They have four children.[12]

Ironically, years after the bruising campaign, both Baxley and Graddick had similar perspectives on how it affected their lives. Both professed to be glad they lost, citing business successes and satisfying family lives that might have eluded them had they served as governor.[13]

Guy Hunt entered the 1986 campaign with no realistic chance of victory. He had been out of the public's view since his lopsided loss in 1978. His campaign was underfunded and understaffed, and his own party indicated no interest in his candidacy, choosing instead to concentrate on the U.S. Senate race. Moreover, Hunt was limited as a campaigner and as a candidate. He played no role in Bill Baxley's challenging the results of the runoff election. Nor did he do anything to convince the public that the Democratic Party was wrong in selecting Baxley as its nominee. Hunt also did little to cause the runoff election controversy to continue throughout the late summer and fall or to convince the public to have increasingly negative opinions about Baxley and Graddick. Further, during the campaign, Hunt failed to cultivate any intense personal following through either his presence or the force of his ideas. In fact, evidence suggests that Hunt, like Baxley and Graddick, was losing favor with the public at the end of the campaign. Still, despite both the obstacles he faced and the limits of his campaign, Hunt took advantage of the self-destruction of the Democratic Party and its candidates to become Alabama's first Republican governor since Reconstruction.

In 1990 Hunt was narrowly reelected governor, defeating Democrat Paul Hubbert. This campaign, which Hunt won by a 52 to 48 margin, was far less eventful than the 1986 contest. Still, questions about Hunt's personal finances did briefly reappear as a campaign issue. In particular, the *Montgomery Advertiser* published a story detailing how Hunt, while in office, has managed to pay off a large personal debt. Soon afterwards, however, the *Advertiser* retracted the story, saying it was based on errors and inaccurate reading of documents.[14]

While the newspaper's retraction pushed the issue of Hunt's finances off the election agenda, questions about the topic reemerged once the campaign ended. As a result, the state's attorney general, Democrat Jimmy Evans, began an investigation of Hunt. (Evans had pursued the case of the stolen Baxley tax records as Montgomery County district attorney.) This investigation ultimately resulted in Hunt's being convicted in April 1993 of misusing $200,000 of the money donated to the 1987 funds for the inauguration.[15] With the conviction, Hunt was automatically removed from office and replaced by Lieutenant Governor Jim Folsom Jr., a Democrat (who was first elected to this position in 1986).

Folsom, the son of former governor "Big" Jim Folsom, won the 1994 Democratic gubernatorial nomination over former nominee Paul Hubbert and was then defeated by Fob James in the general election. Hunt, meanwhile, sought in a variety of venues to have his conviction overturned. Finally, shortly before the 1998 primary filing deadline, the state Board of Pardons and Paroles voted to grant Hunt a pardon, on the grounds of innocence.[16] Following this, Hunt entered the 1998 Republican primary election for governor. This effort was unsuccessful. Hunt finished third in the race, receiving only about 8 percent of the vote.

After the primary, Hunt threw his support to Winton Blount. This action, though, had little effect, because Fob James defeated Blount in GOP runoff. Despite these setbacks, Hunt did not totally leave Alabama politics. In 2002 he suffered another electoral defeat, this time in a bid for a state senate seat. Several years later he was reportedly writing his memoirs.[17]

State Politics

In addition to affecting the candidates, the 1986 election has also had a continuing impact on the state as a whole.[18] In particular, the 1986 election introduced an era of increased Republican strength and heightened party competition within the state. This transformation of Alabama's partisan politics was not solely the result of the 1986 campaign. Signs that the state was moving away from its solidly Democratic past, in the form of Republican victories in presidential and congressional elections, were evident well before Baxley, Graddick, and Hunt began their campaigns. Still, the 1986 election did affect the pace and scope of electoral change within Alabama. As a result, Alabama's state elections are now more closely and consistently contested than they were at any time during the last century, and perhaps at any time in its history.

Indicators of Alabama's new partisan balance and political competitiveness are abundant. Before 1986, Democrats had controlled the Alabama's governorship for more than a century. Few of the gubernatorial elections held during this post-Reconstruction period were even marginally competitive. In the sixty-year period between the first state election held after the ratification of the women's suffrage constitutional amendment and the last Wallace victory in 1982, no Democratic gubernatorial candidate received less than 60 percent of Alabama's two-party vote.[19]

The 1986 election not only broke the Democratic monopoly over the Alabama governorship but also marked the beginning of a period of closely fought gubernatorial contests. Following Hunt's 1986 victory, Republicans won three of the state's next four gubernatorial elections. Reflecting the state's new competitiveness, however, the GOP's average margin of victory—about 2 percent—in these contests is quite small. Similarly, even the one Democratic gubernatorial victory during this period—Don Siegelman's win in 1998—was based on a margin substantially smaller than that won by most earlier Democratic candidates.[20]

The results of recent elections for state constitutional offices such as lieutenant governor or secretary of state provide another indicator of Alabama's new politics. As was the case with the governorship, before 1986 Democrats had long held a monopoly over these offices. Between 1966 and 1982, each of the Democratic candidates for these offices received at least 70 percent of the vote (table 9.1).

Despite the upheavals of the gubernatorial contest, the 1986 Graddick-Baxley dispute did not immediately alter this situation. Instead, Democrats easily won all six of the state constitutional offices up for election in 1986. In four of these contests, for attorney general, state treasurer, state auditor, and commissioner of agriculture, there was no Republican candidate on the November ballot.

Nor did the GOP win any of the state constitutional positions in 1990. Unlike previous years, however, in 1990 a Republican candidate was on the ballot for all but one of the constitutional offices up for election. Most notable among defeated GOP candidates in 1990 was Perry Hand, whom Hunt had appointed to fill an unexpired term as secretary of state. Despite already being in office, Hand lost to former Wallace aide Billy Joe Camp by a 55 to 45 percent margin.

The GOP's efforts did, however, pay off in 1994. In that year's election not only was Fob James elected governor as a Republican, but the GOP also won the contests for attorney general, state auditor, and commissioner of agriculture.[21] Again, however, these initial Republican victories were not a signal that state's formerly solidly Democratic politics was being replaced by an equally strong Republican dominance. Instead, the initial GOP victories showed that contests for state constitutional offices had become quite competitive. Democrats reclaimed the state auditor and commissioner of agriculture positions in 1998, but lost the races for lieutenant governor and secretary of state. In 2002 and 2006, the parties split the six constitutional offices up for election. Further, as table 9.1 shows, not only have both parties won recent elections for these positions, but these contests have generally been quite close. Rarely do any of the winning candidates, including those who are incumbents, win more than 60 percent of the vote.

Another sign of Alabama's new political balance and competitiveness is found in state legislative elections. Entering 1986, Democratic control over the legislature was nearly as strong as its dominance over other parts of the state government. Typically, there were then few contested general elections for seats in the state legislature. In 1982, for example, Democrats ran unopposed in more than 70 percent of the state house and senate races. In 1986, Republicans contested less than half the seats for both the state house and the state senate (table 9.2).

Since 1986, however, a greater number of GOP candidates have entered

Table 9.1

Democratic percent of two-party vote for Alabama constitutional offices, 1966–2006

	Lieutenant Governor	Attorney General	Secretary of State	State Treasurer	State Auditor	Commissioner of Agriculture
1966	100.0%	73.9%	100.0%	73.5%	75.7%	100.0%
1970	71.4	100.0	100.0	100.0	100.0	100.0
1974	100.0	100.0	100.0	100.0	100.0	100.0
1978	86.5	100.0	82.1	100.0	78.22	100.0
1982	100.0	100.0	100.0	100.0	100.0	100.0
1986	61.8	100.0	61.3	100.0	100.0	100.0
1990	67.3	64.6	55.2	100.0	62.9	55.6
1994	62.2	43.1	53.3	50.0	48.9	48.9
1998	49.6	49.7	49.5	64.6	54.1	51.1
2002	52.4	39.8	50.0	48.0	47.0	52.6
2006	50.7	46.9	42.4	39.4	45.9	59.1

Source: Alabama Secretary of State

Table 9.2

Competitiveness of general elections for Alabama legislature, 1982–2006

	Percent Contests with Democratic but no Republican candidate	Percent Contests with both Democratic and Republican candidate	Percent Contests with Republican but no Democratic candidate
Alabama House of *Representatives* (N = 105)			
1982	70.5	29.5	0.0
1986	53.3	43.8	2.9
1990	47.6	45.7	6.7
1994	43.8	46.7	9.5
1998	28.6	52.4	19.0
2002	28.6	50.5	21.0
2006	34.3	42.9	22.9
Alabama State *Senate* (N = 35)			
1982	71.4	28.6	0.0
1986	65.7	31.4	2.9
1990	31.4	57.1	11.4
1994	40.0	48.6	11.4
1998	17.1	77.1	5.7
2002	22.9	57.1	20.0
2006	17.1	65.7	17.1

Source: Alabama Secretary of State; "Candidates for State Legislature," *Birmingham News*, April 8, 2006, A11.

state legislative races. This shift has not necessarily resulted in an increase in the number of contested general elections for state legislative seats. In fact, while there has been a year-to-year fluctuation, the number of two-party-contested seats has remained relatively stable. What has occurred, in what is another (perhaps perverse) indicator of Alabama's new competitiveness, is an increase in the number of uncontested Republican seats. For example,

Table 9.3

Percent Republican of Alabama house and senate, 1980–2006

	House of Representatives (N = 105)	State Senate (N = 35)
1980	4.0	0.0
1984	12.1	12.5
1988	16.2	17.1
1992	21.9	20.0
1996	31.4	35.3
2000	34.3	35.3
2004	40.0	28.6
2006	40.0	28.6

Source: *Statistical Abstract of the United States* (Washington, D.C., Bureau of the Census), relevant years

in the last several election cycles Democrats did not contest about one-fifth of the state house seats. Still, the overall level of competition has increased. Through a combination of uncontested and contested seats, each party in recent years has entered a candidate for more than half of the state legislative seats. Further, the uncontested positions are now as likely to be a Republican as a Democratic seat.

With the greater competition has come an increase in the number of Republicans within the state legislature (table 9.3). When Guy Hunt was first elected governor in 1986, Republicans held only about 10 percent of the seats in the state legislature. In 2006 the GOP controlled about a third of the seats.

A final indicator of Alabama's new competitiveness is found in the party identifications of the state's citizens.[22] In the Alabama surveys, respondents were asked about both their national and state party identifications.[23] Figures 9.1 and 9.2 show that throughout the period under study there were generally more Democrats and fewer Republicans at the state than at the national level. Both measures, however, show roughly the same direction and magnitude of change over time. In particular, Democrats held a clear advantage over Republicans during the early 1980s (information about the party

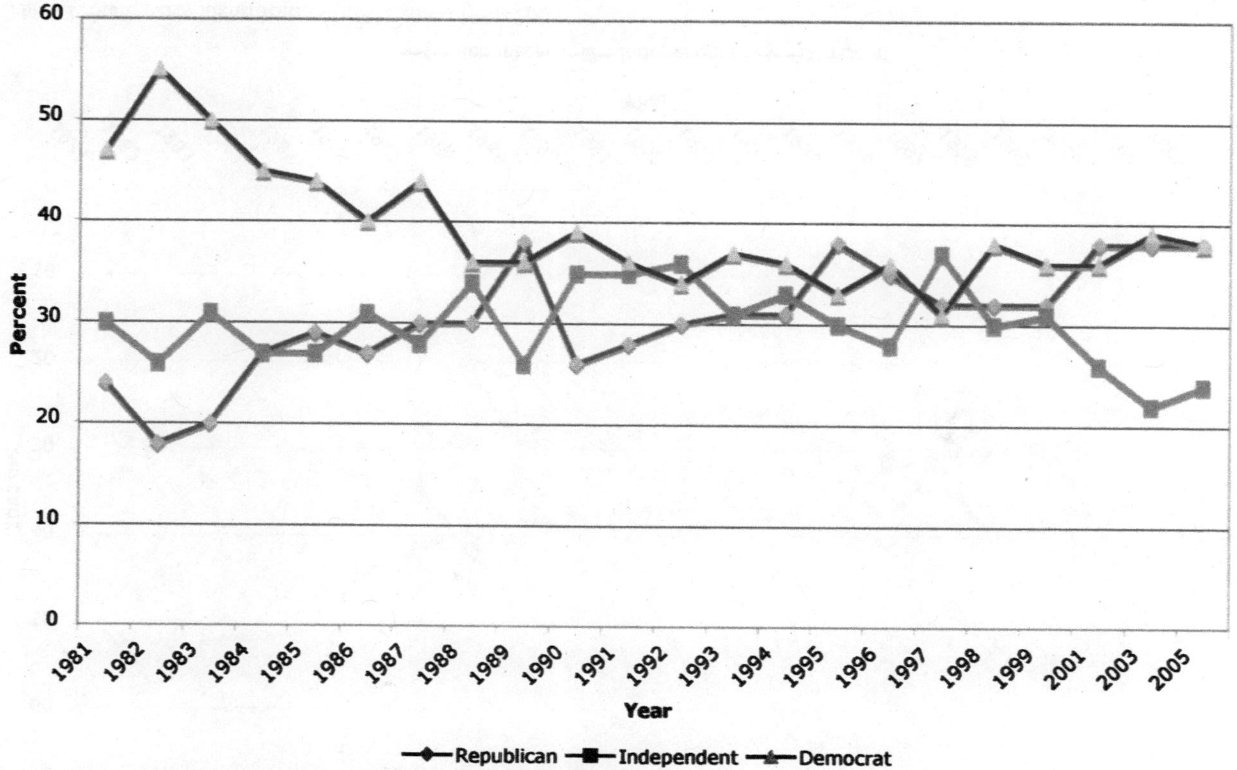

Fig. 9.1. National party identification in Alabama, 1981–2005.

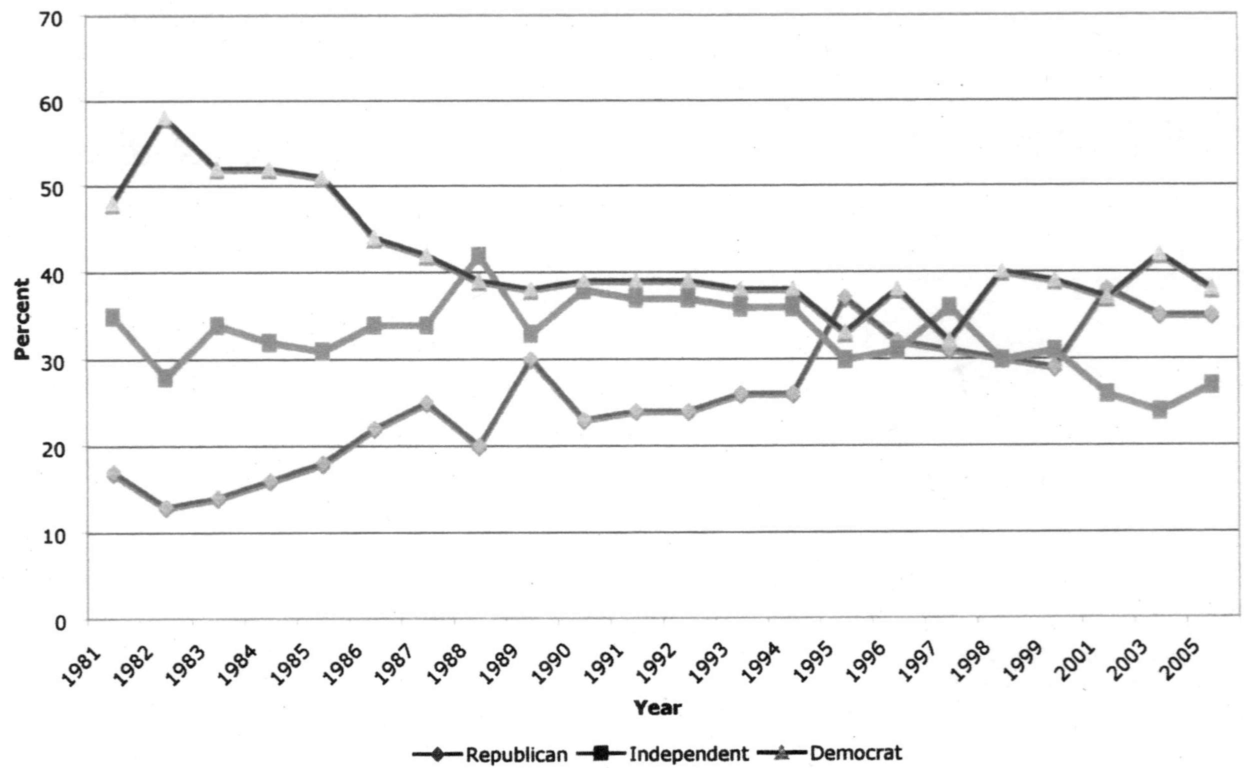

Fig. 9.2. State party identification in Alabama, 1981–2005.

identifications of Alabamians is not readily available before this time). After 1986, the number of national and state Democratic Party identifiers declined while the number of GOP supporters increased. As a result, there is now a rough parity in the number of Republican and Democratic Party identifiers in the state.[24]

The outcome of recent elections for governor, state constitutional offices, and state legislature, plus the changes that have occurred in the party identifications of Alabama citizens, show that the partisan balance is now quite different than it was before 1986. The generally narrow results of recent state elections and the equal number of Democratic and Republican Party identifiers also show that the level of party competition within Alabama is much higher now than it was before 1986. Thus, at the state government level, 1986 marks an end to Alabama's membership in the Solid Democratic South.

10
Explanations

Politically, 1986 was a remarkable year in Alabama. It began with speculation about George Wallace's possible retirement and ended with Guy Hunt's election as the first Republican governor in the state since Reconstruction. In between was a hard-fought Democratic primary election, a bitter runoff contest, and a seemingly endless round of court cases and hearings trying to decide who the party's nominee was. In the end, the Baxley-Graddick nomination struggle split the party and led to Hunt's victory. With this outcome, Democratic dominance over Alabama's state politics ended.

The events and consequences of this remarkable year naturally raise many questions. Why was the 1986 campaign conducted the way it was? Why did this type of contest occur in 1986? And, why did the election have the impact it did on Alabama's politics? No single consideration provides an answer to these questions. Nor are the characteristics, timing, and impact of the 1986 election solely or primarily the result of forces first emerging within Alabama in that year. Instead, we have concluded, answers to the Alabama-related questions raised by the 1986 contest rest upon the intersection of preexisting forces that became connected to one another during that year's campaign.

In particular, the conduct, occurrence, and impact of the 1986 election was the product of a confluence of various demographic, economic, and political forces that were undermining the foundations for Solid South throughout the region; the political vacuum created by Wallace's retirement; and the emergence of a viable alternative to continued Democratic control. Our analysis of Alabama's 1986 election suggests that significant partisan political change in the state required not only the presence of conditions encouraging the undermining of established patterns but also an opportunity for these conditions to come into play, and, finally, the availability of a viable alternative to the status quo.

Conditions of Change

As noted earlier in discussing the longevity of George Wallace's career, Alabama's one-party, solidly Democratic partisan politics developed and most effectively operated at a time when the state had a rural, poor, and near racially balanced population and a predominantly agriculture-based economy. Moreover, the state's one-party system was associated with the adoption and enforcement of restrictive suffrage laws, resulting in a relatively small and socially homogeneous electorate. However, by the time Wallace retired and Bill Baxley, Charlie Graddick, and Guy Hunt entered the 1986 race for governor, each of these conditions had changed dramatically. Compared to earlier conditions, Alabama in the mid-1980s had a more urban, wealthier, and economically varied population as well as a considerably larger and more heterogeneous electorate. As a result, the conditions that fostered Alabama's membership in the one-party South were no longer present within the state.

These demographic, economic, and electoral alterations were not unique to Alabama; rather, they had occurred to varying degrees in each state within the region. Moreover, these changing conditions, by altering the demands made and the voices raised in the electoral arena, had affected partisan politics throughout the region.[1] Alabama was not immune to these changes. In national politics beginning in the 1950s, Republicans had become competitive within Alabama in presidential and, to a lesser extent, congressional contests. When it came to state-level politics, however, the impact of social, economic, and enfranchisement changes had, as the 1986 campaign began, yet to register. Still, the conditions for change were ripe.

Opportunities for Change

It was largely because of the continuing presence of George Wallace that partisan change had not yet come to Alabama's state-level politics. Wallace's supporters, as well as his opponents, included a varied set of groups. What held these groups together was their like or dislike of Wallace. By being the central line of political division within the state, Wallace kept all his various supporters and opponents within the "big tent" of the Democratic Party.

As Alabama changed demographically and economically during the postwar years, the state's expanding and more varied electorate became increasingly difficult to contain under the Democratic Party's big tent. Some groups, such as African Americans, which were once outside the political arena, were now under the canopy. At the same time, other groups, such as business or economic conservatives more generally, which were once a dominating part of the party, were losing influence and becoming marginalized. Still, with Wallace on the scene, feeling about him, which cut across economic, ideological, and racial lines, managed to maintain conflicts as intraparty conflicts.

When Wallace withdrew from the 1986 campaign, the major force both unifying the Democratic Party and maintaining its dominance over state politics was removed. A winner-take-all fight over which groups would control the Alabama Democratic Party was not the necessary outcome of Wallace withdrawal. His earlier retirement, in 1978, did not lead to a particularly bitter primary election or to deep divisions within the party. Rather than a divisive intraparty struggle, the 1986 campaign could have resulted in either the crowning of a Wallace successor or, as in 1978, a more or less temporary truce among competing factions.

Such peaceful outcomes, as we have seen, did not emerge in 1986. Instead, Wallace's "final" retirement deeply split Alabama's Democratic Party. Perhaps the difference in outcomes between 1978 and 1986 was due to the cast of characters involved (particularly the victories of the familiar Charles Graddick versus the then-less-well-known Fob James). Or perhaps the population and economic changes Alabama continued to experience between 1978 and 1986 made the pressure for change too strong to resist.

The Democratic Party's Decision

The action that ultimately shattered the party was the decision to make Baxley the Democratic nominee. Electorally, the decision to name Baxley the party's nominee makes little sense. The state of public opinion at the time of the party committee's hearings, in addition to Alabama's well-recognized pro-democracy, anti-institution, populist tradition, meant that the negative consequences of Baxley's selection were highly predictable. Moreover, during the South's post–World War II "Second Reconstruction," the first notable Republican success in several of the region's other states had occurred following an exceptionally divisive Democratic primary or the nomination of a scandal-plagued Democratic candidates.[2] There was little reason to believe that the Alabama Democratic Party would avoid the same fate if it experienced a similar internal division.

Explanations offered at the time for the party's decision are also difficult to understand. One tried to explain the decision on procedural grounds, noting the expense involved in holding a new runoff and the lack of time before the November general election. This explanation is not very persuasive, however. Given the public's substantial interest in the controversy and the existing court involvement in the protest, it is highly probable that the Democratic Party committee could have called a new runoff without generating much public hostility concerning costs, even if this meant postponing the general election.

Another, somewhat more persuasive, argument the party offered for declaring Baxley its nominee was that they did not want Graddick to benefit from his illegal actions. This is also a rationale the federal court used in stripping Graddick of his nomination in its August 1 ruling. Clearly, Graddick's actions warranted the overturning of his runoff victory. Why his campaign took the actions it did during the final days of the runoff campaign, other than in response to a fear that some of Baxley's supporters would somehow "steal" the election, remains unclear.

The desire to prevent Graddick from gaining an unjust reward does not, however, automatically lead to a decision that Baxley should be the party's nominee without holding a new election. In particular, it ignores the fact that the party's most effective means of preventing Graddick from benefiting from illicit activities was to disqualify him as a candidate. It chose not to do this. As a result, the party could not argue, as the facts of the case showed, that Baxley was its nominee because his opponent was a cheat and a crook; rather, it had to make the more complex and less substantiated argument that, in the party's opinion, Baxley probably won the election.

More importantly, this explanation ignores the fact that the party very likely could have avoided rewarding Graddick for his improper actions and still obtained legitimacy for its nominee by calling for a new election. While it would have not been easy, Baxley had an excellent chance to win a new election, even if Graddick was allowed to be a candidate. The electorate in the new election would have changed with the enforcement of the runoff rule. If Baxley and his supporters really believed that they gained a majority of the legally cast votes in the first runoff, then they certainly could have done it again in a new runoff. Moreover, Graddick would have entered the contest after a federal court had forcefully stated in public that he had broken the law. The campaign would also have begun after a week of well-publicized committee hearings in which Graddick's misdeeds had been further documented. For Baxley to have lost under these circumstances assumes that he would have run a highly incompetent campaign.

Neither a concern about process nor a desire to avoid rewarding the sinner adequately explains the party's decision. Instead, it is better seen as a product of the struggle that had developed during the campaign over which groups then under the Democratic big tent would control the party (and presumably the state government) and which ones would be outside the circle of influence in the post-Wallace era.

The Desire for "Change"

During the primary and runoff election campaigns, Charles Graddick came to represent the factions and groups at that time outside the party's inner circle. He had few ties to the party's organization. Indeed, Graddick went out of his way to demonstrate his disregard for the party and for the liberal, black, and labor groups that then composed its core. Throughout his campaign, Graddick made it clear that things were going to change if he was elected.

Bill Baxley, in contrast, was the candidate of the groups and factions within the party's current establishment. Baxley was closely tied to the current party leaders and organization. Similarly, he was seen as an ally of the liberal, black, and labor organizations in the state. In holding these disparate groups together, Baxley tried to inherit the mantle of George Wallace and ultimately became the candidate of the status quo. During the primary and runoff campaigns, he was unable to define himself otherwise.

The emphasis on change during the primary and runoff campaigns put Baxley and his supporters on the defensive. They represented the kind of politics and politicians that their opponents said the state needed to be rid of. Consequently, the stakes in the election became very high. For Baxley and his supporters, losing the nomination was more serious than simply not winning one particular election. It meant losing power and control of the party to groups and individuals with whom they had little in common and who threatened to eliminate all the "progress" the Baxley forces had achieved.[3]

The stakes became so high and the wounds suffered during the campaign became so deep that the warring elements of the party could not reunite following the runoff. None of the competitors took the symbolic or substantive steps necessary to unify the party. Even after his "victory," Graddick continued to display his disregard for the party. He refused to endorse the entire ticket. He met with some of the Democratic members of the state legislature but pointedly ignored others. Similarly, leaders of black and labor groups were slow to pledge their support for Graddick.

Unfortunately for Graddick and fortunately for his opponents, the attorney general's campaign had included activities that brought a federal court into the conflict. The court's actions allowed the competition for control of the party to continue. It also permitted the current party leadership, rather than voters, to decide the outcome of the dispute. Not surprisingly, the party leadership, even admitting the weakness of the evidence, supported Baxley in the controversy, thus preserving their position of influence.

Added to these actions was a belief that no matter what the Democratic Party did, Alabamians in the end would not elect a Republican governor. This belief may have been based on the experience of 1983, when the party had succeeded despite the criticisms over its "hand-picking" candidates. It ignored, however, differences between gubernatorial and state legislative elections. It also ignored the experience of Alabama's regional neighbors.

In the end, whatever the reason, naming Baxley the nominee without holding a second election created an opportunity for change in Alabama's state politics.

A Viable Alternative

The 1986 election was not the first time opportunity for change had emerged in Alabama. The state had been experiencing important social, economic, and enfranchisement changes for a considerable period before 1986.

Nor was 1986 the first time George Wallace had left the state's political scene. Many, apparently including Wallace, thought that his career was at an end in 1978.

Nor was 1986 the first time deep conflicts had developed within the Alabama Democratic Party. The 1983 "hand-picking" of state legislative candidates had generated much disagreement and even outright bolts within the party. Earlier conflicts over religion and the nomination of Catholic Al Smith as the Democratic presidential candidate in 1928, civil rights in the 1940s and 1950s, and the bitter 1970 contest between Albert Brewer and George Wallace had also deeply divided the state's Democrats.[4]

Nor was 1986 the first time in recent years that the GOP had experienced electoral success in Alabama. Republicans had been doing well in the state's presidential elections since the 1950s. In U.S. Senate elections, Republican Jim Martin nearly won in 1962, while Jeremiah Denton did gain a seat for the GOP in 1980.[5] Republicans had also held several seats in the U.S. Congress since the mid-1960s. Finally, the GOP had mounted serious (but ultimately losing) efforts for governor in 1966 and most recently in 1982.

Yet, all these previous events had not produced more than minor (and, in some cases, temporary) modifications in the Democrats' dominance over Alabama's state government. Why, then, did the 1986 contest have such an impact on Alabama's state politics?

Two closely related factors offer explanations. The first involves the electoral calculations of the state's strategic politicians.[6] Specifically, before Hunt's victory, previous contests for governor, state constitutional offices, or state legislature had attracted relatively few qualified Republican candidates. The reason for this situation, of course, was that Alabama's electoral history convincingly showed that Republican candidates for these positions had little prospect for success. A politician seriously interested in winning office would either run as a Democrat or, if philosophically loyal to the GOP, seek a position in national politics.

The 1986 election, however, provided a different lesson. Guy Hunt won. This victory strongly suggested that other Republicans now could win election for state offices in Alabama. No longer was it necessary, as it had been earlier for Fob James and Charles Graddick, former Republicans, to run as a Democrat in order to have a chance for victory. Following 1986, the Republican Party now also offered an avenue to success. As a result, an increasing number of the state's strategic politicians may have determined that it was now worthwhile to enter electoral politics on the GOP side, or, in the case of current officeholders, to switch to the Republican side of the ticket. If this occurred, then, following 1986, an increasing number of credible candidates would campaign for local and statewide offices as Republicans.

The previously observed increase in the number of GOP candidates running for state constitutional offices (table 9.1) and state legislature (table 9.2) suggests that the electoral calculations of Alabama politicians did change after Hunt's victory. The growth in the number of qualified Republican candidates running led, in turn, to an increase in GOP support and victories, and thus a changed partisan balance and a heightened level of party competition within the state.[7]

The second, and related, factor offering an explanation for the impact of the 1986 election on Alabama's politics involves the organizational development of the state's Republican Party. Research has shown that there is a relationship between the strength of party organizations and the level of party competition. Strong party organizations can recruit good candidates, effectively manage campaigns, and mobilize supporters. As a result, when party organizations are strong, competition is high.[8]

During the era of the Solid South, Republican Party organizations within the region were particularly weak. Indeed, in his midcentury analysis of the region's politics, V. O. Key asserted that the GOP then "scarcely deserves the name of party. It wavers somewhat between an esoteric cult on the order of a lodge and a conspiracy for plunder in accord with the accepted customs of our politics." He went on to say that "Republican organizations in the South—save perhaps those in Virginia and North Carolina—make little effort to get people into the habit of voting Republican."[9]

Later writers found a somewhat different situation. In particular, beginning in the 1950s, the Republican Party throughout the region began to develop more effective, professional, and permanent organizations and to become more concerned with actually winning elections.[10]

Unfortunately, it is not possible retroactively to construct measures of party organizational strength. Thus, it is not possible to trace the actual organizational development of Alabama's Republican Party. Still, it is reasonable to believe that, unlike the case earlier, by 1986 the state's GOP had developed organizationally to a point where it could take advantage of Hunt's unexpected victory and become a viable alternative to the Democratic Party. In particular, Hunt's victory provided Alabama Republicans with news resources in the form of such things as campaign volunteers and easier access to the media and financial contributors. In earlier years, the state's Republican organization may not have been able to effectively absorb such resources. By 1986, however, it is likely that they could.

Perhaps more importantly, Hunt's victory gave Republicans access to the governor's appointment powers for the first time. The authority permitted Hunt to fill positions in state and local governments with other Republicans. As a result, the state Republican organization was now in the position to offer potential, calculating candidates the resources needed to mount serious campaigns. It also was in a position to put its followers into office and thus make them credible candidates for future elections. As a result, the number of Republican electoral victories increased and the state's partisan balance changed.

One indicator of the impact of the 1986 election on the GOP's organizational development is found in the results of a survey of local party activities.[11] In this 1991 survey of county party committee members, respondents were asked if they had ever belonged to another party. If they had, they were asked when they had switched to their current party. Additionally, respondents who had not switched parties were asked when they had become active in politics beyond voting. In combination, these items can be used to calculate when Republican activists first became involved in party activities.

If the 1986 election affected the organizational strength of the Alabama's

GOP by attracting new volunteers, then a substantial number of Republican activists should have first become involved with the party at that time or later. The results presented in table 10.1 suggest that such a change did occur. At the time of the 1991 survey, slightly more than one in five Republican activists said that they had first become involved in party activities in 1986 or later. This proportion of "new" recruits is slightly lower than that found for Georgia and slightly higher than the results for Arkansas and South Carolina. The remaining southern states all had fewer "new" activists than did Alabama.

The 1986 election provided the Alabama GOP with resources that, possibly unlike the past, it could use to its long-term advantage. As a consequence, Alabama's 1986 gubernatorial election had a major impact on the state's electoral politics. The contest ended one-party politics at the state level. In its place, a more evenly balanced and competitive politics has emerged.

Southern Politics

The primary purpose of this book has been to describe and analyze Alabama's remarkable 1986 election for governor. While our approach has been narrow and inductive, our findings still provide, we believe, a useful insight into the more general study of southern politics. In particular, our study of Alabama's 1986 election suggests an alternative approach for studying partisan change within the region.

The political change that followed Alabama's 1986 election is only one late example of the broader transformation in partisan politics that took place throughout the South in the post–World War II years. Researchers have devoted considerable energy studying the demise of the Solid Democratic South and the development of a more competitive, even Republican-leaning, politics within the region.[12] These investigations include examinations of the types and sources of the region's political change.[13] More important for our purposes, investigators have also sought to identify the causes for the South's political transformation. These studies have focused on determining what issues led southern voters to shift their partisan allegiances. While all recognize that multiple factors are involved, some researchers have concluded that race played an especially important role in altering the party affiliations of southerners.[14] Others believe that economic, class, or other nationalizing forces best explain the changing party identifications of southerners.[15]

By extension, then, the individual-level approach employed by most pre-

Table 10.1

Proportion of southern Republican Party activitists becoming involved in party affairs since 1986

	Switched to Republican Party after 1986	Never switched parties, became active in GOP after 1986	Total	N
Alabama	6.2	15.2	21.4	593
Arkansas	4.5	15.3	19.8	464
Florida	6.8	9.2	16.0	368
Georgia	3.4	20.6	23.9	447
Louisiana	7.6	7.2	14.8	236
Mississippi	3.0	9.2	12.3	660
North Carolina	4.8	12.1	16.9	413
South Carolina	2.7	17.5	20.2	486
Tennessee	0.4	8.2	8.6	244
Texas	2.8	11.5	14.3	781
Virginia	1.8	12.7	14.5	165

Source: 1991 Southern Grassroots Party Activists Study

vious researchers suggests that explaining the conduct and outcome of Alabama's 1986 election should begin by examining the issue positions and voting behavior of the state's voters. This analysis would show what preferences or orientations distinguish one candidate's supporters from others', and what type of coalitions the competing candidates and parties constructed during the campaign.

The data needed for such an investigation are available in the surveys we conducted during the campaign. The analysis of this information would undoubtedly produce interesting and useful results. Our observations, however, raise questions about the value of employing the individual-level approach as a means for understanding Alabama's 1986 election. The primary source of this reservation is that the story of the campaign provides little reason for believing that the conduct, timing, or impact of the campaign originated in a mass-based, bottom-up movement by voters.

Instead, the story of Alabama's 1986 election shows that the character and impact of the campaign was the result of a post-Wallace retirement struggle among competing candidates, activists, and groups. The fight over the Democratic gubernatorial nomination split the party, leading to temporary and then permanent increases in campaign-relevant resources available to the Republican Party. Thus, the story of Alabama's 1986 gubernatorial election suggests a possible alternative and potentially more fruitful approach for explaining the conduct and impact of the campaign (and possibly for understanding the broader topic of southern political changes). This approach involves investigating the goals, strategies, tactics, and calculations of political elites.

Focusing on the objectives and actions of elites will in some ways returns the study of southern politics to its roots. Specifically, Key attributes the Solid South political systems to the prowess of a relatively small group of activists—Black Belt whites and their conservative allies—who, through appeals to white supremacy and regional loyalty, fraud, intimidation, and other devices, created a system that for a half-century or more "managed to subordinate the entire South to the service of their peculiar local needs."[16]

More generally, focusing on the objectives and actions of elites builds on research demonstrating the important role played by political activists in affecting the partisan politics of a state, region, or nation.[17] Electoral outcomes and partisan alignments, this research argues, are affected by the alternatives with which mass publics are presented. Moreover, citizens, while not totally powerless or passive, generally do not directly or immediately control the number or character of the options presented to them. Rather, the actions of political elites largely, though not completely, determine the choices presented to citizens. Citizens typically select from the available choices; leaders, within limits, determine what the alternatives will be.

This research further argues that if the choices offered to voters undergo a persistent and fundamental shift (i.e., one extended over several elections and changing in the number of credible options or a change in the division distinguishing the options), then the character of an area's electoral politics will change. Thus, for example, if voters are consistently presented with contests in which no viable Democratic or Republican candidates appear, one-party politics will occur. However, if both parties begin to present credible candidates, then competitive politics are likely to follow.

The choices offered citizens reflect elites' calculation of how best to satisfy or meet their electoral and policy goals.[18] Various members of the elite may of course differ over what are the desired electoral or policy goals. These differences result in competition among elites over the character and number of alternatives offered to voters. Moreover, when situations change, then calculations of elites regarding what type of alternatives to offer may also shift.[19]

This "elite" approach offers a potentially useful method for understanding the scope, type, and pace of partisan changes in the South. Moreover, our observations concerning the importance of conditions, opportunities, and alternatives in Alabama's 1986 election identify possible factors affecting elites' calculations and recalculations. Specifically, more than the presence of conditions encouraging change is required. Also needed is an opportunity for these change forces to manifest themselves. Even this combination, however, is not sufficient for change to occur. The presence of a viable alternative to the political status quo must also exist. Without such an alternative, calculating politicians will not willingly shift their political affiliations, no matter how uncomfortable current conditions may be.

Appendix A: Survey Methodology

The survey data presented here come from three sources: 1986 election-related surveys conducted for the *Birmingham News* and the *Anniston Star* (table A.1); public affairs surveys conducted by the Capstone Poll between 1980 and 1987 (table A.2); and a series of statewide surveys conducted by Southern Opinion Research between 1988 and 2005 (table A.3).

The Capstone Poll and Southern Opinion Research data presented here are based on telephone surveys of random samples of either adult Alabama citizens or Alabama registered voters. A multi-stage, random-digit-dialing method of sample was used in each of the surveys. Specific information about each of the surveys employed is presented below.

The 1986 election survey results presented here are based on the responses of all respondents rather than on those of likely voters only. The items needed to identify likely voters are not available for all these surveys. Moreover, some of the 1986 surveys were conducted weeks or months prior to an election. The accuracy of identifying likely voters in surveys conducted well before an election is questionable. Finally, focusing on likely voters when they can be reasonably identified has little substantive impact on results.[1] For example, tables A.4 and A.5 show the results for candidate preference and candidate evaluation items in the pre-primary, pre-runoff and pre-general-election surveys for all respondents and for likely voters only. Examination of these tables shows little difference between the two groups.

Table A.1

Capstone Poll election surveys

Studies conducted for the *Birmingham News*

Study	*Date*	*Sample size*
148	10/14–10/23/85	416 registered
160	1/23–1/30/86	418 registered
169	4/16–4/23/86	483 registered
175	5/22–6/1/86	798 registered
176	6/15–6/22/86	934 registered
181	7/8–7/12/86	440 adults
(398 registered)		
185	8/7–8/11/86	487 registered
188	9/8–9/11/86	501 registered
191	10/6–10/9/86	530 registered
193	10/27–11/2/86	973 registered

Study conducted for *Anniston Star*

Study	*Date*	*Sample size*
178	6/24–7/7/86	499 adults

Table A.2

Capstone Poll semi-annual public affairs surveys

Study	*Date*	*Sample size*
02	9/24–10/16/80	670 adults
08	5/10–5/21/81	552 adults
13	10/26–11/9/81	494 adults
23	3/14–3/29/82	523 adults
45	11/4–11/18/82	511 adults
59	4/27–5/12/83	515 adults
76	10/6–10/30/83	528 adults
94	4/23–5/8/84	554 adults
116	11/29–12/13/84	519 adults
131	5/6–5/19/85	508 adults
154	11/6–11/17/85	508 adults
167	3/17–3/24/86	506 adults
194	11/16–11/24/86	499 adults
211	5/20–6/2/87	488 adults
221	10/1–10/11/87	502 adults

Table A.3

Southern Opinion Research surveys

Study	*Date*	*Sample size*
06	8/27–8/31/88	502 registered voters
10	12/4–12/12/88	645 adults
16	7/9–7/18/89	415 adults
50	7/25–8/5/90	424 adults
51	9/30–10/6/90	563 registered voters
53	10/28–11/2/90	772 registered voters
54	1/20–1/23/91	519 adults
56	4/3–4/8/91	503 adults
57	6/22–7/3/91	395 adults
79	6/17–6/23/92	408 adults
82	7/6–7/10/92	416 adults
102	4/12–4/20/93	409 adults
109	6/20–6/25/93	401 adults
140	8/24–9/6/94	404 adults
145	9/25–9/30/94	427 registered voters
148	10/27–11/5/94	734 registered voters
153	2/16–2/26/95	385 adults
157	6/20–7/1/95	405 adults
169	1/4–1/8/96	405 registered voters
170	1/23–2/1/96	525 registered voters
171	2/8–2/22/96	408 adults
179	4/11–4/18/96	508 registered voters
185	5/24–6/1/96	1035 registered voters
187	6/14–6/22/96	1011 registered voters
192	9/7–9/12/96	400 registered voters
196	10/25–11/2/96	640 registered voters
208	8/5–8/9/97	407 adults

Study	*Date*	*Sample size*
215	2/25–2/26/98	500 adults
232	7/21–8/24/98	400 adults
234	9/3–9/4/98	500 registered voters
235	9/10–9/14/98	400 adults
237	10/1–10/2/98	501 registered voters
240	10/21–10/23/98	500 registered voters
241	10/29–10/31/98	600 registered voters
242	11/4–11/5/98	500 adults
248	8/8–9/5/99	404 registered voters
255	1/8–1/9/01	400 adults
259	10/28–11/1/01	500 registered voters
267	4/3–4/6/03	501 registered voters
293	6/28–6/30/05	500 registered voters

Table A.4

Pre-election candidate preferences for all respondents and likely voters only

	All respondents	Likely voters
Pre-primary	N = 798	N = 484
Baxley	28%	32%
Graddick	32	33
James	21	20
McMillan	9	10
Don't know/No answer	10	5
Pre-runoff	N = 934	N = 705
Baxley	45%	47%
Graddick	48	50
Don't know/No answer	7	4
Pre-general	N = 973	N = 739
Baxley	40%	40%
Hunt	52	56
Don't know/No answer	8	4

Source: Capstone Poll 175, 176, 193

Table A.5

Pre-election candidate evaluations for all respondents and likely voters only

	Primary		Runoff		General	
	All resp.	Likely voters	All resp.	Likely voters	All resp.	Likely voters
Baxley						
Positive	42%	43%	35%	38%	30%	31%
Neutral/Don't know	30	24	34	30	18	15
Negative	28	33	31	31	52	54
Graddick						
Positive	44%	43%	41%	43%		
Neutral/Don't know	35	30	29	26		
Negative	21	26	30	31		
James						
Positive	30%	29%				
Neutral/Don't know	30	25				
Negative	40	46				

Continued on the next page

Table A.5. *Continued*

	Primary		Runoff		General	
	All resp.	Likely voters	All resp.	Likely voters	All resp.	Likely voters
McMillan						
Positive	32%	36%				
Neutral/Don't know	45	39				
Negative	23	25				
Hunt						
Positive					37%	39%
Neutral/Don't know					31	28
Negative					32	34

Source: Capstone Poll 175, 176, 193

Appendix B: Election Results

The following tables present county-by-county vote totals and percentage results for all of the statewide gubernatorial elections in Alabama in 1986.

Tables B.1 and B.2 show the vote totals for the Democratic and Republican primary elections. While nearly one million people voted in the Democratic primary, fewer than 50,000 voted in the Republican primary. In one county, Greene, no one is recorded as having voted in the Republican primary.

Table B.3 shows the vote totals for the Democratic runoff election. This second election in the Democratic Party drew more than 900,000 voters—nearly as many as the primary election.

Table B.4 shows the vote totals for the general election in November. In this election, more than one million people voted, and the fortunes of the Republicans had shifted substantially.

The figures in all of these tables are the official figures certified by the Alabama secretary of state.

Table B.1

Results, 1986 Democratic gubernatorial primary election

County	Baxley	%	Graddick	%	James	%	McMillan	%	O'Neal	%
Autauga	2,195	28.6	2,163	28.2	2,449	31.9	847	11.0	18	.2
Baldwin	4,107	24.8	6,082	36.7	5,133	30.9	1,206	7.3	61	.4
Barbour	2,931	45.3	1,839	28.4	1,334	20.6	351	5.4	16	.2
Bibb	2,634	43.3	1,470	24.1	1,322	21.7	617	10.1	45	.7
Blount	2,393	26.2	3,614	39.6	1,919	21.0	1,152	12.6	52	.6
Bullock	2,494	54.7	611	13.4	1,050	23.0	384	8.4	17	.4
Butler	2,782	35.8	1,682	21.7	2,110	27.2	1,161	15.0	27	.3
Calhoun	6,860	28.9	7,729	32.5	3,857	16.2	4,984	21.0	330	1.4
Chambers	2,811	29.5	2,875	30.2	3,079	32.4	718	7.5	31	.3
Cherokee	3,524	58.3	1,314	21.7	631	10.4	523	8.7	50	.8
Chilton	2,900	31.1	3,547	38.0	1,910	20.5	920	9.9	57	.6
Choctaw	4,132	59.6	1,745	25.2	791	11.4	234	3.4	33	.5
Clarke	3,326	39.4	2,809	33.3	2,023	23.9	276	3.3	13	.2
Clay	1,218	26.4	1,652	35.8	1,023	22.2	676	14.6	49	1.1
Cleburne	1,289	23.5	1,334	24.3	1,231	22.4	1,572	28.6	62	1.1
Coffee	3,552	37.1	2,394	25.0	2,572	26.9	1,030	10.8	24	.3
Colbert	7,585	50.1	3,340	22.1	1,699	11.2	2,452	16.2	67	.4
Conecuh	2,240	38.4	2,108	36.1	898	15.4	566	9.7	21	.4
Coosa	1,528	40.6	1,086	28.8	799	21.2	331	8.8	24	.6
Covington	3,352	31.1	2,890	26.8	3,050	28.3	1,401	13.0	74	.7
Crenshaw	2,153	39.2	1,395	25.4	1,412	25.7	523	9.5	15	.3
Cullman	5,828	34.0	6,100	35.6	2,929	17.1	2,068	12.1	216	1.3
Dale	3,016	33.3	2,993	33.0	2,189	24.2	848	9.4	17	.2

Dallas	6,418	46.8	2,635	19.2	3,430	25.0	1,199	8.7	32	.2
Dekalb	5,533	43.9	3,162	25.1	2,019	16.0	1,798	14.3	81	.6
Elmore	3,322	28.0	3,185	26.9	3,805	32.1	1,511	12.7	39	.3
Escambia	3,586	33.4	4,332	40.3	1,861	17.3	809	7.5	150	1.4
Etowah	11,705	40.2	8,506	29.2	4,229	14.5	4,330	14.9	315	1.1
Fayette	2,290	31.8	2,903	40.4	1,039	14.4	901	12.5	61	.8
Franklin	3,501	45.3	2,096	27.1	1,104	14.3	980	12.7	53	.7
Geneva	2,754	36.2	2,606	34.3	1,562	20.5	615	8.1	68	.9
Greene	2,788	61.5	716	15.8	656	14.5	346	7.6	31	.7
Hale	2,447	48.0	1,192	23.4	821	16.1	607	11.9	33	.6
Henry	2,044	44.9	1,250	27.4	848	18.6	405	8.9	9	.2
Houston	7,461	41.9	4,348	24.4	4,199	23.6	1,748	9.8	53	.3
Jackson	5,016	45.2	2,702	24.4	1,752	15.8	1,544	13.9	76	.7
Jefferson	50,891	34.2	39,040	26.3	37,307	25.1	20,784	14.0	641	.4
Lamar	2,135	31.9	1,624	24.3	1,193	17.8	1,654	24.7	78	1.2
Lauderdale	7,818	48.0	3,342	20.5	2,215	13.6	2,838	17.4	63	.4
Lawrence	4,704	48.7	2,653	27.4	1,160	12.0	1,074	11.1	76	.8
Lee	4,308	28.6	3,460	23.0	4,320	28.7	2,935	19.5	34	.2
Limestone	5,877	44.6	3,783	28.7	1,966	14.9	1,479	11.2	60	.5
Lowndes	2,547	60.7	407	9.7	787	18.7	454	10.8	3	.1
Macon	4,314	62.1	803	11.6	950	13.7	850	12.2	29	.4
Madison	13,028	34.8	10,295	27.5	6,521	17.4	7,404	19.8	225	.6
Marengo	3,663	46.9	1,764	22.6	1,876	24.0	475	6.1	25	.3
Marion	4,188	38.6	3,560	32.8	1,458	13.5	1,489	13.7	143	1.3
Marshall	5,240	32.2	5,800	35.6	3,032	18.6	2,095	12.9	106	.7
Mobile	17,251	28.3	30,159	49.4	8,849	14.5	4,630	7.6	127	.2

Continued on the next page

Table B.1. *Continued*

County	Baxley	%	Graddick	%	James	%	McMillan	%	O'Neal	%
Monroe	3,278	40.4	2,884	35.5	1,280	15.8	605	7.5	66	.8
Montgomery	18,135	38.7	8,723	18.6	13,456	28.7	6,447	13.8	92	.2
Morgan	8,116	35.6	6,147	27.0	5,294	23.2	3,052	13.4	169	.7
Perry	2,642	51.8	855	16.8	867	17.0	724	14.2	8	.2
Pickens	3,321	41.6	2,254	28.2	1,464	18.3	891	11.2	61	.8
Pike	3,516	38.5	2,233	24.4	2,555	28.0	798	8.7	33	.4
Randolph	1,661	30.7	1,630	30.1	1,278	23.6	791	14.6	54	1.0
Russell	3,450	45.0	2,335	30.5	1,478	19.3	371	4.8	26	.3
St. Clair	2,678	29.0	3,386	36.7	1,947	21.1	1,144	12.4	81	.9
Shelby	3,174	22.8	4,392	31.6	4,801	34.5	1,478	10.6	67	.5
Sumter	3,881	61.2	741	11.7	1,273	20.1	409	6.4	40	.6
Talladega	5,185	34.4	4,225	28.1	4,196	27.9	1,299	8.6	148	1.0
Tallapoosa	3,760	30.2	3,943	31.7	3,529	28.4	1,158	9.3	40	.3
Tuscaloosa	10,658	36.2	9,858	33.5	3,868	13.1	4,936	16.8	102	.3
Walker	5,978	33.0	7,353	40.6	2,236	12.3	2,258	12.5	302	1.7
Washington	2,817	40.8	3,112	45.1	606	8.8	342	5.0	29	.4
Wilcox	2,259	50.3	1,005	22.4	834	18.6	387	8.6	10	.2
Winston	1,797	42.2	1,543	36.3	513	12.1	374	8.8	29	.7
TOTAL	**345,985**	**36.8**	**275,714**	**29.3**	**195,844**	**20.8**	**117,258**	**12.5**	**5,287**	**.6**

Source: Elections Division, Office of the Secretary of State

Table B.2

Results, 1986 Republican gubernatorial primary

County	Carter	%	Hunt	%	Votes
Autauga	37	37.8	61	62.2	98
Baldwin	694	41.6	973	58.4	1,667
Barbour	8	42.1	11	57.9	19
Bibb	8	50	8	50	16
Blount	53	18.7	231	81.3	284
Bullock	2	40	3	60	5
Butler	7	36.8	12	63.2	19
Calhoun	163	39.2	253	60.8	416
Chambers	35	58.3	25	41.7	60
Cherokee	7	33.3	14	66.7	21
Chilton	75	28.3	190	71.7	265
Choctaw	0	0	2	100	2
Clarke	12	50	12	50	24
Clay	2	13.3	13	86.7	15
Cleburne	22	57.9	16	42.1	38
Coffee	58	49.2	60	50.8	118
Colbert	19	38	31	62	50
Conecuh	1	10	9	90	10
Coosa	10	23.8	32	76.2	42
Covington	13	44.8	16	55.2	29
Crenshaw	5	33.3	10	66.7	15
Cullman	72	11.7	544	88.3	616
Dale	44	30.1	102	69.9	146
Dallas	36	37.9	59	62.1	95
DeKalb	142	20	568	80	710
Elmore	61	45.9	72	54.1	133
Escambia	20	40.8	29	59.2	49
Etowah	66	26.8	180	73.2	246
Fayette	9	47.4	10	52.6	19
Franklin	10	25.6	29	74.4	39
Geneva	7	33.3	14	66.7	21
Greene	0	.	0	.	0
Hale	4	33.3	8	66.7	12
Henry	2	25	6	75	8
Houston	150	32.5	311	67.5	461
Jackson	20	47.6	22	52.4	42
Jefferson	2,006	22.9	6,737	77.1	8,743
Lamar	4	40	6	60	10
Lauderdale	233	55.6	186	44.4	419
Lawrence	1	25	3	75	4
Lee	66	46.8	75	53.2	141

Continued on the next page

Table B.2. *Continued*

County	Carter	%	Hunt	%	Votes
Limestone	32	36.8	55	63.2	87
Lownes	7	77.8	2	22.2	9
Macon	1	10	9	90	10
Madison	623	28.3	1,576	71.7	2,199
Marengo	9	36	16	64	25
Marion	11	33.3	22	66.7	33
Marshall	33	37.1	56	62.9	89
Mobile	1,288	31.8	2,767	68.2	4,055
Monroe	5	23.8	16	76.2	21
Montgomery	0	0	1,515	100	1,515
Morgan	87	28.9	214	71.1	301
Perry	5	38.5	8	61.5	13
Pickens	0	0	5	100	5
Pike	7	25.9	20	74.1	27
Randolph	15	32.6	31	67.4	46
Russell	21	58.3	15	41.7	36
St. Clair	53	21.9	189	78.1	242
Shelby	357	27.3	950	72.7	1,307
Sumter	0	0	5	100	5
Talladega	109	39.4	168	60.6	277
Tallapoosa	20	37.7	33	62.3	53
Tuscaloosa	286	39.3	441	60.7	727
Walker	83	28.3	210	71.7	293
Washington	4	57.1	3	42.9	7
Wilcox	1	20	4	80	5
Winston	374	19.4	1,551	80.6	1,925
Total	**7,615**	**28.7**	**20,824**	**71.3**	**28,439**

Source: Elections Division, Office of the Secretary of State

Table B.3

Results, 1986 Democratic runoff

County	Baxley	%	Graddick	%
Autauga	3,322	41.7	4,641	58.3
Baldwin	5,846	33.9	11,389	66.1
Barbour	3,703	56.5	2,848	43.5
Bibb	2,849	54.8	2,352	45.2
Blount	3,194	36.0	5,674	64.0
Bullock	3,305	72.0	1,288	28.0
Butler	3,625	50.4	3,565	49.6
Calhoun	10,750	44.5	13,416	55.5
Chambers	3,270	40.5	4,811	59.5
Cherokee	3,412	67.2	1,664	32.8
Chilton	3,514	38.7	5,555	61.3
Choctaw	3,927	64.2	2,188	35.8
Clarke	4,097	48.4	4,360	51.6
Clay	1,423	38.6	2,263	61.4
Cleburne	2,002	42.2	2,746	57.8
Coffee	4,152	47.8	4,536	52.2
Colbert	8,968	65.4	4,745	34.6
Conecuh	3,322	51.1	3,181	48.9
Coosa	1,715	49.8	1,726	50.2
Covington	3,965	43.6	5,129	56.4
Crenshaw	2,792	49.7	2,821	50.3
Cullman	6,675	47.7	7,317	52.3
Dale	3,461	42.5	4,688	57.5
Dallas	8,470	61.0	5,406	39.0
Dekalb	6,376	56.9	4,839	43.1
Elmore	4,913	42.6	6,622	57.4
Escambia	4,160	44.6	5,176	55.4
Etowah	14,825	56.0	11,652	44.0
Fayette	2,996	41.2	4,274	58.8
Franklin	3,133	61.2	1,989	38.8
Geneva	2,908	46.6	3,332	53.4
Greene	3,244	75.8	1,034	24.2
Hale	2,858	59.6	1,939	40.4
Henry	2,883	58.8	2,017	41.2
Houston	8,384	50.6	8,191	49.4
Jackson	4,783	54.3	4,031	45.7
Jefferson	77,086	49.0	80,310	51.0
Lamar	2,897	47.6	3,195	52.4
Lauderdale	10,135	63.6	5,811	36.4
Lawrence	6,672	63.7	3,794	36.3
Lee	6,348	42.9	8,442	57.1

Continued on the next page

Table B.3. *Continued*

County	Baxley	%	Graddick	%
Limestone	6,279	58.9	4,374	41.1
Lowndes	3,303	79.8	836	20.2
Macon	5,891	83.7	1,150	16.3
Madison	19,083	48.8	20,037	51.2
Marengo	3,830	56.8	2,908	43.2
Marion	3,967	50.2	3,929	49.8
Marshall	6,983	43.6	9,051	56.4
Mobile	30,812	39.0	48,285	61.0
Monroe	4,126	50.8	3,996	49.2
Montgomery	29,070	55.5	23,354	44.5
Morgan	10,900	49.3	11,229	50.7
Perry	3,302	68.5	1,515	31.5
Pickens	3,454	53.8	2,971	46.2
Pike	3,803	51.7	3,548	48.3
Randolph	2,255	41.1	3,235	58.9
Russell	4,266	54.1	3,614	45.9
St. Clair	3,286	37.4	5,501	62.6
Shelby	4,737	31.7	10,203	68.3
Sumter	3,449	71.1	1,400	28.9
Talladega	7,074	45.9	8,337	54.1
Tallapoosa	4,780	40.6	7,000	59.4
Tuscaloosa	14,496	50.6	14,153	49.4
Walker	7,081	47.0	7,988	53.0
Washington	3,062	49.1	3,176	50.9
Wilcox	3,664	71.9	1,431	28.1
Winston	1,982	51.4	1,873	48.6
Total	**461,295**	**49.5**	**470,051**	**50.5**

Source: Elections Division, Office of the Secretary of State

Table B.4

Results, 1986 general election for governor

County	Baxley	%	Hunt	%
Autauga	3,763	35.3	6,889	64.7
Baldwin	7,829	26.2	22,072	73.8
Barbour	4,155	54.9	3,409	45.1
Bibb	2,629	51.0	2,521	49.0
Blount	3,635	28.5	9,133	71.5
Bullock	3,441	71.4	1,375	28.6
Butler	3,658	48.8	3,838	51.2
Calhoun	12,343	40.9	17,811	59.1
Chambers	3,675	38.2	5,934	61.8
Cherokee	4,696	67.0	2,315	33.0
Chilton	3,915	34.2	7,521	65.8
Choctaw	3,409	61.0	2,182	39.0
Clarke	4,283	46.3	4,968	53.7
Clay	1,840	34.3	3,528	65.7
Cleburne	1,238	32.9	2,523	67.1
Coffee	4,751	41.0	6,839	59.0
Colbert	11,794	68.4	5,440	31.6
Conecuh	3,154	50.3	3,121	49.7
Coosa	1,813	46.5	2,090	53.5
Covington	4,421	37.3	7,417	62.7
Crenshaw	2,619	47.4	2,901	52.6
Cullman	7,042	27.9	18,238	72.1
Dale	3,499	32.0	7,444	68.0
Dallas	10,467	58.8	7,338	41.2
Dekalb	7,602	44.9	9,314	55.1
Elmore	5,448	35.5	9,893	64.5
Escambia	3,700	39.1	5,753	60.9
Etowah	17,571	55.5	14,081	44.5
Fayette	2,441	38.0	3,984	62.0
Franklin	4,631	58.2	3,321	41.8
Geneva	2,994	40.3	4,433	59.7
Greene	3,535	78.7	954	21.3
Hale	3,482	64.1	1,946	35.9
Henry	2,497	46.4	2,883	53.6
Houston	8,759	36.7	15,134	63.3
Jackson	5,645	54.9	4,631	45.1
Jefferson	98,569	42.1	135,692	57.9
Lamar	1,848	41.3	2,626	58.7
Lauderdale	14,304	63.1	8,369	36.9
Lawrence	5,677	63.1	3,316	36.9
Lee	7,133	36.8	12,228	63.2

Continued on the next page

Table B.4. *Continued*

County	Baxley	%	Hunt	%
Limestone	7,107	52.0	6,570	48.0
Lowndes	3,977	75.9	1,261	24.1
Macon	6,746	85.2	1,171	14.8
Madison	22,918	37.9	37,553	62.1
Marengo	4,511	53.5	3,921	46.5
Marion	4,199	45.3	5,065	54.7
Marshall	6,811	38.1	11,055	61.9
Mobile	38,023	36.1	67,405	63.9
Monroe	3,898	48.7	4,106	51.3
Montgomery	34,520	48.9	36,144	51.1
Morgan	13,273	41.4	18,801	58.6
Perry	3,519	65.8	1,831	34.2
Pickens	3,166	49.8	3,193	50.2
Pike	4,156	46.1	4,856	53.9
Randolph	2,684	36.6	4,652	63.4
Russell	4,542	56.5	3,493	43.5
St. Clair	3,874	30.3	8,895	69.7
Shelby	6,170	23.5	20,125	76.5
Sumter	4,123	73.5	1,490	26.5
Talladega	7,854	40.9	11,343	59.1
Tallapoosa	4,438	37.0	7,543	63.0
Tuscaloosa	17,882	48.0	19,396	52.0
Walker	9,190	47.1	10,326	52.9
Washington	2,922	49.6	2,972	50.4
Wilcox	3,760	69.9	1,620	30.1
Winston	2,995	33.3	6,011	66.7
TOTAL	**537,163**	**43.6**	**696,203**	**56.4**

Source: Eections Division, Office of the Secretary of State

Notes

Preface

1. For descriptions of Wallace's retirement see, for example, Lloyd Rohler, *George Wallace: Conservative Populist* (Westport: Praeger, 2004); Dan T. Carter, *The Politics of Rage*, 2nd ed. (Baton Rouge: Louisiana State University Press, 2000); Frederick Burger, "Wallace Says Goodbye," *Anniston Star*, April 3, 1986, A1; Amy Herring, "Tearful End for Wallace Era," *Montgomery Advertiser*, April 3, 1986, A1; Ray Locker, "Wallace Kept Plans Secret from Family, Close Friends," *Montgomery Advertiser*, April 3, 1986, A11; Bill Person, "Wallace Closes the Door on Politics," *Washington Post*, April 3, 1986, A1; William E. Schmidt, "Ending an Era, Wallace Announces He Will Retire," *New York Times*, April 3, 1986, A1.

2. Capstone Poll survey 167. The wording of the party-identification question asked in the Alabama surveys was, "When it comes to national politics, do you consider yourself to be a Republican, a Democrat, an Independent, or what?" In this survey, respondents were also asked about their "state" party identification. On this measure, Democrats outnumbered Republicans among Alabama citizens by an even wider 47 to 18 percent margin.

3. Southern Opinion Research survey 293. This study also found an even balance of Democrats (35 percent) and Republicans (33 percent) when respondents were asked about their "state" party identification.

Similarly, an averaging of 2006 Gallup Poll results found slightly more Democratic (49 percent) than Republican (46 percent) party identifiers in Alabama (Jeffrey M. Jones, "Democratic Edge in Partisanship in 2006 Evident at National, State Level," Gallup Poll Briefing, January 2007, 108–11). Other studies have found that Republicans currently outnumber Democrats within Alabama. (See, for example, "Party ID: Red States Still Red, Swing States Deadlocked, Blue States Get Even More Democratic," Pew Research Center for the People & the Press, September 27, 2006 http://people-press.org/commentary/pdf/140.pdf.) The changes occurring in the party identifications of Alabama citizens are examined more thoroughly in chapter 9.

4. The *Birmingham News* endorsed Fob James in the Democratic primary, Charles Graddick in the runoff, and Guy Hunt in the general election. Both the *Montgomery Advertiser* and the *Anniston Star* supported George McMillan in the primary and Bill Baxley in the runoff. Neither newspaper made an endorsement in the 1986 general election for Alabama governor.

5. Those interviews included the following: John Baker, Paul Hubbert, Chris Grimshawe, Charles Graddick, Tom Coker, Glenn Stephens, Bill Baxley, and Jack Drake.

Chapter 1

1. For information about Wallace's life and political career see Marshall Frady, *Wallace* (New York: New American Library, 1968); Jody Carlson, *George C. Wallace and the Politics of Powerlessness* (New Brunswick, N.J.: Transaction, 1981); Stephan Lesher, *George Wallace: American Populist* (Reading, Pa.: Addison-Wesley, 1994); Dan T. Carter, *The Politics of Rage: George Wallace, the Origins of the New Conservatism, and the Transformation of American Politics* (New York: Simon and Schuster, 1995); Anne Permaloff and Carl Grafton, *Political Power in Alabama: The More Things Change . . .* (Athens: University of Georgia Press, 1995).

2. For discussions of southern, and Alabama, politics during this period see V. O. Key, *Southern Politics* (New York: Knopf, 1949); J. Morgan Kousser, *The Shaping of Southern Politics: Suffrage Restrictions and the Establishment of the One-Party South, 1880–1910* (New Haven: Yale University Press, 1974); Paul Lewinson, *Race, Class, and Party: A History of Negro Suffrage and White Politics in the South* (New York: Russell and Russell, 1963); Michael Perman, *Struggle for Mastery: Disfranchisement in the South, 1888–1908* (Chapel Hill: University of North Carolina Press, 2001); Alexander Keyssar, *The Right to Vote: The Contested History of Democracy in the United States* (New York: Basic Books, 2000); Jerrold G. Rusk and John J. Stucker, "The Effect of the Southern System of Election Laws on Voting Participation: A Reply to V. O. Key, Jr.," in *The History of American Electoral Behavior,* ed. Joel H. Silbey, Allan G. Bogue, and William H. Flanigan (Princeton: Princeton University Press, 1978), 198–250; William Warren Rogers, Robert David Ward, Leah Rawls Atkins, and Wayne Flynt, *Alabama: The History of a Deep South State* (Tuscaloosa: University of Alabama Press, 1994); Sheldon Hackney, *Populism to Progressivism in Alabama* (Princeton: Princeton University Press, 1969); Samuel L. Webb, *Two-Party Politics in the One-Party South* (Tuscaloosa: University of Alabama Press, 1997).

3. Key, *Southern Politics*, 37.

4. Ibid., 42.

5. William Barnard, *Dixiecrats and Democrats: Alabama Politics, 1942–1950* (Tuscaloosa: University of Alabama Press, 1974); George E. Sims, *The Little Man's Big Friend* (Tuscaloosa: University of Alabama Press, 1985); Carl Grafton and Anne Permaloff, *Big Mules and Branchheads: James Folsom and Political Power in Alabama* (Ath-

ens: University of Georgia Press, 1985); Permaloff and Grafton, *Political Power in Alabama.*

6. Culpepper E. Clark, *The Schoolhouse Door: Segregation's Last Stand at the University of Alabama* (New York: Oxford University Press, 1993).

7. For discussions of this period in southern politics see Numan Bartley, *The Rise of Massive Resistance: Race and Politics in the South during the 1950s* (Baton Rouge: Louisiana State University Press, 1965); Numan V. Bartley and Hugh D. Graham, *Southern Politics and the Second Reconstruction* (Baltimore: Johns Hopkins University Press, 1975); Jack Bass and Walter DeVries, *The Transformation of Southern Politics* (New York: Basic Books, 1976); Alexander Lamis, *The Two-Party South* (New York: Oxford University Press, 1988); Earle Black and Merle Black, *Politics and Society in the South* (Cambridge: Harvard University Press, 1987); Kari Frederickson, *The Dixiecrat Revolt and the End of the Solid South, 1932–1968* (Chapel Hill: University of North Carolina Press, 2001); Bernard Cosman, *Five States for Goldwater: Continuity and Change in Southern Presidential Voting Patterns* (University: University of Alabama Press, 1966); Dewey W. Grantham, *The Life and Death of the Solid South* (Lexington: University of Kentucky Press, 1988); Richard M. Valelly, *The Two Reconstructions: The Struggle for Black Enfranchisement* (Chicago: University of Chicago Press, 2004); Jason Sokol, *There Goes My Everything: White Southerners in the Age of Civil Rights, 1945–1975* (New York: Knopf, 2006); Donald Strong, "Alabama: Transition and Alienation," in *The Changing Politics of the South*, ed. William C. Harvard (Baton Rouge: Louisiana State University Press, 1972), 446–50; Barnard, *Dixiecrats and Democrats;* Sims, *The Little Man's Big Friend;* Grafton and Permaloff, *Big Mules and Branchheads;* Robert J. Norrell, "Labor at the Ballot Box: Alabama Politics from the New Deal to the Dixiecrat Movement," *Journal of Southern History* 57 (1991): 201–34; Diane McWhorter, *Carry Me Home: Birmingham, Alabama: The Climatic Battle of the Civil Rights Revolution* (New York: Simon and Schuster, 2001); J. Mills Thornton III, *Dividing Lines: Municipal Politics and the Struggle for Civil Rights in Montgomery, Birmingham, and Selma* (Tuscaloosa: University of Alabama Press, 2002).

8. Bob Ingram, "Wallace Bears Down on Race Issue in Opening Campaign," *Montgomery Advertiser*, February 16, 1958, A1.

9. The large number of candidates reflects both the disorganization of Alabama's partisan politics and the fact that during the Solid South era the "real" election in the region was the Democratic primary. Winning the party's nomination in the primary (or in a runoff election between the top two finishers if no candidate received a majority of the primary vote) was tantamount to ultimate victory.

10. "Governor Race Ends as Voters Ballot Today," *Montgomery Advertiser*, June 3, 1958, A1.

11. George Patterson, "Patterson, Wallace Map Stump Tours in Runoff," *Montgomery Advertiser*, May 11, 1958, A1; "Patterson Gains Alabama Victory," *New York Times*, June 4, 1958, 16; Bob Ingram, "Patterson Nominated for Governor," *Montgomery Advertiser*, June 4, 1958, A1. For later commentary and analysis of the 1958

campaigns, reaching similar conclusions about the sources of Patterson's victory, see James S. Taylor, "John M. Patterson and the 1958 Alabama Gubernatorial Race," *Alabama Review* 23 (1970): 226–34; Ted Bryant, "Patterson Recalls Start of Career," *Birmingham Post-Herald,* December 13, 1982, A9.

12. For the different accounts of this incident see Carter, *The Politics of Rage,* 96.

13. Wire reports, "Jefferson Vote Asked by Wallace," *Anniston Star,* May 16, 1962, A1.

14. "'Capital Day' for Children DeGraf Plan," *Montgomery Advertiser,* April 19, 1962, A1.

15. "State Waste of Money Hit by Wallace," *Birmingham News,* April 20, 1962, 18.

16. For information about Wallace's presidential campaigns and the type of voters he attracted in both his state and national efforts, see Michael Rogin, "Wallace and the Middle Class: The White Backlash in Wisconsin," *Public Opinion Quarterly* 30 (1966): 98–108; Robert Sherrill, *Gothic Politics in the Deep South* (New York: Grossman, 1968); Philip E. Converse, Warren E. Miller, Jerrold G. Rusk, and Arthur C. Wolfe, "Continuity and Change in American Politics: Parties and Issues in the 1968 Election," *American Political Science Review* 63 (1969): 1083–1103; Michael Rogin, "Politics, Emotion, and the Wallace Vote," *British Journal of Sociology* 20 (1969): 27–49; Eitzen D. Stanley, "Status Inconsistency and Wallace Supporters in a Midwestern City," *Social Forces* 48 (1970): 493–98; Seymour Martin Lipset and Earl Raab, *The Politics of Unreason* (New York: Harper and Row, 1970); Anthony M. Orum, "Religion and the Rise of the Radical White: The Case of Southern Wallace Support in 1968," *Social Science Quarterly* 51 (1970): 674–88; Irving Crespi, "Structural Sources of the George Wallace Constituency," *Social Science Quarterly* 52 (1971): 115–32; Robert A. Schoenberger and David R. Segal, "The Ecology of Dissent: The Southern Wallace Vote in 1968," *Midwest Journal of Political Science* 15 (1971): 583–86; Yung Wie and H. R. Mahood, "Racial Attitudes and the Wallace Vote: A Study of the 1968 Election in Memphis," *Polity* 3 (1971): 532–49; Strong, "Alabama: Transition and Alienation"; Earl Black and Merle Black, "The Wallace Vote in Alabama: A Multiple Regression Analysis," *Journal of Politics* 35 (1973): 730–36; Lewis Bowman and Guy Peters, "Alabama," in *Explaining the Vote: Presidential Choices in the Nation and States,* ed. David M. Kovenock, James W. Prothro, and Associates (Chapel Hill: Institute for Research in Social Science, 1973), 466–513; James C. Rawls, C. Wade Harrison, Donna J. Rawls, Robert L. Hayes, and August W. Johnson, "Comparison of Wallace, Nixon and Humphrey Supporters along Certain Demographic, Attitudinal, and Value-System Dimensions," *Psychological Reports* 32 (1973): 35–39; Robert D. Wrinkle and Jerry L. Polinard, "Populism and Dissent: The Wallace Vote in Texas," *Social Science Quarterly* 54 (1973): 306–20; Earl Black, "The Militant Segregationist Vote in the Post-Brown South: A Comparative Analysis." *Social Science Quarterly* 54 (1973–74): 66–84; Harold G. Grasmick, "Rural Culture and the Wallace Movement in the South," *Rural Sociology* 39 (1974): 454–70; J. Michael Ross, Reeve D. Vanneman, and Thomas F. Pettigrew, "Patterns of Support for George Wallace: Implications for Racial Change," *Journal of Social Is-*

sues 36 (1976): 69–91; Gerald C. Wright, "Contextual Models of Electoral Behavior: The Southern Wallace Vote," *American Political Science Review* 71 (1977): 497–508; Robert Oldenick and Stephen E. Bennett, "The Wallace Factor: Constancy and Cooptation," *American Politics Quarterly* 6 (1979): 469–84; Ira M. Wasserman, "A Reanalysis of the Wallace Movement," *Journal of Political and Military Sociology* 7 (1979): 243–56; Carlson, *Wallace and the Politics of Powerlessness.*

17. David J. Garrow, *Protest at Selma: Martin Luther King, Jr., and the Voting Rights Act of 1965* (New Haven: Yale University Press, 1978); Harold W. Stanley, *Voter Mobilization and the Politics of Race: The South and Universal Suffrage* (New York: Praeger, 1987). See also Brian K. Landsberg, *Free at Last to Vote: The Alabama Origins of the 1965 Voting Rights Act* (Lawrence: University Press of Kansas, 2007).

18. Earl Black, *Southern Governors and Civil Rights: Racial Segregation as a Campaign Issue in the Second Reconstruction* (Cambridge: Harvard University Press, 1976).

19. See, for example, Thomas Byrne Edsall with Mary D. Edsall, *Chain Reaction* (New York: Norton, 1991); Martin Gilens, "Racial Attitudes and Opposition to Welfare," *Journal of Politics* 57 (1995): 994–1014; Martin Gilens, "'Race Coding' and White Opposition to Welfare," *American Political Science Review* 90 (1996): 593–604; Tali Mendelberg, "Executing Hortons: Racial Crime in the 1988 Presidential Campaign," *Public Opinion Quarterly* 61 (1997): 134–57; Matthew J. Streb, *The New Electoral Politics of Race* (Tuscaloosa: University of Alabama Press, 2002). For a discussion of the relationship between race and voting in the 1966 Alabama election see Jason J. Battles, "Racial Politics and the 1966 Alabama Gubernatorial Election," *Alabama Review* 49 (1996): 108–22.

20. Joe McFadden, "Wallace Bandwagon Rolls over South Alabama Area," *Montgomery Advertiser*, April 21, 1966, A1.

21. "Lurleen Brings Campaign to Shopping Center Here," *Montgomery Advertiser*, November 6, 1966, A1.

22. Don F. Wasson, "Wallace Touches All Bases in Big Rally at Bessemer," *Montgomery Advertiser*, April 26, 1970, A2.

23. Milo Dakin, "Wallace Returns to South Alabama to Open Final Week of Campaign," *Montgomery Advertiser*, April 28, 1970, 2.

24. "Gubernatorial Hopefuls Break into Run," *Birmingham News*, May 1, 1970, 2.

25. Lawrence C. Falk, "Wallace to Drive on Racial Issue," *Anniston Star*, May 8, 1970, A1.

26. "Wallace Confident at Talladega Rally," *Anniston Star*, May 24, 1970, A1.

27. Ed Williams, "Wallace Quitting Political Scene after 3 Terms and 37 Years," *Montgomery Advertiser*, May 17, 1978, A1.

28. Mike Sherman, "Wallace Appears in Good Mood, Giving No Reason on Withdrawal," *Anniston Star*, May 18, 1978, B5.

29. "Wallace Lauds Race Relations in Final Speech," *Anniston Star*, January 11, 1979, D1. For a discussion of Alabama politics at what looked like the end of Wallace's career see Margaret K. Latimer, "'No-party' Politics at the End of the Wallace Era," *Publius* 9 (1978): 215–27.

Chapter 2

1. For newspaper profiles of Baxley see Ralph Holmes, "Baxley Sets Sights on Legislature, Says He Will Change Things," *Birmingham News*, July 17, 1978, A4; "Baxley Started Out Young in Politics, Took on Foes," *Birmingham News*, September 24, 1978, A31; Ray Locker, "Mellower Baxley Hopes Second Time the Charm," *Montgomery Advertiser*, May 21, 1986, A1; Ray Locker, "Traditional Populist Cloak of Wallace, Folsom Fits Baxley," *Montgomery Advertiser*, May 19, 1986, A1; Murphy Evans, "Dothan Watched Baxley Change," *Anniston Star*, June 16, 1986, A1; Frederick Burger, "Political Ads on TV Often Stretch Truth," *Anniston Star*, June 22, 1986, A1; Paul Rilling, "Baxley and Graddick: A Tale of Two AGs," *Anniston Star*, June 22, 1986, A1.

2. Locker, "Traditional Populist Cloak," A1.

3. Al Fox, "James Won More Than Half of State's Counties in Ballot," *Birmingham News*, September 17, 1978, F1; Ralph Holmes, "Ignored James Got to Grass-roots with His Campaign," *Birmingham News*, September 28, 1978, A1; "From Almost Unknown, James Has Erupted into the Man to Beat," *Birmingham News*, September 24, 1978, A31; Brett Guge and Boone Aiken, "If There Has Ever Been Storybook Life, It Is Fob James'," *Birmingham News*, October 1, 1978, A2; "James: Outsider Runs Once More," *Anniston Star*, March 2, 1986, A1; Sam Duvall, "James Wants Voters to Make Him Their Pick," *Birmingham News*, May 11, 1986, A1; Amy Herring, "Homespun James Sets Sights on Repeat of 1978 Campaign," *Montgomery Advertiser*, May 22, 1986, A1.

4. V. O. Key, *Southern Politics* (New York: Knopf, 1949), 36.

5. For example, the results of a survey conducted in March 1986—just before the intense campaigning got under way that year—found that when Alabama citizens were asked if the state government is run for the benefit of all the people or for just a few big interests, 49 percent said "big interests" and just 38 percent said "all the people." Similarly, about 30 percent said they trusted government to do the right thing "almost all of the time" or "most of the time," while nearly 70 percent said they trusted the state government only "some of the time" or "almost none of the time." This survey also found that Alabamians, for the most part, tended to believe that governmental officials were not so much crooked as they were dumb. A little more than 30 percent said that "quite a few" people in government were crooked, while 60 percent said there were "not many" or "hardly any" crooked people in government. But more than half said that those in government did not know what they were doing most of the time, while about 34 percent said that smart people were running the government. Nearly half of those in the survey said they felt that the state government wasted "a lot" of money. Very similar results were found in other University of Alabama public affairs surveys conducted between 1980 and 1986.

6. For example, surveys conducted in the 1980s typically found that only about 30 percent of Alabamians said that the state legislature was doing an "ex-

cellent" or "good" job, while about six in ten said that the legislature was doing a "fair" or "poor" job. When the Alabama results are compared to the findings of surveys conducted elsewhere, it is found that Alabamians are somewhat more dissatisfied with the quality of their state government than are citizens of these other states. Patrick R. Cotter, James G. Stovall, and Samuel H. Fisher III, *Disconnected: Public Opinion and Politics in Alabama.* (Northport, Ala.: Vision Press, 1994); Patrick R. Cotter, "Legislatures and Public Opinion," *State Government* 59 (1986): 46–51.

7. James's shift to the Republican Party was noted during the 1978 campaign. For example, in the last days of the runoff campaign, Baxley referred to James as "my millionaire Republican opponent." Ron Thomas, "Candidates in Stretch for Tuesday Showdown," *Montgomery Advertiser and Alabama Journal,* September 24, 1978, A1. Apparently there was also some recognition that Republican primary voters were participating in the Democratic runoff election. Olivia Barton, "Challenge Filed in Mountain Brook against Republicans Voting in Democratic Runoff," *Birmingham News,* September 16, 1978, A2. Still, possibly reflecting the GOP's weak position in state politics, analysis of the 1978 primary and runoff elections did not attribute James's success to his support among Republican identifiers. See, for example, Holmes, "Ignored James Got to Grass-roots."

8. Press reports of the anti-crossover rule's adoption simply noted the party's action. Information about any debate concerning the rule or its implication was not presented. Jim Earnhardt, "Democrats Change Rules to Stop Crossover Second Primary Voting," *Montgomery Advertiser,* April 22, 1979, A3; Associated Press, "Demo Committee Turns Down August Primary," *Birmingham News,* April 23, 1979, A2.

9. For a newspaper profile of Hunt see Tom Gordon, "Hunt: 'We've Got a Shot at It in '86,'" *Birmingham News,* May 22, 1986, A1.

10. Frederick Burger, "McMillan Running for a Change," *Anniston Star,* March 16, 1986, A1; Michele MacDonald, "McMillan: Hard Work Is 'Only Thing I Know,'" *Birmingham News,* May 18, 1986, A1; Mark Alpert, "McMillan Confident of Making Runoff," *Montgomery Advertiser,* May 23, 1986, A1.

11. Frederick Burger, "Graddick–The Tough-Talking AG," *Anniston Star,* February 23, 1986, A1; Sam Duvall, "Graddick's 'New Face' Races against Three Vets," *Birmingham News,* May 20, 1986, A1; Pamela Grundy, "Mobile's Graddick 'Polite, Aggressive,'" *Anniston Star,* June 15, 1986, A1; Rilling, "Baxley and Graddick"; Peggy Wilhide, "Graddick Gains Momentum in Campaign's Final Weeks," *Montgomery Advertiser,* May 21, 1986, A1; Burger, "Political Ads on TV Often Stretch Truth."

12. "Wallace Best Known, Liked Says UA Poll," *Birmingham News,* April 3, 1982, A2.

13. Sam DuVall, "Wallace Makes It Official–He Wants Old Job," *Montgomery Advertiser and Alabama Journal,* May 23, 1982, A1.

14. Olivia Barton, "McCorquodale Focuses on State's Image and Jobs," *Birming-*

ham News, August 30, 1982, A1; Phillip Rawls, "McCorquodale Seeks Governor's Chair," *Montgomery Advertiser and Alabama Journal*, May 30, 1982, A1.

15. Ralph Holmes, "McCorquodale Endorses Folmar: 'Too Much at Stake in Alabama,'" *Birmingham News*, September 30, 1982, A1.

16. Associated Press, "McMillan Says He's in Governor Race," *Montgomery Advertiser*, May 27, 1982, A1; Sandra Baxley Taylor and Kitty Frieden, "McMillan's Home in South Alabama, Heart in Politics," *Birmingham News*, September 26, 1982, A1; Kitty Frieden, "McMillan Works Hard for Image as Progressive," *Birmingham News*, August 31, 1982, A1.

17. Kitty Frieden, "Folmar Keeps Eye on Road—No Looking Back," *Birmingham News*, September 13, 1981, A1; Kitty Frieden, "Folmar's Always Been Leader, and Wants to Keep It That Way," *Birmingham News*, October 3, 1982, A1.

18. "Wallace Defends His Record," *Anniston Star*, October 21, 1982, A7.

19. Olivia Barton, "ADC Unanimous: McMillan, Baxley for Top Spots in Primary," *Birmingham News*, August 22, 1982.

20. Tim Funk, "Appeal to Blacks New Twist in Wallace Pitch," *Anniston Star*, August 23, 1982, A1.

21. Olivia Barton, "Tammy Stands by Wallace at Rainsville Political Rally," *Birmingham News*, September 1, 1981, A3.

22. "Folmar, Wallace Stump State for Votes," *Montgomery Advertiser*, October 28, 1982, A11.

23. Kitty Frieden, "Wallace, McMillan to Square Off: Both Promise Clean Race, Some Politicos See Dogfight," *Birmingham News*, September 8, 1982, A1.

24. Kitty Frieden and Olivia Barton, "McMillan Win Seen Hanging on Who Gets Their Vote Out," *Birmingham News*, September 26, 1982, A1.

25. Olivia Barton, "Wallace, Folmar Were Glued to TV Sets," *Birmingham News*, September 29, 1982, A2; William Bunch, "Egg on Faces, 2 TV Stations Here Try to Wipe It Off," *Birmingham News*, September 30, 1982, A2.

26. Patrick R. Cotter and Harvey Kline, "George Wallace and the Changing Party Politics of Alabama" (paper delivered at the Southern Political Science Association Meeting, Charlotte, North Carolina, 1983).

27. Dave White, "Alabamians Choose Wave of Democrats," *Birmingham News*, November, 3, 1982, A18; "GOP Candidates Generally Take It on Chin in Alabama," *Birmingham News*, November 3, 1982, A18.

28. Mark J. Skoneki, "Democrats Choose State Candidates," *Montgomery Advertiser*, October 2, 1983, A1; Michele MacDonald, "Eleven Incumbents Axed from Demo Tree," *Birmingham News*, October 2, 1983, A1; Ted Bryant, "Democrats Face Dumping Party Veterans," *Birmingham Post-Herald*, October 1, 1983, A1; Kendal Weaver, "Remapping Divides Democrats, Boosts GOP," *Anniston Star*, October 9, 1983, A5.

29. Frederick Berger, "Tuesday Outcome Could Tilt Legislative Balance of Power," *Anniston Star*, November 6, 1983, A1.

30. Ted Bryant, "Vote to Have Little Effect on Session," *Birmingham Post-Herald,* November 10, 1983, A1; Frederick Berger, "New Coalition Could Emerge: Alabama Vote Cuts into Democratic Lead," *Anniston Start,* November 9, 1983, A1; Mark J. Skoneki, "Hooper Claims House 73 Victory: Hand-picking Issue Plagues Democrats," *Montgomery Advertiser,* November 9, 1983, A1; Michelle MacDonald, "Independents and GOPers Profit from Backlash," *Birmingham News,* November 9, 1983, A1.

31. See, for example, Ted Bryant, "Politicians Lining up '86 Backers," *Birmingham Post-Herald,* January 14, 1985, A1.

32. Michele MacDonald, "Governor May Run: I'll Check the Polls," *Birmingham News,* September 1, 1985, A2.

33. Another health-related item included in the October 1985 survey asked respondents, "Does the condition of his health make you more or less likely to vote for him?" Some 59 percent said they were less likely to vote for Wallace because of his health problems; 29 percent said his health would have no effect on how they voted; and 8 percent said they were more likely to vote for him because of his health problems.

34. Michele MacDonald and Sam Duvall, "Despite Doubts Public Still Prefers Wallace," *Birmingham News,* October 27, 1985, A1.

35. Sam Duvall, "Hints, but That's All from Wallace Talk," *Birmingham News,* December 13, 1985, A1.

36. Staff and Associated Press reports, "Was Governor's Talk a Kickoff to Campaign?" *Birmingham News,* January 15, 1986, A1.

37. Sam Duvall, "Camp to Resign, Planning to Enter Race for Governor," *Birmingham News,* January 22, 1986, A1.

38. Associated Press, "Camp Decides He Won't Be Running in Governor's Race," *Birmingham News,* April 4, 1986, A2.

Chapter 3

1. William E. Schmidt, "Ending an Era, Wallace Announces He Will Retire," *New York Times,* April 3, 1986, A1.

2. See, for example, V. O. Key, *Southern Politics* (New York: Knopf, 1949); Earl Black and Merle Black, *Politics and Society in the South* (Cambridge: Harvard University Press, 1987); Gavin Wright, *Old South, New South: Revolutions in the Southern Economy since the Civil War* (New York: Basic Books, 1986).

3. Alexander Keyssar, *The Right to Vote: The Contested History of Democracy in the United States* (New York: Basic Books, 2000); Philip A. Klinkner with Rogers M. Smith, *The Unsteady March: The Rise and Decline of Racial Equality in America* (Chicago: University of Chicago Press, 1999); J. Morgan Kousser, *The Shaping of Southern Politics: Suffrage Restrictions and the Establishment of the One-Party South, 1880–1910* (New Haven: Yale University Press, 1974); Paul Lewinson, *Race, Class, and Party: A*

History of Negro Suffrage and White Politics in the South (New York: Russell and Russell, 1963); Donald Matthews Donald and James W. Prothro, *Negroes and the New Southern Politics* (New York: Harcourt, Brace and World, 1966); Michael Perman, *Struggle for Mastery: Disfranchisement in the South, 1888–1908* (Chapel Hill: University of North Carolina Press, 2001); Kent Redding, *Making Race, Making Power: North Carolina's Road to Disfranchisement* (Urbana: University of Illinois Press, 2003); Richard M. Valelly, *The Two Reconstructions: The Struggle for Black Enfranchisement* (Chicago: University of Chicago Press, 2004).

4. Nicholas Lemann, *The Promised Land: The Great Black Migration and How It Changed America* (New York: Knopf, 1991); Neil Fligstein, *Going North: Migration of Blacks and Whites from the South, 1900–1950* (New York: Academic Press, 1981).

5. See, for example, Alexander Heard, A *Two-Party South?* (Chapel Hill: University of North Carolina Press, 1952); Kevin J. McMahon, *Reconsider Roosevelt on Race: How the Presidency Paved the Road to Brown* (Chicago: University of Chicago Press, 2004); Harvard Sitkoff, "Harry Truman and the Election of 1948: The Coming of Age of Civil Rights in American Politics," *Journal of Southern History* 37 (1971): 597–616; Nancy J. Weiss, *Farewell to the Party of Lincoln: Black Politics in the Age of FDR* (Princeton: Princeton University Press, 1983).

6. For general discussions about factors affecting political participation see Sidney Verba, Kay Lehman Schlozman, and Henry E. Brady, *Voice and Equality* (Cambridge: Harvard University Press, 1995); Sidney Verba and Norman H. Nie, *Participation in America* (New York: Harper and Row, 1972); Steven J. Rosenstone and John Mark Hansen, *Mobilization, Participation, and Democracy in America* (London: Longman, 1993); Raymond E. Wolfinger and Steven J. Rosenstone, *Who Votes?* (New Haven: Yale University Press, 1980); Pippa Norris, *Democratic Phoenix: Reinventing Political Activism* (New York: Cambridge University Press, 2002).

7. For discussions about the operation and repeal of various disfranchising devices see, for example, Darlene Clark Hine, *Black Victory: The Rise and Fall of the White Primary in Texas*, new ed. (Columbia: University of Missouri Press, 2003); Frederic D. Ogden, *The Poll Tax in the South* (University: University of Alabama Press, 1958); Charles L. Zelden, *The Battle for the Black Ballot:* Smith v. Allwright *and the Defeat of the Texas All-White Primary* (Lawrence: University Press of Kansas, 2004); Sarah Wilkerson-Freeman, "The Second Battle for Woman Suffrage: Alabama White Women, the Poll Tax, and V. O. Key's Master Narrative of Southern Politics," *Journal of Southern History* 68 (2002): 333–74; Brian K. Landsberg, *Free at Last to Vote: The Alabama Origins of the 1965 Voting Rights Act* (Lawrence: University Press of Kansas, 2007).

8. Harold W. Stanley, *Voter Mobilization and the Politics of Race: The South and Universal Suffrage, 1952–1984* (New York: Praeger, 1987).

9. David J. Garrow, *Protest at Selma: Martin Luther King, Jr. and the Voting Rights Act of 1965* (New Haven: Yale University Press, 1978), 7, 19, 189, 200.

10. Jeffrey E. Cohen, Patrick R. Cotter, and Philip B. Coulter, "The Changing Structure of Southern Political Participation: Matthews and Prothro Twenty Years Later," *Social Science Quarterly* 64 (1983): 536–49.

11. Patrick R. Cotter, Samuel H. Fisher III, and Felita T. Williams, "Changes in the Composition of Political Activists," in *Southern Parties and Elections*, ed. Robert P. Steed, Laurence W. Moreland, and Tod A. Baker (Tuscaloosa: University of Alabama Press, 1997), 63–77.

12. Key, *Southern Politics*, chapter 3.

13. H. Brandt Ayres, "Qualified Praise for Wallace," *New York Times*, April 11, 1986, A35.

14. It should be noted that these survey results are from one survey at a time when Wallace was exiting the state's political stage. The fact that he was leaving, that he was old and infirm, and that he had been the visible victim of an assassination attempt for nearly a quarter of a century may well have smoothed some of the rough edges of public opinion about him that would have been present in his more active years.

Chapter 4

1. As mentioned in the previous chapter, Billy Joe Camp, Wallace's press secretary, was briefly a Democratic candidate for governor. Barbara Evans O'Neil, a Bessemer businesswoman, was also a candidate in the Democratic primary. She received less than 1 percent of the vote in the primary. Because Camp and O'Neil had little effect on the 1986 election, their activities are not discussed here.

2. Ted Bryant, "Politicians Lining Up '86 Backers," *Birmingham Post-Herald*, January 14, 1985, A1.

3. Michele MacDonald, "McMillan Launches Bid for Governor," *Birmingham News*, September 11, 1985, A1.

4. Ibid.

5. Michele MacDonald, "Baxley and McMillan Clash over Proposed Teacher Basic Skills Test," *Birmingham News*, December 6, 1985, A5.

6. Ibid.

7. Michele MacDonald, "McMillan: Hard Work Is 'Only Thing I Know,'" *Birmingham News*, May 18, 1986, A1.

8. Mark Alpert, "McMillan Confident of Making Runoff," *Montgomery Advertiser*, May 23, 1986, A1.

9. Sam Duvall, "Graddick in Race for Governor," *Birmingham News*, January 16, 1986, A1.

10. Sam Duvall, "James Dishes up Fish and Spreads the Word He'll Run for Governor," *Birmingham News*, November 7, 1985. A5.

11. Elaine Etheridge, "Fob James Wants to Finish Work He Started," *Birmingham News*, February 25, 1986, A5.

12. Michele MacDonald, "McMillan, James Blast Tax Package," *Birmingham News*, March 12, 1986, A2.

13. Michele MacDonald, "Candidates for Governor Put Their Cases to Alabama Cattlemen's Association," *Birmingham News*, February 13, 1986, A2.

14. Michele MacDonald, "Baxley Blitz: Campaign Is 'Raring to Go,'" *Birmingham News*, March 17, 1986, A1.

15. Ibid.; Michele MacDonald, "On the Trail, a Week to Go: Stop Sparring, Says Baxley, Talk Issues," *Birmingham News*, May 28, 1986, A2; Ray Locker, "Mellower Baxley Hopes Second Time's the Charm," *Montgomery Advertiser*, May 20, 1986, A1.

16. Michele MacDonald and Tom Gordon, "State Cars Put to Private Use for Lt. Gov. Baxley," *Birmingham News*, March 30, 1986, A2.

17. The authors had a number of informal conversations with *Birmingham News* editors and reporters during this controversy and for several years afterward. In 1994 we formally interviewed Glenn Stephens, state editor of the *Birmingham News*, about this matter for this book. Our discussion herein reflects all of those conversations.

18. In 1987 former Colorado senator Gary Hart set off a long and heated political debate when he was observed spending the night with Donna Rice, a woman who was not his wife. Guido H. Stempel and John W. Windhauser, eds., *The Media in the 1984 and 1988 Presidential Campaigns* (Westport, Conn.: Greenwood, 1991); Jack W. Germond and Jules Witcover, *Whose Broad Stripes and Bright Stars: The Trivial Pursuit of the Presidency, 1988* (New York: Warner Books, 1989).

19. Interview with Bill Baxley, September 25, 2001; interview with Glenn Stephens, September 24, 1994.

20. Michele MacDonald, "Citizens Group Asks for Probe of Baxley," *Birmingham News*, April 11, 1986, A2.

21. Locker, "Mellower Baxley Hopes Second Time's the Charm."

22. Ray Locker, "Baxley Says Sign-Painters Not Part of His Campaign," *Montgomery Advertiser*, April 24, 1986, A2; Associated Press, "Cabinet Ignores Warnings, Aids Baxley," *Anniston Star*, May 5, 1986, A7; Sam Duvall, "Guard Officer Solicits Funds for Baxley," *Birmingham News*, May 8, 1986, A2.

23. Kathy Roe, "Candidates Court Vote of Coalition at Political Rally," *Birmingham News*, April 26, 1986, A2.

24. Ray Locker, "Baxley Says One Candidate Will Tear Apart Progress," *Montgomery Advertiser*, April 26, 1986, A2.

25. Dave White, "Seven Running for No. 1 Mix It Up Verbally in Florence," *Birmingham News*, May 2, 1986, A2; Associated Press, "Candidates for Home Rule, Highway Funds," *Birmingham News*, May 10, 1986, A2.

26. Michele MacDonald, "McMillan Targets Baxley," *Birmingham News*, May 14, 1986, A2.

27. Michele MacDonald, "Front Runners Thinking of Runoff: McMillan, James Go on Attack," *Birmingham News*, May 14, 1986, A2.

28. Interview with Charles Graddick, December 1, 1994.

29. MacDonald, "McMillan Targets Baxley."

30. Associated Press, "Baxley Blames Foes for State Problems," *Birmingham News*, May 20, 1986, A4.

31. Locker, "Mellower Baxley Hopes Second Time's the Charm."

32. Michele MacDonald, "McMillan Bases His Strength in Race on 12 Opinion Polls," *Birmingham News*, January 19, 1986, C1.

33. Michelle MacDonald, "Alabama Heads on New Course with Today's Vote," *Birmingham News*, June 3, 1986, A1. By 1986, Alabama had come of age politically in many ways, one being the ubiquitous presence of public-opinion pollsters. Most of the candidates had invested a part of their campaign resources in survey research, and a number of polls were being conducted by nonpartisan organizations and special-interest groups. The *Birmingham News* retained the University of Alabama's Capstone Poll (which the authors of this book co-directed) for a series of election surveys beginning in August 1985. The *Birmingham Post-Herald*, under the direction of reporter Tom Hargrove, produced its own series of public-opinion polls. The Birmingham firm of Davis-Penfield, headed by Birmingham Southern political scientist Natalie Davis, was hired by the Alabama Education Association to do tracking polls that were eventually used by Baxley's campaign. The Alabama Voice, the public-opinion survey unit of Auburn University at Montgomery, under the direction of Jerry Ingram, conducted a number of surveys throughout the year. Marketing Research Institute of Jackson, Mississippi, surveyed Alabamians for the Farm Bureau Association, which contributed to a number of campaigns but was noted most for its opposition to Baxley. These were just some of the organizations that engaged in gathering public opinion during 1986.

34. MacDonald, "McMillan Bases His Strength."

35. Michele MacDonald, "Black Group Ponders 'Principles' or Polls," *Birmingham News*, May 10, 1986, A2.

36. Ibid.

37. Michele MacDonald, "Coalitions; Choice: Vision or Victory," *Birmingham News*, May 12, 1986, A1.

38. "McMillan Calls It 'Wide Open': Predicts He Will Make Runoff," *Birmingham News*, May 13, 1986, A2.

39. Sam Duvall, "ADC Backs Bill Baxley Candidacy," *Birmingham News*, May 18, 1986, A1.

40. Dean Barber, "Labor Group Votes to Back Baxley," *Birmingham News*, April 20, 1986, A13.

41. The survey's results may have underrepresented the support Baxley received from African-American voters. One explanation for the discrepancies between the results of the survey and the outcome of the primary is a shift in black support to Baxley as a result of the campaigning that took place the weekend before the election. White voters were more likely to support Graddick than any other candidate. Republican identifiers who said they would vote in the Democratic primary were

most likely to support either James (34 percent) or Graddick (30 percent). Baxley was the leading vote-getter among Democratic identifiers, with 34 percent, while Independents were most likely to support Graddick (35 percent).

42. The "positive-negative" questions were asked in each election survey because of the importance of candidate evaluations on voter behavior and the outcome of elections (Angus Campbell, Philip E. Converse, Warren E. Miller, and Donald E. Stokes, *The American Voter* [New York: Wiley, 1960]). These questions only asked respondents for their overall evaluations of the candidates. In none of the election surveys was it possible to ask citizens why they felt positively or negatively about a candidate.

43. Michele MacDonald, "Three Demo Candidates for Governor Aim Barbs at Baxley," *Birmingham News*, April 3, 1986, A4.

44. Associated Press, "Candidates for Home Rule, Highway Funds."

45. Associated Press, "Baxley Blames Foes for State Problems."

Chapter 5

1. Terri Troncale, "Baxley and Graddick Smile, Then Tear into Each Other," *Birmingham News*, June 8, 1986, A2.

2. Michele MacDonald and Sam Duvall, "Baxley, Graddick: Focus on the Issues," *Birmingham News*, June 5, 1986, A1.

3. Troncale, "Baxley and Graddick Smile."

4. Frederick Burger, "Graddick Throws First Jabs," *Anniston Star*, June 5, 1986, A1.

5. Ibid.; MacDonald and Duvall, "Baxley, Graddick: Focus on the Issues"; Troncale, "Baxley and Graddick Smile."

6. Burger, "Graddick Throws First Jabs."

7. Michele MacDonald, "Candidates Swap Knocks in First Debate," *Birmingham News*, June 9, 1986, A1; Frederick Burger, "No Clear Winner in First Debate," *Anniston Star*, June 9, 1986, A1; Amy Herring, "Baxley Takes Offensive in First Debate," *Montgomery Advertiser*, June 9, 1986, A1.

8. Michele MacDonald, "Baxley Questions Graddick's Allegiance to the Demo Party," *Birmingham News*, June 14, 1986, A1; Amy Herring, "Businessmen Raise Funds for Graddick," *Montgomery Advertiser*, June 14, 1986, A1.

9. Michele MacDonald and Sam Duvall, "Tough Talk: 'A Puppet'–'An Opportunist': Graddick, Baxley Swap Harshest Words of Campaign," *Birmingham News*, June 16, 1986, A1; Amy Herring, "Candidates Trade Shots in Debate," *Montgomery Advertiser*, June 16, 1986, A1; Frederick Burger, "Candidates Swap Charges in Round Two," *Anniston Star*, June 16, 1986, A1.

10. Sam Duvall, "Friends' Rides in State Cars Ruled Illegal," *Birmingham News*, June 6, 1986, A2.

11. Much of the information on the *Birmingham News* was gathered in talking with *News* reporters Michele MacDonald, Tom Gordon, and Sam Duvall during and after the campaign. During 1986 the authors were the directors of the Univer-

sity of Alabama's Capstone Poll, which had been contracted by the *News* to do a series of public-opinion surveys about the election. Their work with the *News* brought them into contact with all of the reporters covering the campaign at various times through the year.

12. Interview with Bill Baxley, September 25, 2001.

13. Michele MacDonald and Tom Gordon, "Graddick: Ethics, *News* Should Release Baxley Info," *Birmingham News*, June 17, 1986, A2.

14. Ibid.

15. Ibid.

16. Ibid.

17. Amy Herring and Mark Alpert, "Baxley Aide: McMillan Sought Cash," *Montgomery Advertiser*, June 17, 1986, A1.

18. Amy Herring, "James Refuses to Choose Sides, but Key Staffer Aligns with Baxley," *Montgomery Advertiser*, June 10, 1986, A1.

19. Herring and Alpert, "Baxley Aide: McMillan Sought Cash."

20. Ibid.; Baxley's version of his contact with the McMillan campaign officials is presented in an interview published in the *Anniston Star* on June 20, 1986, A11.

21. "Mitchem Gets on Graddick Bandwagon," *Birmingham News*, June 17, 1986, A2.

22. Staff and wire reports, "Graddick Kills Debate: Baxley Wants Him on Lie Detector," *Montgomery Advertiser*, June 18, 1986, A1.

23. James E. Jacobson, "The State Car: An Editor's Explanation," *Birmingham News*, June 18, 1986, A2. The fact that the *News* did not have pictures of a state-owned auto outside Baxley's apartment made life more uncomfortable for the newspaper. It gave Baxley some room to deny all of the allegations against him, and it produced some doubts among other media about the strength of the evidence against Baxley (Staff and wire reports, "Newspaper Photos Don't Link Baxley to Misuse of State Cars," *Montgomery Advertiser*, June 19, 1986, A1). Reporters believed Baxley had indeed used state cars to transport Prat to his apartment. They had been watching this happen for several days. The day a photographer was summoned to take pictures of the event, however, Baxley stopped using his state-owed car and began using a campaign vehicle.

24. Michele MacDonald, Sam Duvall, and Tom Gordon, "'Truth' a Central Issue, Says Graddick," *Birmingham News*, June 19, 1986, A1.

25. Staff and wire reports, "Newspaper Photos Don't Link Baxley."

26. MacDonald, Duvall, and Gordon, "'Truth' a Central Issue."

27. Murphy Evans, "Baxley Says Pictures Irrelevant," *Anniston Star*, June 19, 1986, A1.

28. "Baxley: Questions and Answers," *Anniston Star*, June 20, 1986, A11.

29. MacDonald, Duvall, and Gordon, "'Truth' a Central Issue."

30. Frederick Burger, "Graddick Pushes Tax Return Issue," *Anniston Star*, June 19, 1986, A1; MacDonald, Duvall, and Gordon, "'Truth' a Central Issue."

31. Burger, "Graddick Pushes Tax Return Issue."

32. MacDonald, Duvall, and Gordon, "'Truth' a Central Issue."

33. Staff and wire reports, "Newspaper Photos Don't Link Baxley."

34. Staff and wire reports, "Issue Fading as Candidates Repeat 'Dirty Accusations,'" *Montgomery Advertiser*, June 20, 1986, A1; Michele MacDonald, "McMillan: Baxley Lied about Debt," *Birmingham News*, June 20, 1986, A1.

35. Staff and wire reports, "Issue Fading."

36. Ibid.

37. MacDonald, "McMillan: Baxley Lied about Debt."

38. Ibid.

39. Murphy Evans, "Baxley Releases '79–84 Tax Returns," *Anniston Star*, June 21, 1986, A1; Peggy Wilhide, "Baxley Discloses Taxes for the Past Six Years," *Montgomery Advertiser*, June 21, 1986, A1.

40. Baxley always maintained that he paid all of his taxes, although sometimes he was late. Occasionally, he would miss even the extension deadlines and would then pay "horrendous penalties." He cited the theft of his tax returns as more evidence that the *Birmingham News* reporters had turned against him in the campaign, saying the reporters were not just observers but rather "participants" in the controversy. Interview with Bill Baxley, September 25, 2001.

41. Sam Duvall and Michele MacDonald, "Campaigning for Top Post on Final Lap," *Birmingham News*, June 22, 1986, A1.

42. Ray Locker, "Baxley, Graddick Both Predict Run-off Victory," *Montgomery Advertiser*, June 24, 1986, A1.

43. Ray Locker, "Baxley Shows Up Anyway," *Montgomery Advertiser*, June 23, 1986, A1; Sam Duvall and Michele MacDonald, "Final Pitches from Baxley and Graddick," *Birmingham News*, June 23, 1986, A1.

44. Jamie Creamer, "BOE Runoff Declared for District 5," *Montgomery Advertiser*, June 17, 1986, A1.

45. Interview with John Baker, November 1994.

46. Amy Herring, "Graddick Lists $252,700 in Gifts since June 3," *Montgomery Advertiser*, June 21, 1986, A2.

47. Interview with John Baker, November 1994.

48. For a recap of these events and the candidates' statements see Tom Gordon, "The Burning Question: Will They, Won't They, Can They Cross Vote?" *Birmingham News*, June 22, 1986, A2; Mark Alpert, "GOP Voters in Dark for Runoff," *Montgomery Advertiser*, June 24, 1986, A1; Paul Newberry, "Crossovers Become Issue in Election," *Anniston Star*, June 24, 1986, A6; Associated Press, "GOP's Sullivan Sees Crossover to Graddick," *Birmingham News*, June 17, 1986, A4.

49. Interview with Charles Graddick, December 1, 1994.

50. This sequence of events is described in several of the subsequent court decisions that resulted from these actions.

51. Michael Gordon and Greg Garrison, "Graddick Asks Poll Watchers," *Anniston Star*, June 21, 1986, A1.

52. Interview with Bill Baxley, September 25, 2001.

53. Hunt defeated businessman Doug Carter in the largely ignored Republican primary.

Chapter 6

1. Alabama law does not require that voters register their party affiliation before going to vote in a primary election.

2. Interview with Ed Patridge, 1987.

3. Sam Duvall, "Count Close: Some Ballots Impounded," *Birmingham News* June 26, 1986, A1.

4. Ray Locker and Peggy Wilhide, "Graddick Has 'Inspirational' Talk with Gov. Wallace," *Montgomery Advertiser*, June 26, 1986, A1.

5. Duvall, "Count Close."

6. Frederick Burger and Murphy Evans, "It's Graddick by a Hair: Ballots Impounded after Bitter Race," *Anniston Star*, June 25, 1986, A1.

7. Mark Albert, "Baxley Urged to Challenge Run-off Vote," *Montgomery Advertiser*, June 27, 1986, A1.

8. In the room where the meeting between Graddick and the legislators took place, a videoscreen displayed the message "Welcome Gov. Graddick" (Frederick Burger, "Graddick Meets with Lawmakers," *Anniston Star*, June 27, 1986, A1). For other accounts of this meeting see Ray Locker, "Graddick Meets with Legislators," *Montgomery Advertiser*, June 27, 1986, A1; Sam Duvall, "Graddick Mends Fences, Begins Laying Groundwork," *Birmingham News*, June 27, 1986, A2.

9. Alvin Benn, "Sullivan Says Republicans Were Key to Run-off Win," *Montgomery Advertiser*, June 26, 1986, A1; similarly, the executive director of the Alabama Republican Party, Marty Connors, said that Graddick won because of his support from GOP voters. "They were panicked that a liberal like Baxley might win," Connors said (Wire reports, "Baxley May Ask Recount," *Anniston Star*, June 26, 1986, A1). See also Tom Gordon and Sam Duvall, "Conservatives Pleased with Results, GOP Official Says," *Birmingham News*, June 25, 1986, A2.

10. In an election-night interview with a Huntsville television station, Graddick said that he encouraged people who voted in the GOP primary to support him in the Democratic runoff. "I think they really played a part. I don't know how many Republicans crossed over, but obviously . . . they voted 30 something though on June 3, so obviously they made a difference and I want to tell them how much I appreciate it." Bill Poovey, "Court May Make Final Decision," *Montgomery Advertiser*, August 11, 1986, A1. See also Burger and Evans, "It's Graddick by a Hair."

11. Duvall, "Count Close"; Amy Herring, "Graddick Criticized for Action Taken," *Montgomery Advertiser*, June 26, 1986, A1; Pamela Gundy, "Spokesmen Expound on Impounding Votes," *Anniston Star*, July 1, 1986, A2.

12. Interview with John Baker, November 1994.

13. Interview with Bill Baxley, September 25, 1994. Baxley said he thought he would be able to keep Graddick from getting the nomination. "The one chance I thought I had" for winning the election, he said, "was that if Guy Hunt would stay in the race," the Republicans would replace Hunt as the nominee when they thought there was a chance for a Republican to be elected. He laughed at the irony of that calculation.

14. Interview with John Baker, November 1994.

15. Curt Anderson, "Democrats Nominate Graddick," *Montgomery Advertiser*, June 29, 1986, A1; Michele MacDonald, "Baxley Backers Contest Runoff," *Birmingham News*, June 29, 1986, A1.

16. Tom Gordon, "The Pikes' Challenge: Madison Pair Say They Acted on Their Own," *Birmingham News*, August 15, 1986, A1.

17. MacDonald, "Baxley Backers Contest Runoff."

18. Ibid.

19. The Hubbert-Graddick meeting later grew to legendary status. Graddick partisans believe that the powerful and influential Hubbert had indeed threatened Graddick and that the seeds of the challenge were sown there. When Graddick told his version of the meeting in 1989, as Hubbert was preparing his gubernatorial bid, Hubbert shot back that Graddick should "pull out his tapes of the meeting" to hear what really happened—a reference to the charge that Graddick had used his power as attorney general to bug Baxley's campaign headquarters. Reference to the meeting also appeared in a newspaper profile of Graddick when he was running for lieutenant governor in 1994 (Tom Lindley, "Get Ready for Down and Dirty Lieutenant Governor's Race: Graddick's Rival Says He's Cutthroat When He's Campaigning for Office," *Birmingham News*, October 9, 1994, A1).

20. The night of the runoff election, Graddick told his supporters, "The ADC (the Alabama Democratic Conference) and the AEA (Alabama Education Association) are going to be diminished quite a bit in their voice in the Legislature if I have anything to do about it." Sam Duvall and Michele MacDonald, "Graddick: Changes on the Way," *Birmingham News*, June 25, 1986, A1.

21. Interview with Charles Graddick, December 1, 1994; interview with Paul Hubbert, October 20, 1994.

22. MacDonald, "Baxley Backers Contest Runoff."

23. Staff and wire reports, "Manager Says Baxley Won't Concede Race," *Montgomery Advertiser*, June 30, 1986, A1; Sam Duvall, "Graddick Blasts Demo Leaders," *Birmingham News*, June 30, 1986, A1.

24. Ray Locker, "Baxley Claims He's Nominee for Governor," *Montgomery Advertiser*, July 1, 1986, A1; Michele MacDonald and Sam Duvall, "Who Won? Demos Face a Choice," *Birmingham News*, July 1, 1986, A1.

25. Locker, "Baxley Claims He's Nominee"; MacDonald and Duvall, "Who Won?"

26. For information about the origins of the federal lawsuits see Associated

Press, "Attorney Believes Suit Will Succeed," *Anniston Star*, July 11, 1986, A2; Associated Press, "Demos May Hear 1,000 Witnesses," *Birmingham News*, July 11, 1986, A1.

27. The legal proceedings involving the challenge were covered extensively by the state's newspaper. These accounts document the strategies being used by the Graddick and Baxley camps.

28. Kendal Weaver, "Graddick Says Throw Out Challenges," *Montgomery Advertiser*, July 3, 1986, A1; see also Frederick Burger, "Runoff Charges Swapped," *Anniston Star*, July 15, 1986, A1.

29. Staff and wire reports, "McMillan, Brewer Chide Baxley for Challenge to Graddick Victory," *Birmingham News*, July 3, 1986, A1.

30. Amy Herring, "Group Says Baxley Nod Will Hurt Party," *Montgomery Advertiser*, July 9, 1986, A1; Amy Herring, "Graddick, Baxley Use PR Tactics," *Montgomery Advertiser*, July 10, 1986, A1; Associated Press, "Califano: Challenge to Graddick Not Valid," *Anniston Star*, July 9, 1986, B4.

31. Michele MacDonald, "Graddick Meets with Top Nominees," *Birmingham News*, July 12, 1986, A1; Frederick Burger, "I Am a Democrat, Graddick Asserts," *Anniston Star*, July 12, 1986, B1.

32. Associated Press, "Demos to Hear 1,000 Testify," *Anniston Star*, July 11, 1986, A1; see also Staff and Associated Press reports, "Baxley Seeks Delay in Challenge Hearing," *Birmingham News*, July 14, 1986, A1.

33. Herring, "Group Says Baxley Nod Will Hurt Party"; Herring, "Graddick, Baxley Use PR Tactics."

34. Staff and Associated Press reports, "Baxley Seeks Delay in Challenge Hearing"; Michele MacDonald, "Panel Ready to Hear Contests for Governor," *Birmingham News*, July 13, 1986, A1; Amy Herring, "Attorneys Can Prove Republicans Cast Ballots Illegally, Baxley Says," *Montgomery Advertiser*, July 14, 1986.

35. For accounts of the arguments in the federal court hearings, and Judge Johnson's comments, see Stan Bailey and Sam Duvall, "Judge Orders GOP to Turn Over Voting Records by Monday," *Birmingham News*, July 25, 1986, A1; Stan Bailey, "U.S. Judges Set Sunday Deadline for List of Voters," *Birmingham News*, July 26, 1986, A1; Michele MacDonald and Sam Duvall, "Baxley and Graddick Go to Battle in Different Courts for Demos' Bid," *Birmingham News*, July 30, 1986, A1; Stan Bailey, "Opinion Poll after Primary 'Unworkable,'" *Birmingham News*, July 31, 1986, A2; Michele MacDonald and Sam Duvall, "Baxley, Graddick Argue Count on Crossover Voters," *Birmingham News*, July 31, 1986, A1; Amy Herring, "Assistant AG Consulted Campaign before Issuing Crossover Warning," *Montgomery Advertiser*, July 24, 1986, A1; Amy Herring, "Judges Hear Counts Differ on Crossover," *Montgomery Advertiser*, July 31, 1986, A1; Frederick Burger, "Federal Panel Delays Challenge Suit," *Anniston Star*, July 31, 1986, D1.

36. Stan Bailey and Sam Duvall, "Judges: New Runoff or Baxley," *Birmingham News*, August 2, 1986, A1; Frederick Burger, "Federal Judges Tell Democrats: A New Runoff or Nominate Baxley," *Anniston Star*, August 2, 1986, A1.

37. Graddick's spokesman, Chris Grimshawe, argued that the decision "is the reaction of a liberal federal court in support of a liberal candidate." Bailey and Duvall, "Judges: New Runoff or Baxley"; see also Sam Duvall and Michele MacDonald, "'Don't Look Good for You,' Baxley Tells Graddick," *Birmingham News*, August 2, 1986, A2; Sam Duvall and Michele MacDonald, "Graddick: 'Circle Them Again, Bill,'" *Birmingham News*, August 3, 1986, A1.

38. Staff and Associated Press reports, "No Second Chance for Graddick, Says Winner in Lawsuit," *Birmingham News*, August 4, 1986, A1.

39. Ibid.

40. Duvall and MacDonald, "'Don't Look Good for You.'"

41. Michele MacDonald, "Graddick Faces Disqualification Hearing," *Birmingham News*, August 12, 1986, A1.

42. Amy Herring, "Panel Hears Crossover Voting Data," *Montgomery Advertiser*, August 12, 1986, A1. How Henderson was able to distinguish crossover votes from those coming to the runoff candidates from previous James and McMillan voters was not reported. Nor, apparently, was any attention given to the problem of making inferences about the behavior of voters based on an analysis of precincts.

43. MacDonald, "Graddick Faces Disqualification Hearing"; Tom Gordon and Michele MacDonald, "Demo Panel Weighing Decision: Hearings Draw the Committed and the Curious," *Birmingham News*, August 14, 1986, A1.

44. Michele MacDonald, "Baxley Forces Say AG's Staff Conspired to Allow Crossovers," *Birmingham News*, August 13, 1986, A1; Michele MacDonald "Demo Panel Weighs Decision: 'May Come Today,' Says Party Chairman," *Birmingham News*, August 14, 1986, A1.

45. Macdonald, "Baxley Forces Say AG's Staff Conspired."

46. MacDonald, "Demo Panel Weighs Decision."

47. Interview with John Baker, November 1994.

48. Michele MacDonald, "Baxley Declared Demo Nominee: 'Atrocity,' Says Graddick Lawyer," *Birmingham News*, August 15, 1986, A1; Tom Gordon and Michele MacDonald, "Baxley, Graddick Faces Foretold Demo Committee's Final Decree," *Birmingham News*, August 16, 1986, A2.

Chapter 7

1. Amy Herring, "Baxley Wins, Graddick Appeals," *Montgomery Advertiser*, August 16, 1986, A1; Michele MacDonald and Tom Gordon, "Baxley 'Relieved': Graddick Heads Back to Court," *Birmingham News*, August 16, 1986, A1; Frederick Burger, "Graddick to Appeal Demos' Ruling," *Anniston Star*, August 16, 1986, A1.

2. Michele MacDonald, "Baxley Asks for Demo Unity as Graddick Weighs Options," *Birmingham News*, August 17, 1986, A1; see also Frederick Burger, "GOP Scents Victory in Baxley Pick," *Anniston Star*, August 17, 1986, A1.

3. Herring, "Baxley Wins, Graddick Appeals"; MacDonald and Gordon, "Baxley 'Relieved'"; Burger, "Graddick to Appeal Demos' Ruling."

4. Michele MacDonald, "U.S. Judges Indicate They Will Side with Baxley Lawyers, Party," *Birmingham News*, August 22, 1986, A1; Frederick Burger, "Judges Hear Graddick," *Anniston Star*, August 22, 1986, A1.

5. Stan Bailey, "Graddick Takes Fight to Highest Courts," *Birmingham News*, August 28, 1986, A1.

6. Michele MacDonald, "No Ruling, but Graddick Set for a Write-in," *Birmingham News*, August 23, 1986, A1. George McMillan also attended the rally and spoke in support for Graddick. McMillan also supported Graddick through helping form an "Alabamians for Democracy" group (Sam Duvall, "McMillan Group Urges Graddick Write-in Campaign," *Birmingham News*, August 21, 1986, A1). See also Frederick Burger, "Citizens Group Urges Graddick Write-in," *Anniston Star*, August 21, 1986, D1; Curt Anderson, "Graddick to Run as Write-in If Appeal Fails," *Anniston Star*, August 23, 1986, A1.

7. Michele MacDonald, "Baxley Predicts Graddick Will Drop Write-in Plans," *Birmingham News*, August 24, 1986, A1.

8. Ibid.; Amy Herring, "Baxley Predicts Graddick Will Give Up Write-in Bid," *Montgomery Advertiser*, August 24, 1986, A2. See also Michele MacDonald and Tom Gordon, "Democratic Leaders Re-elect John Baker as Party Chairman," *Birmingham News*, August 24, 1986, A7.

9. Sam Duvall and Associated Press, "Baxley Turns to TV Ads to Combat Voters Doubts," *Birmingham News*, August 18, 1986, A1; Frederick Burger, "Baxley Goes on TV to Explain Why He Is Democrat Winner," *Anniston Star*, August 19, 1986, A12.

10. For background on this suit see Michele MacDonald, "Graddick Asks Judge to Order New Elections," *Birmingham News*, September 6, 1986, A2; Frederick Burger, "Justices Refuse Graddick," *Anniston Star*, September 4, 1986, A1.

11. Stan Bailey, "Denied New Runoff, Graddick Mulls Options," *Birmingham News*, August 27, 1986, A1; Frederick Burger, "Graddick Plans Further Appeals," *Anniston Star*, August 27, 1986, A1; Amy Herring, "Baxley Wins Another Fight in U.S. Court," *Montgomery Advertiser*, August 27, 1986, A1.

12. Sam Duvall, "Graddick Rejected, Eyes U.S. Supreme Court," *Birmingham News*, September 4, 1986, A1; Burger, "Justices Refuse Graddick"; Amy Herring, "Court: Choice Up to Demos," *Montgomery Advertiser*, September 4, 1986, A1.

13. Frances Spotswood, "Court Offers Graddick Runoff Deal," *Birmingham News*, September 17, 1986, A1; Murphy Evans, "Judge Orders New Runoff," *Anniston Star*, September 18, 1986, A1; Amy Herring, "Judge Orders New Runoff," *Montgomery Advertiser*, September 18, 1986, A1.

14. Jack Wheat, "Graddick Says He Wants New Runoff," *Tuscaloosa News*, September 18, 1986, A1.

15. Herring, "Judge Orders New Runoff"; see also Staff writers, "Fight Goes to Appeal in Atlanta," *Birmingham News*, September 18, 1986, A2; Staff writers, "Graddick, Baxley Set to Run Again, but Appeals Continue," *Birmingham News*, September 18, 1986, A1; Michele MacDonald, "Graddick Looks at Legal Options," *Birmingham News*, September 22, 1986, A1.

16. Bill Poovey, "Judge Vance Refuses to Vacate Seat on Panel," *Anniston Star*, September 25, 1986, A7.

17. Michele MacDonald, "Next Stop: Supreme Court," *Birmingham News*, October 2, 1986, A1; Michele MacDonald, "Graddick Pleads for New Election," *Birmingham News*, October 4, 1986, A1; Frederick Burger, "Graddick to Appeal to Supreme Court," *Anniston Star*, October 4, 1986, A1; Staff writers, "Graddick Appeal Turned Down by Powell," *Birmingham News*, October 8, 1986, A1.

Chapter 8

1. Frederick Burger, "Everyone in Holly Pond Knows GOP's Hunt," *Anniston Star*, October 1986,.A1; Rick Bragg, "Hunt's Spot in Front Surprises Even GOP," *Birmingham News*, October, 28, 1986, A1.

2. Associated Press, "GOP Expresses Support Anew for Guy Hunt," *Birmingham News*, August 1, 1986, A2.

3. Tom Gordon, "GOP's Guy Hunt 'Finding Groundswell,'" *Birmingham News*, August 7, 1986, A2; Tom Gordon, "Demo Logjam May Be Hunt's Kindling," *Birmingham News*, August 10, 1986, A1.

4. Curt Anderson, "GOP: Graddick Should Join Us," *Anniston Star*, August 17, 1986, A17.

5. Sam Duvall, Michele MacDonald, and Robert Dunnavant, "GOP Leaders Deny Baxley Claim of Plot to Replace Nominee—Hunt," *Birmingham News*, September 5, 1986, A1.

6. Curt Anderson, "Dump Hunt Effort Revealed by Aide," *Anniston Star*, September 5, 1986, A1; Frederick Burger, "Hunt Says He Will Ignore Controversy," *Anniston Star*, September 7, 1986, A9; Associated Press, "Bachus Says Graddick Team Tried to Oust Hunt," *Birmingham News*, September 6, 1986, A2; Frank Sikora, "Hunt in Running, Cannot Be Bought," *Birmingham News*, September 9, 1986, A2; Ted Bryant, "Attempts Made to Get Hunt Out of Race, Bachus Says," *Birmingham Post-Herald*, September 6, 1986, A1; Ted Bryant, "Hunt Doesn't Deny That Some Want to Buy Nomination from Him," *Birmingham Post-Herald*, September 7, 1986, B1.

7. The state and national party organization were also recognizing the possibility of a Hunt victory. Michael Brumas, "Reagan May Plug Hunt's Candidacy," *Birmingham News*, August 26, 1986, A2; Michael Brumas, "Hunt War Chest Swells after New Runoff Denied," *Birmingham News*, October 9, 1986, A2; Frederick Burger, "National GOP Giving to Hunt," *Anniston Star*, October 22, 1986, A10.

8. Frederick Burger, "Graddick Hopes Earlier Ruling Is Overturned," *Anniston Star*, August 30, 1986, A5; Associated Press, "Write-in Restrictions Set by State Election Officials," *Birmingham News*, September 5, 1986, A4; George Vlahakis, "Graddick to Ask Court to Detail Rules for His Write-in Election Bid," *Birmingham News*, September 11, 1986, A2.

9. Michele MacDonald, "Baxley Predicts Graddick Will Drop Write-in Plan," *Birmingham News*, August 24, 1986, A1.

10. Frederick Burger, "Graddick Pollster Feels Time Ripe for Write-in," *Anniston Star*, August 19, 1986, A1; Michael Jennings, "Survey Shows Graddick Has Support as Write-in Candidate," *Birmingham News*, August 19, 1986, A2; Amy Herring, "Graddick Eyeing Write-in Campaign," *Montgomery Advertiser*, August 19, 1986, A1.

11. "The Aaron Burr of Alabama Politics," *Anniston Star*, September 10, 1986, A4.

12. "Look at Both," *Montgomery Advertiser*, September 28, 1986, B3.

13. "Playing into Baxley's Hands," *Birmingham News*, September 10, 1986, A10.

14. Interview with Charles Graddick, December 1, 1994; Sam Duvall, "Graddick in Last of Long-Shot Battles," *Birmingham News*, October 28, 1986, A1.

15. Norman Zumwalt, "Baxley Plan Is Finding Wide Support," *Tuscaloosa News*, September 14, 1986, A1.

16. For information about the special legislative session see Jay Reeves, "Wallace to Call Special Session," *Anniston Star*, September 4, 1986, B1; Frederick Burger, "Special Session: Many Lawmakers Leery of Tax Package," *Anniston Star*, September 9, 1986, A1; Frederick Burger, "Baxley Tells Non-taxing Alternatives," *Anniston Star*, September 11, 1986, A1; Philip Rawls, "No Tax Plan in Legal Study," *Anniston Star*, September 12, 1986, A1; Associated Press, "Legislators Pass Concession Sales Tax," *Anniston Star*, September 25, 1986, B9.

17. Frederick Burger, "Baxley Tax Returns Fuel Controversy," *Anniston Star*, September 23, 1986, A1.

18. Sam Duvall and Michele MacDonald, "Baxley Acknowledges Being Tardy on Taxes," *Birmingham News*, September 25, 1986, A1.

19. Frederick Burger, "Graddick Aide Says He Distributed Returns," *Anniston Star*, September 25, 1986, A1; Thomas Hargrove, "Graddick Not Consulted on Tax Return, Aide Says," *Birmingham Post-Herald*, September 26, 1986, A1.

20. Ted Bryant, "'Cracker Barrel Caper' Adds Mystery," *Birmingham Post-Herald*, September 25, 1986, A4.

21. Duvall and MacDonald, "Baxley Acknowledges Being Tardy on Taxes."

22. Michele MacDonald and Sam Duvall, "Records Show Baxley Slow Several Times to Pay Taxes," *Birmingham News*, September 24, 1986, A1.

23. Sam Duvall and Michele MacDonald, "Baxley Late Every Year Paying Federal Income Taxes," *Birmingham News*, October 24, 1986, A2; Duvall and MacDonald, "Baxley Acknowledges Being Tardy on Taxes."

24. Amy Herring, "Evans Agrees to Investigate Theft of Baxley's Tax Records," *Montgomery Advertiser*, October 2, 1986, A1; Michael Jennings, "Montgomery Grand Jury Postpones Baxley Probe," *Birmingham News*, October 30, 1986, A2.

25. The investigation of the release of Baxley's tax returns continued after the election. Eventually, both Harry Michael Yeomans and Pat Robinson were convicted on criminal charges related to the event. Stan Bailey, "Former Revenue Clerk

Found Guilty of Releasing Baxley's Tax Records," *Birmingham News*, June 5, 1987, A1; Staff and Associated Press reports, "Robinson Pleads Guilty in Baxley Tax Return Case," *Birmingham News*, August 31, 1987, A2.

The investigation also revealed that listening devices were taken from Graddick's attorney general's office and used to "bug" the state Democratic headquarters and a Baxley telephone bank. The motivation for bugging the phone bank was a rumor that it was being used to tell black voters that Graddick was linked to the Klan. In 1989, Andy Yeomans and Don Bekurs, an executive assistant to Graddick, pleaded guilty to misdemeanor charges related to the use of the listening equipment. Stan Bailey and Tom Gordon, "DA: Bug from Graddick Office Used to Spy on Demos, Baxley," *Birmingham News*, May 7, 1987, A1; Sam Duvall, "Indictments of His Ex-workers Has Political Taint, Graddick Says," *Birmingham News*, February 27, 1989, C2; Frederick Burger, "Graddick Aides Likely to Get Minor Fines," *Anniston Star*, July 18, 1989, A7; Shelton Foss, "Graddick Aides Accept Plea Bargain," *Montgomery Advertiser*, July 18, 1989, A1.

Uncertainty remains, for both the tax and "bugging" incidents, over what Graddick knew and when he knew it. Staff and Associated Press reports, "Ex-aide: Graddick Discussed Divulging Baxley's Tax Records," *Birmingham News*, June 4, 1987, A2; Tom Gordon and Stan Bailey, "Graddick: I Didn't Do Wrong," *Birmingham News*, June 11, 1987, A1; Stan Bailey, "Ex-aides Diff on What Graddick Knew," *Birmingham News*, July 18, 1989, 1E; Stan Bailey, "Graddick Denies Knowing State Equipment Used to Spy," *Birmingham News*, July 19, 1989, A1; Shelton Foss, "Former Graddick Aide Gets $500 Fine," *Montgomery Advertiser*, August 25, 1989, C1.

26. John Archibald and Associated Press, "Baxleys' '85 Income Shown as $193,625 from Tax Returns," *Birmingham News*, October 22, 1986, A2.

27. Amy Herring, "Employee Admits Taking Tax Records, Commissioner Says," *Montgomery Advertiser*, September 24, 1986, A1.

28. MacDonald and Duvall, "Records Show Baxley Slow Several Times"; interview with Bill Baxley, September 25, 2001.

29. MacDonald and Duvall, "Records Show Baxley Slow Several Times."

30. "Responsible Steward," *Birmingham News*, September 26, 1986, A16.

31. The State Ethics Commission eventually ruled that there was insufficient evidence to rule that Baxley violated state law. Sam Duvall and Stan Bailey, "Ethics Commission Drops Baxley Investigation," *Birmingham News*, October 9, 1986, A2.

32. Interview with Bill Baxley, September 25, 2001.

33. Michael Bennighof, "Hunt Commercials Fire Salvos at Graddick," *Birmingham Post-Herald*, October 24, 1986, C1.

34. Michele MacDonald, "Baxley Only Candidate Seeking Debate," *Birmingham News*, September 30, 1986, A2; Robert Dunnavant and Dennis Love, "Hunt: Might Debate Baxley If Certain Conditions Are Met," *Birmingham News*, October 3, 1986, A2.

35. Michele MacDonald, Tom Gordon, and Robert Dunnavant, "Hunt the Tar-

get of Attack in Ads," *Birmingham News*, October 11, 1986, A1; Frederick Burger, "Democrats Unveil New Ad Campaign," *Anniston Star*, October 11, 1986, A5.

36. William E. Schmidt, "Alabama Democratic Fight Aids G.O.P. Candidate," *New York Times*, October 25, 1986, I:7.

37. Amy Herring, "Democrats Don't Need to Panic over Public Relations Beating," *Montgomery Advertiser*, September 21, 1986, C1.

38. Tom Gordon, "Closer Contest: Poll Shows Shelby Narrows Denton Lead," *Birmingham News*, October 13, 1986, A1; Thomas Hargrove, "Denton's Big Lead Is Nearly Gone," *Birmingham Post-Herald*, October 29, 1986, A1.

39. John Brinkley and Ted Bryant, "Investigation Dropped When Hunt Left ASCS," *Birmingham Post-Herald*, October 15, 1986, A1; Michael Brumas, Sam Duvall, and Michele MacDonald, "USDA Boss Urged Hunt to Quit Job," *Birmingham News*, October 15, 1986, A1; Murphy Evans, "Hunt Says Charge 'Politics,'" *Anniston Star*, October 16, 1986, A1; Sam Duvall, "Hunt Ex-boss: Didn't Mean to Imply Guilt," *Birmingham News*, October 21, 1986, A1.

40. Staff and wire reports, "Nothing Found in Hunt Probe," *Anniston Star*, October 14, 1986, A1; Associated Press, "Hunt: Report from 'Left Field,'" *Anniston Star*, October 15, 1986, A1; see also Frederick Burger, "Hunt Probe Defended," *Anniston Star*, October 21, 1986, A1.

41. Michele MacDonald, "Baxley Charges Hunt Put Money to Personal Use," *Birmingham News*, October 24, 1986, A1; Ted Bryant, "Pressing the Flesh: Baxley Charges Hunt Used Public Group's Funds," *Birmingham Post-Herald*, October 24, 1986, C1.

42. Michele MacDonald, "Baxley-Approved Ads Blast Hunt as LaPierre Says Demos on Attack," *Birmingham News*, October 23, 1986, A4; Frederick Burger, "Baxley: Hunt's Secrecy a Confession of Guilt," *Anniston Star*, October 30, 1986, A1. To the charge that he lacked experience, Hunt replied, "I'm glad I don't have the experience that some people have in state government. A bank robber has plenty of experience, but you're not going to appoint him the chairman of a bank." Evans, "Hunt Says Charge 'Politics.'"

43. Ted Bryant, "Law Protected Hunt as Probate Judge, Baxley Says," *Birmingham Post-Herald*, October 28, 1986, A3; Frederick Burger, "Baxley Urges Voters to Vote 'Intelligently,'" *Anniston Star*, October 24, 1986, A1; Murphy Evans, "Baxley Fights to Overcome Protest Vote," *Anniston Star*, October 28, 1986, A1.

44. Thomas Hargrove, "Hunt, Baxley in Dead Heat, Survey Shows," *Birmingham Post-Herald*, October 27, 1986, A1.

45. Sam Duvall and Michele MacDonald, "In or Out? Graddick Reconsiders," *Birmingham News*, October 28, 1986, A1; Michele MacDonald and Sam Duvall, "Baxley, Hunt Wait on Word from Graddick," *Birmingham News*, October 29, 1986, A1.

46. Associated Press, "Contributions to Graddick Slowing," *Anniston Star*, October 25, 1986, A5.

47. Associated Press, "Baxley: $10,000 If Graddick Stays in Race," *Anniston Star,* October 25, 1986, A1.

48. Interview with Charles Graddick, December 1, 1994; interview with Tom Coker, December 1994.

49. Mark Alpert, "Graddick Drops Write-in, Doesn't Endorse Candidate," *Montgomery Advertiser,* October 31, 1986, A1; Frederick Burger, "Graddick's Plan: 'Beat Baxley,'" *Anniston Star,* October 31, 1986, A1.

50. Sam Duvall and Michele MacDonald, "Can't Win, Graddick Drops Out," *Birmingham News,* October 30, 1986, A1.

51. Ted Bryant, "How Much Will Graddick Get?" *Birmingham Post-Herald,* August 27, 1986, C2.

52. At the time of his withdrawal, those saying that they supported Graddick in a three-man race found Hunt favored over Baxley by a margin of 68 to 12 percent in a two-man campaign.

53. Michele MacDonald and Michael Brumas, "Voters Hear Candidates' Final Pitches," *Birmingham News,* November 3, 1986, A1. In perhaps the final irony of the campaign, the Baxley campaign aired a radio advertisement during the last weekend of the election in which Governor Wallace (whose presidential campaign's slogan was "Send them a message") told voters, "Don't throw away your future by voting a protest born of frustration."

54. Michele MacDonald, "Gov. Hunt: Alabama Voters Make History," *Birmingham News,* November 5, 1986, A1.

Chapter 9

1. Michael Jennings, "Wallace Bids Teary Farewell at Sendoff," *Birmingham News,* November 23, 1986, A1. For views of Wallace's career at the end of his last term see Michelle MacDonald and Sam Duvall, "Wallace's Political Image, Style Leave Mixed Legacy in State," *Birmingham News,* January 11, 1987, A1.

2. Stephan Lesher, *George Wallace: American Populist* (Reading, Mass.: Addison-Wesley, 1994); Dan T. Carter, *The Politics of Rage: George Wallace, the Origins of the New Conservatism, and the Transformation of American Politics* (New York: Simon and Schuster, 1995).

3. Tom Gordon, "Wallace to Dole: 'I Voted for You,'" *Birmingham News,* October 25, 1996, 2E.

4. Mary Colurso, "Law Firm Puts Names on City Stages," *Birmingham News,* February 6, 2005, A1.

5. Tom Gordon, "Some Democrats May Have Helped GOP Vote Jump," *Birmingham News,* June 4, 1998, A1; Tom Gordon, David White and Mary Orndorff, "James, Blount Fly into Runoff Battle," *Birmingham News,* June 30, 1998, A1.

6. In 2006 the state's Republican Executive Committee considered, but ultimately rejected, an anti-crossover voting rule. Phillip Rawls, "Republicans Laud Riley, Stop Move to Limit Voting," *Birmingham News,* January 15, 2006, A24.

7. Siegelman was elected Alabama secretary of state in 1978 and 1982. In 1986 he was elected state attorney general. In 1990 he lost his bid for the Democratic gubernatorial election, but he came back four years later to claim the lieutenant governor's position.

8. Tom Lindley, "Graddick Dumps Demos for GOP," *Birmingham News*, October 27, 1989, B3.

9. Ragan Ingram, "Graddick Continues Assault on Hubbert," *Montgomery Advertiser*, October 23, 1990, A2. During the campaign, Graddick (while at the same time saying it should not be an issue) also raised questions about Hubbert's health. Hubbert, who had received a liver transplant, denied that he had any health problems. Associated Press, "Hubbert's Health on Graddick's Mind," *Montgomery Advertiser*, October 11, 1990, A2; Associated Press, "Hubbert: Transplant No Obstacle," *Montgomery Advertiser*, October 12, 1990, A3.

10. "Ex-AG Graddick New Circuit Judge," *Birmingham News*, July 16, 2004, C5.

11. Baxley's past record in office, and particularly the cases he pursued as attorney general, also sometimes generate news coverage. This notably occurred in 2001 with the conviction of Thomas Blanton for his role in the civil-rights-era bombing of the Sixteenth Street Baptist Church in Birmingham. As attorney general in the 1970s Baxley had begun an investigation into this case. For Baxley's assessment of the case, and the FBI's involvement in the investigation, see Bill Baxley, "Why Did the F.B.I. Hold Back Evidence?" *New York Times*, May 3, 2001, 25A; Alvin Benn, "Baxley Tells about Church Bombing Trial," *Montgomery Advertiser*, January 20, 2006, C3.

12. Mike Cason, "Confidence Regained, Baxley Aims for Top," *Birmingham News*, May 15, 2006, A1.

13. Interview with Charles Graddick, December 1, 1994; interview with Bill Baxley, September 25, 2001.

14. Amy Herring, "Hunt Repays $650,000 in Four Years," *Montgomery Advertiser*, September 9, 1999, A1; "Stories Were Wrong," *Montgomery Advertiser*, September 13, 1990, A1.

15. Dan Moore, "Folsom Takes Office: Hunt Makes Quick Exit in Face of Felony Ethics Conviction," *Montgomery Advertiser*, April 23, 1993, A1.

16. This action generated considerable controversy in part because Hunt had appointed two of the three members of the board. Malcomb Daniels, "Hunt Pardoned," *Montgomery Advertiser*, April 1, 1998, A1.

17. Tom Gordon, "Hunt Hopes for Fall Finish of Memoirs," *Birmingham News*, April 14, 2005, B1.

18. The political impact of the 1986 election is also examined in a useful and interesting way by Thomas C. Ellington in "The Hidden Realignment: The 1986 Gubernatorial Race and Party Loyalty in Alabama," *American Review of Politics* 20 (1999): 25–47. Ellington's conclusions about the impact of the 1986 election are similar, though not exactly the same, as those presented here. Another interesting analysis of the relationship between George Wallace's career and the rise of the Republican Party in Alabama is found in Gerald R. Webster, "Partisan Shifts in Presi-

dential and Gubernatorial Elections in Alabama, 1932–1994," *Professional Geographer* 48 (1996): 379–91. See also Gerald R. Webster, "Demise of the Solid South," *Geographical Review* 82 (1992): 43–55.

19. Jerrold G. Rusk, *Statistical History of the American Electorate* (Washington, D.C.: Congressional Quarterly, 2001).

20. In 1990, Guy Hunt defeated Paul Hubbert by a 52.1 percent to 47.9 percent margin. Fob James led Jim Folsom Jr. in the 1994 contest 50.4 to 49.6 percent. Siegelman won over James in 1998 by a 57.8 to 42.2 percent margin. Bob Riley defeated Siegelman 50.1 to 49.9 percent in 2002, and Lucy Baxley 58.0 to 42.0 percent in 2006.

The increasing competitiveness of Alabama's general elections is associated with declining turnout in the state's primary elections. A likely reason for this decline is that the increased competitiveness of Alabama politics has led voters to recognize that the Democratic primary is no longer the "real" election in the state. Specifically, between 1966 (the first statewide election following the passage of the Voting Rights Act) and 1986 roughly one-third to one-half of the state's voting-age population participated in the primary election. In more recent gubernatorial primaries, however, less than one in three potential voters have participated. In 2002 only about one in five age-eligible citizens participated in either the Democratic or Republican primary. In 2006, when both parties had competitive gubernatorial contests, turnout in the primary election was 26.5 percent. Unlike Democratic contests, turnout in Republican primaries has increased since 1986. Indeed, turnout in the 1998 GOP primary exceeded (by less than a thousand votes) that of the Democratic primary. Still, despite having a hotly contested campaign for the gubernatorial nomination while the Democratic race was largely uncontested, the GOP managed to attract only about one in ten of the state's potential voters to its primary. While turnout in primaries has declined, participation in the state's general elections has increased. Through 1986, voting turnout in Alabama was often higher in primaries than in general elections. In more recent years, turnout in general elections has increased so that it now consistently exceeds that of primary elections. Moreover, turnout in later Alabama general elections has also exceeded the national rate.

21. The GOP's success in 1994 was further enhanced when U.S. senator Richard Shelby announced the day after the 1994 election that he was switching to the Republican Party. During the next months and years a number of other Democratic officeholders, including Secretary of State Jim Bennett, made the same move.

22. The specific wording of the party-identification questions in the Alabama surveys is:

> "When it comes to (national/state) politics, do you consider yourself to be a Republican, a Democrat, an Independent, or what?"
>
> (If Republican or Democrat) "Do you think of yourself as a strong or not so strong (Republican/Democrat)?"

(If Independent) "Do you think of yourself as closer to the Republican or the Democratic Party?"

In constructing the party-identification measures used here, missing data cases were deleted from the analysis. There is uncertainty among researchers concerning whether "Independent-leaners" should be treated as partisans or as Independents. (See, for example, Warren E. Miller, "Party Identification, Realignment, and Party Voting: Back to the Basics," *American Political Science Review* 85 [1991]: 557–68; and Bruce E. Keith et al., *The Myth of the Independent Voter* [Berkeley: University of California Press, 1992].) Here we have chosen to treat the "leaning" respondents as Independent. Examination of the data shows that the alternative approach would have resulted in findings equivalent to those presented here.

For further information about the Capstone Poll and Southern Opinion Research statewide surveys used to construct the party-identification measures, see appendix 1. The results of multiple surveys are available for some years. When this occurred, for each survey the percentage of respondents falling into each party-identification category was calculated. These results were then averaged. Also see Patrick R. Cotter and James G. Stovall, "Party Identification and Political Change in Alabama: A Mid-1990s Update," *American Review of Politics* 17 (1996): 193–211.

23. For further information about mixed or dual-party identifications see, for example, M. Kent Jennings and Richard G. Niemi, "Party Identification at Multiple Levels of Government," *American Journal of Sociology* 72 (1966): 86–101; Charles D. Hadley, "Dual Partisanship in the South," *Journal of Politics* 47 (1985): 254–68; and Richard G. Niemi, Stephen Wright, and Lynda W. Powell, "Multiple Party Identifiers and the Measurement of Party Identification," *Journal of Politics* 49 (1987): 1093–1103. See also the winter 1992 issue of *Midsouth Political Science Journal*.

24. For more on party identification in Alabama see Cotter and Stovall, "Party Identification and Political Change in Alabama: A Mid-1990s Update"; Patrick R. Cotter, James G. Stovall, and Samuel H Fisher III, *Disconnected: Public Opinion and Politics in Alabama* (Northport, Ala.: Vision Press, 1994); Patrick R. Cotter and James G. Stovall, "Party Identification and Political Change in Alabama," in *The South's New Politics: Realignment and Dealignment*, ed. Robert H. Swansbrough and David M. Brodsky (Columbia: University of South Carolina Press, 1988), 142–57; Patrick R. Cotter, "Alabama: The Unsettled Electorate," in *Party Realignment in the American States*, ed. Maureen Moakley (Columbus: Ohio State University Press, 1992), 91–105.

Chapter 10

1. See, for example, Earl Black and Merle Black, *Politics and Society in the South* (Cambridge: Harvard University Press, 1987); Earl Black and Merle Black, *The Vital South: How Presidents Are Elected* (Cambridge: Harvard University Press, 1992);

Earl Black and Merle Black, *The Rise of Southern Republicans* (Cambridge: Harvard University Press, 2002).

2. For example, the first post-Reconstruction Republican governor of South Carolina was selected in 1974 following a bitter Democratic nomination struggle in which the winner of the runoff election was removed from the ballot because he did not meet the state's residency requirements. Similarly in Georgia, Republican Matt Mattingly won after incumbent U.S. senator Herman Talmadge encountered both strong intraparty competition and a series of ethics charges concerning his financial affairs. In Louisiana, Republican David Treen was elected governor following a Democratic nomination contest which was so bitter that the losers of this struggle endorsed Treen rather than the nominee of their own party. For discussions of campaigns in the South during this period see Jack Bass and Walter DeVries, *The Transformation of Southern Politics: Social Change and Political Consequences since 1945* (New York: Basic Books, 1976); Alexander P. Lamis, *The Two-Party South*, expanded ed. (New York: Oxford University Press, 1988).

3. One of this manuscript's reviewers helpfully pointed out that the loss of John Teague—backed by many of the same groups supporting Baxley—to Jim Folsom Jr. in the Democratic runoff for lieutenant governor may have contributed to the threat sensed by Baxley and his supporters.

4. J. Mills Thornton III, "Alabama Politics, J. Thomas Heflin, and the Expulsion Movement of 1929," *Alabama Review* 21 (1968): 83–112; William Barnard, *Dixiecrats and Democrats: Alabama Politics, 1942–1950* (Tuscaloosa: University of Alabama Press, 1974).

5. Walter Dean Burnham, "The Alabama Senatorial Election of 1962: Return of Inter-party Competition," *Journal of Politics* 26 (1964): 798–829.

6. For discussion about the importance of the strategic politician see Gary C. Jacobson and Samuel Kernell, *Strategy and Choice in Congressional Elections*, 2nd ed. (New Haven: Yale University Press, 1983).

7. For research showing a relationship between contesting offices and partisan changes in the South, see, for example, Byron E. Shafer and Richard Johnston, *The End of Southern Exceptionalism: Class, Race, and Partisan Change in the Postwar South* (Cambridge: Harvard University Press, 2006); Joseph A. Aistrup, *The Southern Strategy Revisited: Republican Top-down Advancement in the South* (Lexington: University Press of Kentucky, 1996).

8. Cornelius P. Cotter, James L. Gibson, John F. Bibby, and Robert J. Huckshorn, *Party Organizations in American Politics* (Pittsburgh: University of Pittsburgh Press, 1989); James L. Gibson, Cornelius P. Cotter, John F. Bibby, and Robert J. Huckshorn, "Assessing Party Organizational Strength," *American Journal of Political Science* 27 (1983): 193–222; Samuel C. Patterson and Gregory A. Caldeira, "The Etiology of Partisan Competition," *American Political Science Review* 78 (1984): 691–707.

9. V. O. Key Jr., *Southern Politics* (New York: Knopf, 1949), 277, 295. See also Alexander Heard, *A Two-Party South?* (Chapel Hill: University of North Carolina Press, 1952).

10. For discussions of party organizations in Alabama see Donald S. Strong, "Alabama: Transition and Alienation," in *The Changing Politics of the South*, ed. William C. Havard (Baton Rouge: Louisiana State University Press, 1972), 427–71; Bernard Cosman, "Deep South Republicans: Profiles and Positions," in *Republican Politics: The 1964 Campaign and Its Aftermath for the Party*, ed. Bernard Cosman and Robert J. Huckshorn (New York: Praeger, 1968), 76–118; Samuel L. Webb, *Two-Party Politics in the One-Party South* (Tuscaloosa: University of Alabama Press, 1997). For the recollections of an early postwar activities within Alabama's Republican Party see Winton M. "Red" Blount with Richard Blodgett, *Doing It My Way* (Lyme, Conn.: Greenwich Publishing Group, 1996). Finally, for discussions of Republican organizations in other states see, for example, Frank B. Atkinson, *The Dynamic Dominion: Realignment and the Rise of Virginia's Republican Party since 1945* (Fairfax, Va.: George Mason University Press, 1992); Bruce H. Kalk, *The Origins of the Southern Strategy: Two-Party Competition in South Carolina, 1950–1972* (Lexington, Md.: Lexington Books, 2001); Laura Jane Gifford, "'Dixie Is No Longer in the Bag': South Carolina Republicans and the Election of 1960," *Journal of Policy History* 19 (2007): 207–33.

11. For information about his study see Charles D. Hadley and Lewis Bowman, *Southern State Party Organizations and Activists* (Westport, Conn.: Praeger, 1995).

12. See, for example, Aistrup, *The Southern Strategy Revisited;* Numan V. Bartley and Hugh D. Graham, *Southern Politics and the Second Reconstruction* (Baltimore: Johns Hopkins University Press, 1975); Bass and DeVries, *The Transformation of Southern Politics;* Black and Black, *Politics and Society in the South;* Black and Black, *The Vital South;* Black and Black, *The Rise of Southern Republicans;* Kari Frederickson, *The Dixiecrat Revolt and the End of the Solid South, 1932–1968* (Chapel Hill: University of North Carolina Press, 2001); James M. Glaser, *Race, Campaign Politics, and Realignment in the South* (New Haven: Yale University Press, 1996); William C. Havard, ed., *The Changing Politics of the South* (Baton Rouge: Louisiana University Press, 1972); Heard, *A Two-Party South;* Key, *Southern Politics;* Lamis, *The Two-Party South;* Alexander P. Lamis, ed., *Southern Politics in the 1990s* (Baton Rouge: Louisiana State University Press, 1999); Shafer and Johnston, *The End of Southern Exceptionalism;* Robert H. Swansbrough and David M. Brodsky, eds., *The South's New Politics: Realignment and Dealignment* (Columbia: University of South Carolina Press, 1988).

13. Paul Allen Beck, "Partisan Dealignment in the Postwar South," *American Political Science Review* 71 (1977): 477–96; Bruce A. Campbell, "Change in the Southern Electorate," *American Journal of Political Science* 21 (1977): 37–64; Bruce A. Campbell, "Patterns of Change in the Partisan Loyalties of Native Southerners: 1952–1972," *Journal of Politics* 39 (1977): 730–61; Douglas S. Gatlin, "Party Identification, Status, and Race in the South: 1952–1972," *Public Opinion Quarterly* 39 (1975): 39–51; Warren E. Miller, "Party Identification, Realignment, and Party Voting: Back to the Basics," *American Political Science Review* 85 (1991): 557–70; Tom W. Rice, "Partisan Change among Native White Southerners: 1965–1982," *American Politics Quarterly*

2 (1994): 244–51; Harold W. Stanley, "Southern Partisan Changes: Dealignment, Realignment or Both?" *Journal of Politics* 50 (1988): 64–88; Raymond Wolfinger and Robert B. Arseneau, "Partisan Change in the South, 1952–1976," in *Political Parties: Development and Decay*, ed. Louis Maisel and Joseph Cooper (Beverly Hills, Calif.: Sage, 1978), 179–210.

14. Aistrup, *The Southern Strategy Revisited*; Edward G. Carmines and James A. Stimson, *Issue Evolution: Race and the Transformation of American Politics* (Princeton: Princeton University Press, 1989); Black and Black, *Politics and Society in the South*; Black and Black, *The Rise of Southern Republicans*; Chandler Davidson, *Race and Class in Texas Politics* (Princeton: Princeton University Press, 1990); Glaser, *Race, Campaign Politics, and Realignment in the South*; Nicholas A. Valentino and David O. Sears, "Old Times Are Not Forgotten: Race and Partisan Realignment in the Contemporary South," *American Journal of Political Science* 49 (2005): 672–88.

15. Alan I. Abramowitz, "Issue Evolution Reconsidered: Racial Attitudes and Partisanship in the U.S. Electorate," *American Journal of Political Science* 38 (1994): 1–24; Alan I. Abramowitz and Kyle L. Saunders, "Ideological Realignment in the U.S. Electorate," *Journal of Politics* 60 (1998): 634–52; Richard Nadeau and Harold W. Stanley, "Class Polarization in Partisanship among Native Southern Whites, 1952–1990," *American Journal of Political Science* 37 (1993): 900–919; John R. Petrocik, "Realignment: New Party Coalitions and the Nationalization of the South," *Journal of Politics* 49 (1987): 348–75; Shafer and Johnston, *The End of Southern Exceptionalism*; Jeffrey M. Stonecash, *Class and Party in American Politics* (Boulder: Westview Press, 2000).

16. Key, *Southern Politics*, 666.

17. See, for example, Carmines and Stimson, *Issue Evolution*; Jacobson and Kernell, *Strategy and Choice in Congressional Elections*; V. O. Key Jr. with Milton C. Cumming, *The Responsible Electorate* (Cambridge: Harvard University Press, 1966); V. O. Key Jr., *Public Opinion and American Democracy* (New York: Knopf, 1967); Stuart Elaine MacDonald and George Rabinowitz, "The Dynamics of Structural Realignment," *American Political Science Review* 81 (1987): 775–96; E. E. Schattschneider, *The Semi-Sovereign People* (New York: Holt, Rinehart and Winston, 1960); John R. Zaller, *The Nature and Origins of Mass Opinion* (New York: Cambridge University Press, 1992).

18. Lawrence R. Jacobs and Robert Y. Shapiro, *Politicians Don't Pander: Political Manipulation and the Loss of Democratic Responsiveness* (Chicago: University of Chicago Press, 2000).

19. See, for example, Schattschneider, *The Semi-Sovereign People.*

Appendix A

1. Likely voters are respondents who say that they plan to vote in the upcoming Democratic primary, Democratic runoff, or general election and (a) report that they

voted in the 1984 presidential election and are "very much" or "somewhat" interested in the current campaign, or (b) did not vote in the 1984 presidential election but are "very much interested" in the current campaign. Michael W. Traugott and Clyde Tucker, "Strategies for Predicting Whether a Citizen Will Vote and Estimation of Electoral Outcomes," *Public Opinion Quarterly* 48 (1984): 330–43.

Index

Page numbers in italics refer to figures.